The Universe – Solved!

Thank you for your interest. Enjoy!

- Jo Ellistn

ISBN 978-1-4243-3626-5

To my family, Pauline and Brandon,
for listening, challenging, and supporting

Acknowledgements

First, I must acknowledge the many sources of inspiration for this book. Open-minded "out of the box-thinking" scientists such as Michio Kaku, Brian Green, David Bohm, Kip Thorne, Paul Davies, Lee Smolin, Ervin Laszlo, Fred Hoyle, Andrei Linde, and Alan Guth have always challenged my worldview. Scientists and researchers like Dean Radin, Tom Van Flandern, Jessica Utts, Rupert Sheldrake, Rick Strassman, John Mack, Michael Cremo, Robert Jahn and the rest of the Princeton PEAR lab took great risks with their reputations by opening investigations beyond the status quo. Their efforts were both inspirational as well as contributory to my thesis. Writers like Sidney Kirkpatrick, Michael Talbot, Graham Hancock, Arthur James, and Jim Marrs were never afraid to tackle tough topics, and brought alternative viewpoints and theories to my attention. Deep thinkers, futurists, and philosophers like Nick Bostrom, Ray Kurzweil, Deepack Chopra, Brian Weiss, Frank Tipler, and Neal Stephenson have all shaped my view of reality through their works. Broadcasters like Art Bell and George Noory provided an outlet for many of these people to espouse their views. All of the aforementioned people can be considered inspirational sources to my thesis.

Special thanks to my wonderful wife, my Editor-In-Chief, who helped in so many ways, working tirelessly on the hunt for agents and publishers, providing many thoughtful edits and discussions around the content and cover art, following me to conferences and seminars on topics as diverse as string theory and exopolitics, and, not least, modeling for the Jessica graphics. Thanks also to my talented son Brandon for his graphical contributions to the work, and to Angel Estevez for his generosity in allowing the use of his wonderful artwork on the cover and website.

Finally, I wish to acknowledge all of my friends, colleagues, family members, friends of distant relatives, etc. who expressed an interest in reading, reviewing, and/or editing the manuscript or one of the early printings. Valuable and insightful feedback was provided by Stan Drake, Tracy Hughes, Dana Azar (who provided the real challenge that this book needed), and Ranan Banerji.

TABLE OF CONTENTS

The Universe - Solved!

CHAPTER I

The Universe - Solved!

There is a line from the Wachowski brothers movie, "The Matrix" (1999), which goes like this:

Morpheus: What you know you can't explain, but you feel it. You've felt it your entire life, that there's something wrong with the world. You don't know what it is, but it's there, like a splinter in your mind, driving you mad.

Have you ever felt a similar way about the world we live in? Like there is something about reality that isn't quite random, as it should be? Something a little too organized, a little too planned, a little too programmed?

Yeah, me too!

This book starts by addressing that feeling. Then it plans to take you down the "rabbit hole" of introspection and philosophical inquiry, on a wild roller coaster ride through virtual reality, quantum mechanics, and futurism. And, hopefully, it ends with an answer, which just might make sense of it all – of everything that has occupied philosophers, religious scholars, cosmologists, and coffee shop Bohemians for the past couple thousand years. An answer that is both a perfect fit to virtually every scientific theory and a perfect explanation for every anomalous occurrence.

If not, give it to your dog to chew up – he'll have a blast.

1

Oh no. Not another TOE!

I know what some of you are thinking – not another TOE (Theory of Everything)! For the benefit of those of you who don't typically read material like this, there has been a recent spate of books and articles purporting some wild theory that explains everything known to man; M-Theory, the Turquoise Meme, the Akashic Record, 42, the Holographic Universe, to name a few relevant concepts. You'll find these in the science, new age, and philosophy sections of your favorite bookstores. So, in that sense, yes, this book is another TOE. But before you put it down, I promise you that this is a little different. It is sort of a meta-TOE in that it also explains why everybody and their brother are coming up with different TOE's (the "TOE of TOE's").

So let's begin with an exercise in open-mindedness, as we question reality and truth.

What is Reality, Really?

Let's start with two simple exercises.

For the first one, I ask the question "How do you know that what you perceive is not an illusion?" Your perception of reality is nothing more than electrochemical reactions in your brain. So is it not possible that those perceptions are actually produced by an intelligent computer program that is linked to your gray matter via some wireless network? As we shall see, such a technology is only years away.

Thought experiment #2…

How do we really know what happened 2000 years ago? From what we read in books? Doesn't it seem kind of arbitrary that we might consider some books to be authoritative history and others simply mythology. Theoretically, our history may have been planted into our society and collective consciousness. If so, when did our "real" history start? 500 years ago? 100 years ago? One might argue that it couldn't have started a century ago because we have contemporaries who were alive then. And since they had contemporaries who were alive many years before their birth, and so on back to ancient times, it would seem impossible that an artificial reality could be imposed upon us. However, we are only years away from the ability to upload, download, erase, and restore our brains memory banks. Which makes it possible to be fooled into believing an entirely different reality.

These ideas may seem far-fetched, but I hope to show in this book, that the technology that makes them possible is easily within some of our lifetimes. And if that is the case, who is to say that we are not living a simulated or programmed reality today?

For many people out there, reality is simple, and unquestionable. You are taught what reality is by your parents, teachers, leaders, and friends. It is what you see around you – a continuum of objects at various positions and states, all of which is smoothly moving along in time. You trust the history and sciences that you are taught in school. The winners of the World Wars were the good guys. You obey the laws that your country and religion set forth because they are "right." You trust your recollections from the past. We evolved from apes, time travel is just science fiction, and every human is an independent living being with free will.

Probe a little deeper, however, and things change a bit. Political parties vehemently disagree on policy, different religions disagree on right and wrong, history sometimes turns out to be different than you thought. The same people funded both sides of World War II. Science says that free will is an illusion. Religious leaders and mainstream science disagree on the question of an afterlife. You peer deeper and deeper into space and find strange anomalies that defy explanation with current physical laws. You peer deeper and deeper into the atom and things really get strange. You find that time and space are not really continuous but discreet, like a TV screen.

Probe even deeper, spend some time surfing the web, listening to alternative radio programs like "Coast to Coast AM", reading conspiracy books or new age books, and you may find yourself becoming a truth seeker. If reality is what we perceive, for example, and what we perceive is based on a large set of neural synapse firings, then isn't reality just an artifact of what your brain is doing? And the more you probe, the more you will no doubt be confused by the morass of seemingly conflicting information that is out there. Consider…

1. Standard science taught in American schools, supports Darwin's theory of evolution of life.

BUT, many scientists disagree and embrace an "interventionist" point of view. The late world-renowned astronomer from Cambridge University, Sir Fred Hoyle, once said that the probability of producing life anywhere in the universe from evolutionary processes, was similar to the probability of a whirlwind assembling a fully operational Boeing 747 jumbo jet from its parts.[1]

2. Mainstream scientists say that there is no such thing as paranormal phenomena. Certain well known skeptics have even offered large sums of cash to anyone who can prove paranormal phenomena and, to date, have yet to issue a check.

BUT, alternative viewpoints are supported by strong experimental evidence. State of the art mass consciousness studies by no less of a reputable institution than Princeton University have proven beyond a reasonable doubt that there are phenomena that are completely unexplained by conventional science. A Gallup poll in June 2001 found that 60 percent of Americans believe in extrasensory perception and 65 million Americans have personally experienced ESP. Further, the poll shows that the tendency to believe in ESP increased with intelligence. Allegedly, some attempts to collect on the skeptic offers have been met with changing rules, ignored requests, name calling, and various diversionary tactics.

3. Well respected scientists, such as the late Carl Sagan, deny the existence of UFOs.

BUT, astronauts, such as Edgar Mitchell, scientists such as the late Harvard Professor Dr. John Mack, and respected statesmen, like Jimmy Carter, have seen UFOs, and believe that they are extraterrestrial in origin.

4. The Warren Commission's, and the official US government's position on the assassination of John Fitzgerald Kennedy, is that it was done by a lone gunman.

BUT, 77% of the people in the United States, according to a recent New York Times/CBS poll, disagree with the Warren Report's conclusion, and believe instead that the JFK assassination was a conspiracy, and possibly, a coup d'etat.

5. Conventional wisdom is that the physical world that we experience is exactly what it seems to be; e.g. what you see is what you get.

BUT, some reputable scientists believe that there are many levels of reality. Psychedelic drugs may allow the user to jump between levels. A philosopher from Oxford University has written a paper implying that we are actually living in a simulation, a la "The Matrix."

So, which is it?

Do we live in a world that is exactly as it seems to be? One in which there are no UFOs, no Yetis, no conspiracies, there was no Atlantis, the Egyptians build the pyramids, paranormal experiences are hoaxes or have simple explanations, the earth is 4 billion years old, humans evolved from the apes over the past 2 million years, you can trust your government, we only have five senses, and when a tree falls in the woods, it makes a sound if nobody is there.

OR…

Is our world completely different than what we think we perceive? One in which humans are the result of extraterrestrial genetic experiments, parallel universes exist and can be traveled between by ingesting Ayahuasca or simple remote viewing, there is a huge global conspiracy involving hidden knowledge, with a reptilian shape-shifting power elite at the top, and falling trees only make a sound if observed, although valid observers do include plants and rocks.

Or is it somewhere in between?

And how do we decide where the truth lies?

I propose that the truth is none of the above. It is really way beyond the specifics. All is true and none is true as we shall see!

What is True?

What can we really know with conviction? Nothing! Consider the entire set of things that *could* be true. What about things that you haven't personally experienced, but are commonly accepted as fact. I submit that you should reject them all, for all you need is one example, such as Newtonian Mechanics (accepted as fact by the scientific community for hundreds of years, but shown by Einstein in the early 20th century to be just an approximation at slow speeds), to doubt the credibility of the rest of them. 2+2=4? Not in Base 3, where 2+2=11. In Base 10 (or any base >4), 2+2=4 by convention, but only in an abstract way, and not necessarily always true in the *real* world. If you add 2 puddles of water to 2 puddles of water, you still have 2 (albeit larger) puddles of water. For a more conventional example, a 2-mile straight line laid end-to-end with another 2-mile straight line will not add up to *exactly* 4 miles in length due to relativity and the curvature of space-time in all locales. Therefore, 2+2=4 can not be universally true.

So, in the *real* world, that leaves only things that you have personally experienced. What about dreams you have experienced – are they true, or real? Maybe not, rule them out. What about experiences that you've had where someone else remembers something completely different. Many studies have shown that under certain circumstances (e.g. stress, fatigue) people commonly recollect events differently than how they really happened. So rule them out. What about experiences that we had long ago? We know that time tends to erode the clarity of a memory. How many times have you and a friend argued about what class you were in that time in grade school when Biff had that bladder malfunction? Did you and your spouse ever disagree about what happened yesterday? At least one of you cannot trust their memory entirely. Rule out any personal experience older than… a few minutes ago? What are we left with? Extremely recent personal experiences under non-stressful or non-fatigued conditions? Not so fast, Mario. From our previous thought experiment, what if every single memory you have in your head was planted there through some means, 5 seconds ago. You have no way of knowing the difference between that and your memories, especially if supporting information was injected in the memories of your acquaintances and in the mass media. I will show later that this scenario is not as ridiculous as it sounds. So, maybe all we can know for sure is what is happening to us at this exact instant. Then again, how do we know that we aren't in a dream right now??? So, the set of things that are 100% true is simply the null set!

> "You know one thing I hate? It's how quickly people just forget things these days. I mean, who here still remembers that time a couple of years ago when the whole earth blew up? You don't? When they put us all in the big space ark? And they brought us to this planet? And the government said not to tell the stupid people…"
> - Steve Martin

Back to reality. Most of us are content with what we perceive; what we are taught that reality is. However, a number of people from a variety of academic disciplines are starting to question various aspects of our reality and are taking a crack at digging a little deeper into the topic. The scientific community encourages creative inquiry but only to a limited extent. You can push the envelope a little bit, but too much and you might find yourself acquiring the "pseudoscientist" label. Metaphysical free thinkers don't really much care about labels and feel free to propose all kinds of radical ideas. Unfortunately, the preponderance of inconsistent theories makes them all too easy for the scientific community to dismiss. I like to think of it in terms of the diagram in Figure 1-1. The truth about our reality may be hidden from us by a shell of "The World As We See It," which I like to call the reality shell. Some creative thinkers from various academic disciplines are chipping away at the question from their own perspective. Cosmologists like Andre Linde and Frank Tipler offer ideas like self-replication and anthropic principles to explain the curious nature of the universe. Modern philosophers, like Nick Bostrom, and science fiction writers like the Wachowski brothers ponder the possibility that we are living in some sort of simulation. Quantum physicists, like Hugh Everett and Michio Kaku explore the ideas of parallel universes and the role of the observer in the laws of physics. Futurists like Ray Kurzweil see a man-machine convergence happening in the next 100 years. And metaphysical investigators and writers push the reality envelope with investigations into the paranormal, mass consciousness effects, and man's true evolution. Most biologists, on the other hand, for the most part, seem to prefer the comfort of their highly reductionist Darwinian world, and haven't really taken a bite out of the reality shell.

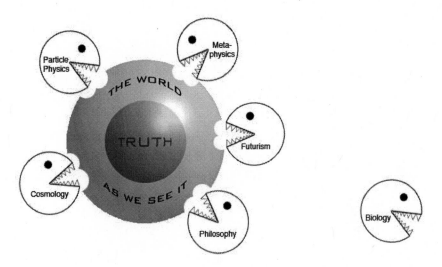

Figure 1-1

All of these groups of people have had some very good ideas to share, some of which overlap nicely. In fact, by taking a step back and viewing the whole "ideascape" of reality-challenging concepts, I've been able to develop a single consistent theory that encompasses all of the research. The fundamental idea is that our reality is programmed. It turns out that such a simple idea is actually enough to effectively drive a wedge through the reality shell, leaving just the truth and a little shell of mystery (see Figure 1-2).

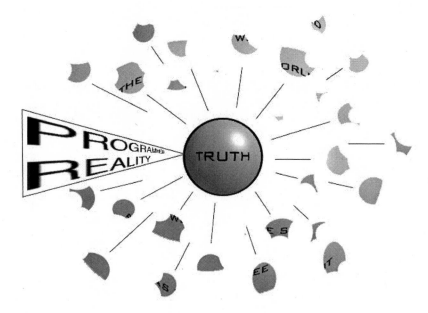

Figure 1-2

The rest of the book will explain the evidence and the implications, show how it is possible, why it is highly probable, and explore the obvious questions:

- *How did it get programmed?*

- *Who programmed it?*

- *Who are you?*

- *When did it start?*

- *How will it end?*

- *How does this explain all of the anomalies and paradoxes of life?*

CHAPTER 2

Food for thought...

Solipsism, Quantum Entanglement, Parallel Universes, and Living in a Hologram

This chapter provides the foundation for the main premise of the book. It is not intended to be an in-depth treatment of philosophy, quantum physics, or cosmology, but rather an overview of the current states of thinking in those fields that are relevant to the premise of this book. If science isn't your bag, feel free to skip those sections, but at least look up "Quantum Mechanics" in your favorite Wiki.

Cogito, Ergo Sum and other assorted Philosophical gems...

Yes, I do recognize the hilarity in attempting to present a few thousand years of worldwide philosophy in a few pages. But if we restrict ourselves to concepts surrounding our central themes – free will, the nature of reality – maybe it is only a little less humorous?

> The First Law of Philosophy: For every philosopher, there exists an equal and opposite philosopher.
>
> The Second Law of Philosophy: They're both wrong.
>
> - Plato and Pasi Kuoppamaki

Reality as an Illusion

Our generation is far from the first to ponder the nature of reality and the possibility that it is illusory. Renaissance French philosopher Rene "I think, therefore I am" Descartes held that perception is unreliable and all that we can know for sure is that we think. 2000 years prior, pre-Socratic Greek philosopher Parmenides believed that the every day world perceived by our senses is not real and only the unchanging "Being" or "Existence" is true reality. Halfway around the world and 600 years earlier, we find a strangely similar Hindu belief that the ordinary world of "things" is an illusion of our minds and that true reality is the eternal and unchanging "One" or "Absolute." Isn't it odd that more than 3000 years later, we are amazed at ourselves for coming up with similar concepts in movies like "The Matrix"?

Free Will

One of the cornerstones of historical philosophical debate has been the concept of free will, or the idea that our choices are up to ourselves. This doctrine has strong (although, not absolute) ties to the idea of a soul and is therefore a core topic for this book. Determinism is the belief that everything that one does is determined by past events. Although some philosophers have argued that determinism can actually be compatible with free will, I believe that they have mistaken free will for the ability to carry out one's choice (every day, things happen to us that are beyond our control, but it is not because we have the capacity to will them away). Furthermore, many of the philosophers who debated the concept did so before much was known about neural activity, or cause and effect in the brain. In effect, modern science, which is deterministic at its core, says that we only have the illusion of a free will due to the rich complexities of neural processes. This seems to be supported by experiments where the subject makes decisions that are shown to be influenced by the presence of magnetic fields, or some other unnoticeable stimuli. The subject believes that they are making conscious decisions. But this doesn't prove anything other than that some of the people can be fooled some of the time.

More interesting, I think, are the experiments that seem to show precognition or the ability to anticipate a stimulus. Scientist Dean Radin (PhD, psychology, University of Illinois) has conducted a number of double blind experiments wherein the subject's EEGs tend to show a response prior to the presentment of a stimulus. The use of a computer to generate the stimulus at random intervals negates the possibility of telepathy. The results seem to indicate that people are able to anticipate events, which is very difficult to explain with deterministic reasoning.[1]

Think about what it means to make a decision. The cashier gave you too much change – do you tell him/her? It seems like you make your choice based on past events (your parents taught you that it was deceitful to take something that shouldn't be yours) or the current state of your mind (the cashier is really cute, maybe I'll get a few points by pointing out the mistake). Upon further analysis, it really seems that the exact state of your brain (memories, neural pathways and triggers) and the state of external stimuli might be fully responsible for each decision and action. However, one could make the same argument for a computer, which function is based on the concept of a finite state machine (each action is fully determined by the state of the machine and its inputs). This idea essentially boils down to us being nothing more than robots. Are you okay with that?

What about the following scenario:

Two kids with the same parents grow up in the same environment. Why do they frequently have a completely different set of values? One gives the money back to the cashier without question; one keeps the money without question. Why? It can't be purely due to genetics. And it can't be purely due to upbringing. Determinists would argue that slight differences in genetics or environment may have a domino effect on the value systems of the individual. But, could it also be due to the possibility that these are two different souls, which have evolved differently? Believers in reincarnation might say that the former has learned a universal lesson in a previous incarnation and is perhaps an older, or more experienced, soul. It is therefore natural for that person to make such a decision, whereas the

Food for thought…

sibling's soul has not yet learned that universal lesson. We can't be sure, but it does seem odd that people often talk of the deep personality differences between their children that are observable at such a young age that environmental differences are precluded. This tends to lend support to the idea that there is a "ghost in the machine."

If the determinists are correct, what's the point in following any laws, or codes of moral responsibility? Everything you do is beyond your control anyway. We would have total chaos if everyone really believed in this. Perhaps that says something about people's deep-seated beliefs.

Religions have an interesting take on free will. Since God is generally considered to be all knowing and all powerful, He must be able to know our choices and make our choices, which is known as theological determinism. Calvinists and similar puritanical theologists believe that we are who we are – stuck in a deterministic destiny toward salvation or damnation. Mormonism and Roman Catholicism teach that humans have free will and can influence their destiny. In Judaism, only humans, and not other animals, have free will.

Strictly speaking, evolutionism is compatible with the idea of free will, but, either we all (all life forms) have it or none of us have it. It doesn't make much sense to assert that an animal with free will evolved from one without it. By extension, every single life form must either be endowed with free will and a soul or simply be deterministic machinery. However, we can relax the strict Darwinist interpretation of evolution by allowing that evolution is a valid process but not necessarily the only process that explains how we got where we are. Think of Voltaire's idea that the universe had a creator that "wound the clock" and set things in motion, but played no further role in the activities of his creation and its creatures. Or Arthur C. Clarke's "2001", in which an extraterrestrial civilization had discrete points of influence in the course of human evolution, but left Darwinistic evolution to run its course in between those points in time. In these cases, one could make an argument that it is possible for a species to be given or not given free will.

Taken to the extreme, Solipsism is the belief that the only thing you can know for certain is yourself. Everyone else is just a projection of your mind. The problem is that it is a lonely philosophy. Why bother to argue it? Does it make sense for a solipsist to have her own website if there is nobody to truly appreciate it?

> "Frank, a philosophy graduate student, was a solipsist. One spring break, all the other graduate students got together a collection, and funded an expensive vacation trip for him. One of the faculty was puzzled by this apparent display of altruism, and asked one of them why they funded a vacation for Frank. The response was: "If Frank goes, everybody goes.""
> - Common Internet joke, source unknown

Where is my mind, anyway?

The standard scientific view (at least that held by most neuroscientists and biologists) is that consciousness is nothing more than an artifact of the complexity of our brain. An artifact? I'm an *ARTIFACT?* Author Adam Gopnik, in stating the position of well-respected cognitive scientist Daniel Dennett, says "There is no "consciousness" apart from the working of all our mental states. Consciousness is not the ghost in the machine; it is the hum of the machinery. The louder the hum, the more conscious you feel."[2] Following this reasoning from a logical standpoint, one would have to conclude that every living thing, including bacteria, has consciousness. In that view of the world, it simply doesn't make sense to assert that there might be some threshold of nervous system complexity, above which an entity is conscious and below which it is not. It is just a matter of degree and you can only argue about aspects of consciousness in a purely probabilistic sense; e.g. "most cats probably do not ponder their own existence." Taking this thought process a step further, one has to conclude that if consciousness is simply a by-product of neural complexity, then a computer that is equivalent to our brains in complexity must also be conscious. Indeed, this is the position of many technologists who ponder artificial intelligence, and futurists, such as Ray Kurzweil. And if this is the case, by logical extension, the simplest of electronic circuits is also conscious, in proportion to the degree in which bacteria is conscious in relation to human consciousness. So, even an electronic circuit known as a flip-flop (or bi-stable multivibrator), which consists of a few transistors and stores a single bit of information, is conscious. I wonder what it feels like to be a flip-flop?

Not all scientists believe in this logic reductio ad absurdum. Former medical school professor and Stanford research scientist, Dr. Bruce Lipton, for example, challenges the prevailing theory that the nucleus of a cell is its "brain." Noting that cells can continue their biological function even with the nucleus removed, his investigations led to the realization that a cell's nucleus in not its control center and that a cell receives its instructions via molecular "antennas" on its surface, or membrane. The signal or instructions to the cell come from outside the cell. This has significant implications to the positioning of our consciousness, especially if you consider that while each of our cells are freestanding intelligent living entities, it is the cooperative community of 50 trillion of them that makes us what we are. So if our cells' behavior is not controlled by the nucleus of the cell, but rather by external signals, how can we, as a collection of these cells, not also be controlled by an external consciousness? Dr. Lipton believes that our "central voice," or our mind and spirit, actually modifies the behavior of genes through intent rather than the other way around. This idea fully explains the many examples of "mind over matter," "spontaneous remissions," and "power of positive thinking, " as well as giving a big Western boost to Eastern philosophies.

THE DEFINITION OF LIFE

Think you know what life is? Guess again.
Conventional biologists typically define life as anything
that generally exhibits all of the following properties:

1. Growth
2. Metabolism
3. Motion
4. Reproduction
5. Homeostasis (or responding to stimuli)

However, it turns out to be surprisingly difficult to
consistently define life according to these or any other
rules. For example, we would all agree that a mule or a
drone bee is alive, although, being sterile, they violate
property 4 above. Viruses have all of the above
properties and are sometimes considered to be living
organisms, but not by certain biologists (aka "cell
bigots") who believe that only cellular organisms can be
considered alive. Fire and crystals have all five life-
defining properties, but most of us would not consider
them to be alive. What about the earth? It certainly
has the properties listed above, with the exception of
reproduction. If one can consider humans nothing more
than a large colony of living cells, then isn't the earth
just a larger such colony? What about the upcoming
marriage of artificial intelligence and nanotech?

I've presented a lot of information and theories thus far. You may be
wondering when I'm going to get to the point. Patience,
Grasshopper.

It depends on what the meaning of the word "is" is...

But, OK, while the main course starts in Chapter 7, for the appetizer,
here is a bona fide opinion...

Food for thought…

I believe that there is something more to me than bio-chemo-electrical processing. The following dialog demonstrates my reasoning:

Jim: If there is no soul, why am I not Fred over there?

Skeptic: Because you are your consciousness, which is a product of your senses and memories. You can't be Fred because you are YOUR senses and memories.

Jim: What if Fred and I swapped brains. Where would "I" be? Wouldn't I now feel like I was simply in Fred's body?

Skeptic: Right, because your consciousness is more defined by your memories than your senses. You are the state of your brain.

Jim: Memories fade and more recent ones are stronger. So, after a while, my brain will be more defined by the memories of the experiences that come into Fred's body than by the memories left over when I was in my body. In that case, hasn't my brain become Fred's brain? Kind of like loading a different operating system into your computer.

Skeptic: Yes, if you define Fred by how he looks, rather than his brain – what used to be Jim's brain is now Fred's brain, but with some of Jim's memories.

Jim: So I have become Fred. And vice versa.

Skeptic: Your use of the word "I" is odd. Your consciousness, or brain state, is in Fred's body.

Jim: Right. And so my consciousness is just as happy being in Fred's body attached to Fred's senses as it was in my body attached to my senses.

Skeptic: Exactly.

Jim: So it seems rather arbitrary where my consciousness is.

Skeptic: I suppose it does.

Jim: Then why wasn't I Fred in the first place?

I believe that there is something unique to us (to me, at least – I can't speak for anyone else, not having been in their shoes) beyond the physical. The plumbing to which biologists refer as defining life is a vehicle for the soul and the soul continues beyond death. I don't know that every living thing has a soul – I can certainly imagine the possibility that sophisticated automatons are part of our reality, in the shapes of wasps, rats, or even humans. Not unlike the NPCs in MMORPGs (see "Games" in Chapter 3 for the definition of these acronyms), or Agent Smith in "The Matrix". But this is nothing new or interesting. 84% of America's population believes in a soul that survives death.[3] The evidence for the existence of the soul is phenomenal. Philosophical arguments aside, I believe that otherwise inexplicable OBEs and NDEs (see "Altered States" in Chapter 3) and Dean Radin's meta-analysis of parapsychological experiments prove beyond a doubt that there is something more to us that body chemistry. Furthermore, consider the following:

The American Heart Association states that brain death and permanent death begin to occur within four to six minutes of a cardiac arrest and that resuscitation rarely succeeds after ten minutes with no heartbeat. There is no scientific evidence of the ability to consistently resuscitate someone who is dead after 10 minutes, despite the availability of heart and lung pumps that are perfectly able to maintain necessary blood and oxygen flow to keep someone alive during surgery. The common reason given for this is that brain cells suffer irreversible damage within minutes of losing blood and oxygen flow. However a study published in The Lancet, a prestigious British medical journal, presented "evidence for survival of human brain neurons up to 8 hours after death such that they still have the potential for recover their functions of energy metabolism and axonal transport."[4] So, if death is irreversible upon permanent neuron damage, which occurs hours after clinical "brain death," why is it impossible to resuscitate someone in the mean time by simply pumping blood through their body? The obvious answer is that death has nothing to do with neuron damage per se. It has to do with a

conscious choice of the soul to leave the body. NDE reports
overwhelmingly support this idea.

> "Yes, we have a soul. But it's made of lots of tiny
> robots."
> - Giulio Giorello

And here's another thought experiment paradox that seems to me to
only be explicable by the existence of a soul:

Given that in the primate world there is a continuum of neural
complexity from lemurs to humans, it is safe to say that somewhere
there is a species with roughly half the neural complexity of a human.
Per the atheistic way of thinking, such a species would therefore have
half the consciousness of a human. Let's arbitrarily define the level
of neural complexity on a scale from 0 to 1, 1 being human. Out
primate friend would then have a neural complexity, and therefore,
consciousness, of .5. Later in this chapter we will present the strong
evidence of the distributed nature of the brain; namely, that there is
no single specific place where a memory resides or a specific
component of a visual image is captured. From the cases involving
brain tumors and brain loss due to injuries, it is clear that we could
remove half of a human's brain and that person would continue to be
conscious. Maybe only half as conscious as before, not unlike
waking up on a beach in Cancun during spring break after a night of
bad tequila.

Here comes the thought experiment part. Imagine the possibility of a
brain transplant. It's not hard to do, given that the brain is simply an
organ, like the many others that are routinely subject to transplant
with today's surgical techniques. There are certainly a lot more
connections to a brain compared with, say, a liver, but it's really just
a matter of time before it is possible and then ultimately perfected.
Just as the cloning procedure is working its way up the species
complexity scale (lab mice, sheep, humans), so will the brain
transplant procedure. A head transplant, for example, was performed

by Case Western Reserve University neurosurgeon Dr. Robert White on a rhesus monkey in 1970. It survived for eight days and exhibited many normal functions. Cross-species transplants, also known as xenotransplants, have long since been proven to be possible, with chimpanzee kidneys in humans, pig livers in humans, cynomolgus monkey hearts in baboons, and baboon hearts in humans all achieving some level of success. The main reasons that experimentation and advances in that field are slow to progress are the controversial ethical issue (it is right for pigs to become organ factories?) and the fear of cross-species viral infections. But, ethical and safety issues aside, it is reasonable to assume that with sufficient technology, it will be possible to transplant a human brain or portion thereof into our primate that nominally has a .5 consciousness level. Let's further imagine that the process could become fairly straightforward, like plugging a new motherboard into a computer. As long as the interfaces line up from a physical and networking standpoint, the procedure is "plug and play."

So let's imagine our human subject, Nick, and 2 lesser primates, Magilla and Kong. We remove Nick's brain and attach it to Magilla's body. Nick should retain his memories and consciousness, but feel really different, since his sensory input is completely new. We would have to conclude that he maintained a continuous, albeit altered, stream of identity. If Karl Pribham and others are right, we could theoretically put half of Nick's brain into Magilla and the other half in Kong. Where is his identity now? Which body does the old Nick feel that he is in? If we took the biological reductionist point of view, we would have to say that his consciousness is in both primates. That must be very confusing, receiving two separate sets of sensory stimuli and two distinct developing sets of new memories. Given that the state of the two primates is fairly consistent with the state of two similar natural primates, namely that they each have a brain of .5 neural complexity, why should there be a single conscious identity occupying both bodies in the case of Kong and Magilla, but two distinct identities in the natural case? My answer is simple, invoking Occam's Razor. Nick's soul simply chose which primate to move into along with his brain. Alternately, his soul could have said,

"This is ridiculous. I'm returning to the spirit domain. Let some other souls fight over those abominations."

What would Ockham have to say about all of these possibilities? Occam's Razor, named after a 14th century logician, William of Ockham, asserts that "Given two equally predictive theories, choose the simpler." Scientists often trump out Occam's Razor to prove a point, such as the belief that there is no need for a God to explain the universe. Ironically, however, as creationists are quick to point out, Ockham himself was a creationist and believed that the unity of the cosmos with God was the simplest possible theory. It is hard to use Occam's Razor to support complex theories like evolution, parallel universes, and hyperinflation. However, and this demonstrates the ultimate flaw of the concept, most scientists universally agree with these complex theories. Ockham never said that the simpler theory was better, just that it might tend to be. By the end of this book, I hope to convince the readers that were Ockham alive today, he would probably have agreed with me.

East Meets West

Quick – name 10 philosophers!

When a "western" person thinks of philosophy, we typically think of the ancient Greeks – Plato, Socrates, Aristotle. Or perhaps, renaissance thinkers like Descartes, Bacon, or Newton. Or maybe even more modern philosophers like Kant, Voltaire, or Nietzsche. How many of us think of Gautama Buddha, Confucius, Lao Zi, or Bodhidharma? We should. It turns out that eastern philosophical concepts have stood the test of time.

After centuries of highly deterministic physics, the 20th century produced a radical departure. Quantum Mechanics taught that nothing was really deterministic, but rather, probabilistic. Particles of matter were not necessarily solid – in fact, depending on how you looked at them or measured them, they might even be waves, like radio waves. There is an obvious similarity between this dual (wave/particle) nature of subatomic matter and the ancient Chinese duality concepts of Yin and Yang, which taught that all things consist of two opposite but complementary forces, which can transform into each other. In addition, physicists strove to develop unified field theories, thinking that all universal forces were actually different manifestations of the same underlying force. Unity or "oneness" is a cornerstone of Hinduism, Taoism, and Buddhism, with the concept of Dharmakaya being equivalent to the unity of the laws of physics. The ancient Chinese medical practice of acupuncture, once labeled as quackery by skeptics, is now an accepted form of treatment in the US. According to various national surveys, usage of alternative medicine increased 45% between 1990 and 1997. Most insurance companies cover several forms of alternative therapies, including massage, homeopathy, meditation, and applied kinesiology, many of which have their roots in Eastern medicinal practices. Many American hospitals are now embracing the Japanese hands-on practice of Reiki as an effective pre- and post-operative treatment. Reiki involves concepts of universal energies, intelligent energy, charkas, and auras, all of which are quite foreign to western scientific beliefs.

Although Frijof Capra popularized the synthesis of modern physics concepts with Eastern philosophies in his book "The Tao of Physics", many of the top physicists of the 20th century had already drawn parallels. A couple examples:

"The great scientific contribution in theoretical physics that has come from Japan since the last war may be an indication of a certain relationship between philosophical ideas in the tradition of the Far East and the philosophical substance of quantum theory."
- Werner Heisenberg

"For a parallel to the lesson of atomic theory...[we must turn] to those kinds of epistemological problems with which already thinkers like the Buddha and Lao Tzu have been confronted, when trying to harmonize our position as spectators and actors in the great drama of existence."
- Neils Bohr

Food for thought…

What interests me most about the Eastern philosophies are two things. One is the concept of enlightenment. Although it has Western analogs such as Christian spiritual rebirth, it is much more of an Eastern idea, and very relevant to our topic of alternate realities, as will become evident in that chapter. I believe that enlightenment, religious ecstasy, psychedelic experiences, shamanic rituals, and savantism are all examples of the glimpse that humans can get into a truer reality. The other important point about Eastern philosophy is simply the manner in which it inspires open-mindedness. Largely separated for millennia by geography and cultural introversion, some eastern and western philosophies can be radically different. And it is critical for anyone who seeks the truth to be able to open his or her mind to alternative viewpoints.

> Zen master steps up to the hot dog cart and says: "Make me one with everything."
>
> The hot dog vendor fixes a hot dog and hands it to the Zen master, who pays with a $20 bill. The hot dog vendor puts the bill in the cash drawer and closes the drawer.
>
> "Where's my change?" asks the Zen master. The hot dog vendor responds: "Change must come from within."
>
> - Common Internet joke, source unknown

Tailgating with Jesus

Life After Death. Is there or isn't there? That's what it's really all about, isn't it? Tightly tied to the concept of the soul, belief in an afterlife is a central part of many world religions and belief systems. However, there are differences. The monotheistic religions (Christianity, Judaism, and Islam) all teach that the soul goes to a heaven (reward) or hell (punishment) for eternity, based on your actions in your life. This means that life is a "one shot deal." Buddhists and Hindus believe in a more cyclical model – one that teaches that reincarnation occurs freely between humans, animals, and spiritual beings. Karma is the sum total of experience in all lives and in various ways helps to determine your next life. Each incarnation is a chance to develop your soul and incarnations occur until one has reached the nirvana state of liberation. It is interesting that the son of a Kentucky farmer named Edgar Cayce came up with the same beliefs with no apparent training in eastern religions, but rather, by slipping into a trance and communicating with so-called spirit entities. Psychologists such as Brian Weiss, Bruce Goldberg, and Erik Fisher have also stumbled upon the same theories while treating patients who "regressed" to previous lives or to the state in between lives. These patients supposedly also had no familiarity with these concepts. So, it seems that there is a confluence of ancient and modern thought from a wide variety of cultures through the world and throughout time. The key points of this collective belief system are:

- *There is a soul and an afterlife.*

- *When you die, you meet with "spirit guides" in the "astral plane" who help you design your next life, the objective being to improve the universal qualities of your soul.*

- *Gender may be swapped from life to life.*

- *The people who play significant roles in your various lives tend to be your soul mates, those who travel from life to life with you; e.g. in this life you are female and have a husband, who may have been your mother or a teacher in a past life, or your twin brother in a future life.*

- *There are multiple levels to the astral planes. In these realms, there is no time. All happens at the same time. Future lives, past lives, are all simultaneous in the spirit realm. Time is a physical construct.*

- *Souls enjoy occupying a body because only then can they have sensory experiences.*

- *The cycle repeats until you achieve spiritual perfection, at which point you may be a spirit guide or become one with the universal spirit, although admittedly this seems to conflict with the idea of timelessness.*

We will later see that there is even a confluence of beliefs between this new age philosophy and some theories of cosmology and directions of technology.

Again, it all comes together in Chapter 7.

The Quantum Mechanical World – Entanglement, Teleportation, and Foam

Background and Walking Through Doors

Quantum Mechanics was one of the two major revolutions (the other being Einstein's relativity) of 20th century physics. It evolved out of the need to explain theoretical anomalies in the behavior of the then newly discovered structure of atoms. Specifically, prior laws of physics can't account for the stability of an atom, which, if left to Newtonian physics, would annihilate itself as negatively charged electrons spiral into the positively charged nucleus of the atom. In addition, experimental anomalies such as the apparent duality of the nature of light were also incorporated into the quantum mechanical theory. Light appeared to act like a wave in the famous double slit experiments, but acted like a particle (or a quantum of energy) in photoelectric experiments. According to QM, light is simultaneously both a particle and a wave, as are other subatomic particles. In fact, depending on the type of measurement technique that you use, one of a particle's distinct personalities emerge. QM explains this by treating all particles as a wave function, which just means that instead of being a rigid fixed object at a specific location, a particle is really just a function of probabilities of being at various positions. And, only when an actual measurement is made, does the wave function "collapse" into an absolute position. While this might sound like an awful lot of hand waving, and one is tempted to ascribe such behavior to "hidden variables," it really doesn't matter, since experimental results are very adequately explained by the model. Figure 2-1 shows how an electron, in Newtonian mechanics, can be stuck on one side of an impenetrable barrier. In QM, however, its wave function can be partly on one side of a barrier and partly on the other side at the same time, which allows for the possibility of "tunneling," a common effect in semiconductors. In fact, were it not for the wave function nature of QM, transistors, and therefore cell phones, computers, satellites, and all other sorts of modern technologies would not even exist!

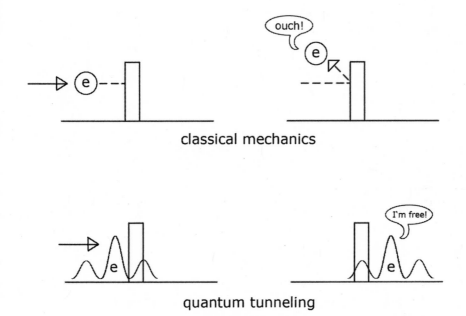

classical mechanics

quantum tunneling

Figure 2-1

Interestingly, this theory does not only apply to subatomic particles, but also to macroscopic objects like me, you, and Donald Trump's hair. Since our bodies are composed of particles, each of which are just wave functions, your body is simply the superposition of these zillions of wave functions, thereby creating its own "macroscopic" wave function. Theoretically, for this reason, you have a finite probability of passing through a wooden door, much like the electron tunneling effect. But, don't try it. Because, when you sum up all of your constituent particles' wave functions, there is a mathematical tendency for the probabilities of large-scale anomalous quantum effects to be extremely small. It is analogous to flipping pennies. The odds that a single penny comes up heads (electron passes through the barrier) is 50-50, but the odds that 1000 pennies all come up heads (you pass through the door) is 2^{1000} (equivalent to a 1 followed by 301 zeros, an impossible to imagine large number) to 1. And you have a helluva lot more than 1000 subatomic particles in your body.

The Observer and Dead-Alive Cats

As alluded to in the last section, the observer is crucial to the functioning of quantum mechanical systems. It is the classic "if a tree falls in the woods, does anyone hear it" situation. In theory, the wave function doesn't collapse until it is observed. One can imagine all kinds of strange scenarios that this gives rise to, and can actually construct an experiment where odd QM effects appear on a macroscopic level. Dozens of books have been written about the famous paradox called "Schrodinger's Cat", which goes something like this: A radioactive atom is placed in a closed box with a Geiger counter, a cyanide capsule, a tiny hammer, and Schrodinger's poor cat (I really hope nobody ever conducted this experiment). The hammer is configured to fall on the capsule when the radioactive atom decays and sets off the Geiger counter. And then, of course, the cat would die. The radioactive atom could decay at any time, depending on its half-life property, but such an event is purely non-deterministic, aka probabilistic. As a result, as long as the box is closed and no attempt has been made to determine the state of the cat, the cat is neither alive nor dead – it is, rather, in a state of alive-dead, which is just a wave function of probabilities that changes as time goes on. Only when the box is opened, is the cat actually alive or dead. When you're done scratching your head on that one, you're ready for our foamy universe…

A Discrete World

As we look around at things, we get the illusion that space is continuous – that, no matter how close together two points are, there are always points between them.

As a thought experiment, imagine an infinitesimally small point near you that we will arbitrarily call Point A and assign it a position = 0. Imagine a second infinitesimally small point called Point B that is 1 meter away from Point A. So, from the perspective of Point A, Point B is at position 1. Now imagine a third infinitesimally small object that is somewhere in between Point A and Point B. Let's try to pinpoint the exact position of the object (see Figure 2-2). Let's say that we have a crude measurement tool called a meter stick, which is 1 meter long and has 10 equally spaced lines on it (so each line is .1 meter apart from the next). Using that tool, let us further imagine that we determine the position of the object to be somewhere between .3 and .4 meters away from Point A. We can't tell more about the position of the object with such a crude device, but we have determined its position to an accuracy of .1 meter.

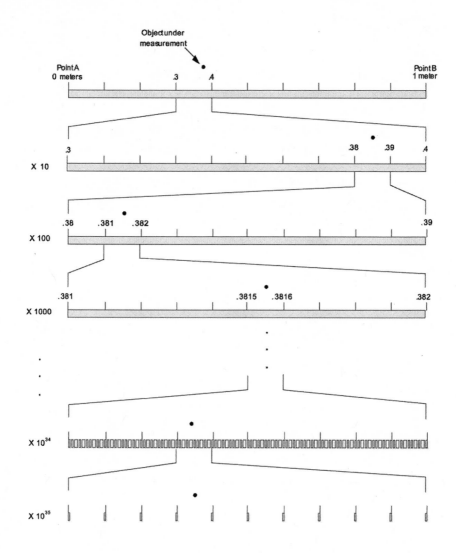

Figure 2-2

However, let say that we take another measurement tool that is 10 times finer, and therefore has lines on it that are separated by .01 meters. We use that device to determine that the position of the object is somewhere between .38 and .39 meters from Point A. If we were to take still another measurement with a device even 10 times finer, we might find the position of the object to be between .381 and

.382 meters and we can now say that we have determined the position of the object to an accuracy of .001 meters.

We can continue this exercise with progressively finer measurement tools, each step using a tool that is 10 times finer than in the previous step. In a continuous world, we will always find that the object is somewhere between the lines on the measurement stick, no matter how fine they are. First, between .3815 and .3816 meters, then between .38150 and .38151 meters, and so on. Further, we can move the object a little bit at each scale such that it changes position but still stays between the lines on the measurement stick. Ultimately, after 35 iterations of this process, we try to measure the position of the object to an accuracy of 10^{-35} meters.

Then, something really strange happens. We find that the object no longer moves continuously, but moves only in discrete jumps of 1.6 x 10^{-35} meters, also known as the Planck length. In fact, not only is it impossible to position the object in between two Planck lengths, nothing even exists there. In fact, space does not even exist between two adjacent points separated by the Planck length. It is sort of analogous to your TV or computer screen. From a distance, you see a nice continuous image. But, when you get close up, you see that the image is nothing but a bunch of dots at discrete positions on the screen and there is actually no part of the image in between two adjacent dots. We therefore say that rather than being continuous, space is discrete, granular, or *quantized*. At this point, our object under measurement can only be exactly at one of those positions, as shown in the bottom of Figure 2-2.

If the TV screen is 18 inches high and the TV is operating in a high definition mode of 1080 lines per screen, then we can say that the vertical resolution or granularity of the TV screen is 1080 lines/18 inches or 60 dots per inch (the horizontal resolution may be similar or slightly different). Compare this to space, which has a resolution or granularity of 1/Planck length or 6 x 10^{35} dots/meter.

Stranger still, it is theoretically impossible to measure something to the accuracy of the Planck length. The very act of attempting to make such a fine measurement invariably causes the object to move, making the measurement indeterminate. It is impossible therefore to simultaneously measure a position of an object and the speed of an object. The more closely you narrow the position, the more information you lose about its speed (this effect will not be lost on photographers who are well aware of the tradeoff between capturing position (clarity) and motion (blurriness) on film). This effect is known as the Heisenberg Uncertainty Principle and is also responsible for some reprehensible physics jokes…

> Heisenberg is out for a drive when he's stopped by a traffic cop.
> The cop says, "Do you know how fast you were going?"
> Heisenberg says, "No, but I know where I am."
> - Common Internet joke, source unknown

Back to our story, the Planck length is where the non-QM world really breaks down. The Planck length, again, is approximately 1.6 x 10^{-35} meters. The Planck time, or the time it takes an object traveling at the speed of light to cross the distance of the Planck length, is about 10^{-43} seconds. It turns out that time, too, is not a continuous property. It is impossible to measure a duration in time to an accuracy greater than the Planck time, or 10^{-43} seconds. So, time is also quantized and moves discretely. This is a very bizarre and counter-intuitive property when you think about it. Subatomic particles, at some position and time (again, which can not be accurately determined), will suddenly disappear, and then reappear a Planck time later at some integral number of Planck lengths away from its last position. Where was it in between the two Planck times? Nowhere, because time was not defined there. How did it get between the two positions? It simply jumped there. This is a somewhat simplified view of QM, but it illustrates an important point – the quantized nature of space-time.

Entanglement and Action at a Distance

Quantum entanglement is a curious property of QM that occurs in certain circumstances when multiple particles physically interact due to the forces between them. Such "entangled" particles thereafter exhibit states and properties (e.g. spin) that are correlated. For example, measuring the state of spin of one entangled particle will cause the spin of the other entangled particle to instantly become known. These particles can be separated by some distance and still remain "coherent." One might expect that the entangled particles in reality share some sort of hidden variable that determines their behavior, but recent experiments have proven this not to be the case. Einstein, bothered by the indeterminism of this effect, once called it "spooky action at a distance."

In the early 1980's, French physicist Alain Aspect conducted a ground breaking experiment that proved the existence of this effect over large distances. Effectively, one entangled particle can be forced to a particular state, resulting in the remote particle being forced into a correlated state at a speed much faster than the speed of light (were there some unknown form of communication between the two). So, either Einstein's theory of relativity needs modification or there is no communication between these particles and they are somehow deeply interconnected in a way that science does not yet understand.

Furthermore, entanglement is not limited to isolated subatomic particles – groups of particles, molecules, and nanostructures can also be entangled according to experimental results by Victor S. Batista of Yale University. If nanostructures, why not macrostructures, like you and I? Indeed, there is a growing school of thought that everything in the universe in interconnected on a fundamental level (there will be much more about this later.)

Finally, a recent entanglement experiment conducted by physicists Markus Aspelmeyer and Anton Zeilinger demonstrated that quantum measurements "do not fit with the idea of an objective reality." It appears that, not unlike the famous "tree falling in the woods" paradigm, reality may not even exist unless observed or measured.[5]

Teleportation

> "Beam me up, Scotty"
> - James T. Kirk, on several episodes of "Star Trek"

It also turns out that it is possible to transport the full state of an unknown particle to a remote location without providing a physical channel for that particle to travel through. In effect, this is like sending a perfect facsimile. Many experiments have now been done to prove this effect. The basic principle is to start with 2 entangled particles and separate them. Then, a third particle (the one whose state will be transported) is brought into contact with one of the two entangled particles. Its state is immediately transferred to the remote entangled particle and the original particle's state is destroyed. Theoretically, the teleportation occurs at instantaneous speed, although, in order for the measurement of the new state to occur, some information has to be sent over standard channels, thereby retaining the Einsteinian law that says that information transfer cannot exceed the speed of light. Progressive experiments have demonstrated the ability to teleport larger and larger objects. In 2004, independent teams from the University of Innsbruck and the US National Institute of Standards and Technology each successfully teleported atoms. Later that year, researchers from the University of Vienna and the Austrian Academy of Science teleported photons across the Danube River.[6] It seems that it is only a matter of time before more macroscopic objects (e.g. your toothbrush) can be teleported over arbitrarily long distances.

This isn't exactly like the teleportation of Star Trek fame. The underlying assumption there was that the actual object was getting teleported. In quantum teleportation, the original object is destroyed and an exact duplicate created at the destination. For those of us who believe that all we are is a pile of subatomic particles, this is good news in that it may allow for speed of light travel to Middletown, China, Mars, Alpha Centauri and beyond. For the rest of us, who believe that we are something more (have a soul, for example), we will probably not opt for this method of transportation until it can be definitively determined that we are not killing people and replacing them with soulless robots many miles away.

The Many Worlds Theory

The idea of the collapsing of a wave function upon observation as a means to explain some of the deterministic paradoxes of quantum mechanics is referred to as the Copenhagen interpretation of quantum mechanics. The name came from the fact that Niels Bohr and Werner Heisenberg worked together in Copenhagen in the 1920's to develop the theory. However, in the 1950's, physicist Hugh Everett developed a radically different interpretation of quantum mechanics that completely avoids the messiness of wave function collapse and replaces it instead with the messiness of parallel universes. In his theory, every time that a probabilistic decision is made at the quantum level (does the photon go through this slit or that slit, or does the radioactive particle decay, killing Schrodinger's cat?) what actually happens is that the universe splits in 2. In one universe, the particle doesn't decay and the cat stays alive. In the other universe, the particle decays and the cat dies. The reason that the cat is alive when you open the box is because we happen to live in the universe in which the cat is alive. Since probabilistic decisions are made at the quantum level zillions of times per second, the Everett interpretation of quantum mechanics says that somewhere there are universes where you are a movie star, universes where you don't exist, universes where you read everything on this page until this exact word and then put down the book forever, universes with no life, and pretty much every other universe that you can possibly imagine. Cosmologist Max Tegmark estimates that there should be $10^{10^{118}}$ total universes, which is an impossible to imagine number.[7] Perhaps even more strange, it turns out that most physicists actually believe this! In 1995, political scientist L. David Raub conducted a poll of 72 of the "leading cosmologists and other quantum field theorists", and found that 58% believed that the Many Worlds Interpretation (MWI) was true, including Stephen Hawking and Nobel Laureates Murray Gell-Mann and Richard Feynman. Another 13% believed that it was possible but that they weren't yet convinced.[8] So where are these universes anyway and can we jump from one to the other? As you might expect, they are not nearby, or even part of our normal 3-dimensional space, but rather exist in an abstract infinite-dimensional space called the Hilbert Space. And no, we can't get there from here, so there goes your bright idea on winning the lottery. We'll come back to this theory in a bit, but first a little about quantum foam.

Quantum Foam and the Birth of the Universe

The concept of quantum foam was developed by physicist John Wheeler in the 1950s. The idea is that, not only is space and time discrete at the Planck lengths and times, but because of the Heisenberg Uncertainty Principle, particles actually pop into and out of existence at Planck time intervals. There is even evidence for this effect in the form of the Casimir effect, which is observed when two metal plates in a vacuum are more attracted to each other as they get closer together. This is due to the fact that only vacuum fluctuations of a wavelength smaller than the distance between the plates should be present between them. So, given that quantum fluctuations are of varying wavelengths, the closer the plates are, the lower the density of allowable fluctuations, or, the less foam there is. This effect was predicted in 1948 by Dutch physicist Hendrik B. G. Casimir, and measured in 1997 by Steve K. Lamoreaux of Los Alamos National Laboratory.[9]

All of this activity occurring so frequently at the Planck level must certainly carry quite a bit of energy, since every particle has mass energy for the duration of its lifetime. Renowned physicists Richard Feynman and John Wheeler once estimated that the energy contained in the vacuum of a light bulb would be sufficient to boil all of the world's oceans.[10] Also know as "zero point energy" because it exists at absolute zero temperature, the idea has spawned a new generation of inventors attempting to tap into this energy and provide the world with a limitless free source of energy.

> "Nature abhors a vacuum."
> - Benedict Spinoza

To the point of our discussion, however, it has been shown by Wheeler, Feynman, and others that it is theoretically possible for a quantum fluctuation to initiate the conditions that create an entire universe. The upcoming section on cosmological theories explores these ideas further as they are important to the thesis of this book, being simultaneously competitive theories to the origin of the universe as well as complementary theories, as we shall see.

Multiple Dimensions and Flatlanders

Hey, what's a science fiction topic doing in the middle of serious scientific discussion? Answer: This is not your father's science.

"Flatland: A Romance of Many Dimensions" was a book written in 1880 by Edwin A. Abbott. In it, he describes a two-dimensional world, called Flatland, inhabited by two-dimensional creatures, all blissfully unaware that their world is really part of a three-dimensional one. Figures 3-3 through 3-7 demonstrate how this is possible. Fred and Barney live in their 2D world and are completely unaware of the sphere hovering in 3D space above their world, but slowly descending through it. (Figure 2-3)

Figure 2-3

As the sphere descends through flatland, all Fred and Barney see is a spot on the ground that grows in circumference and then shrinks and disappears.

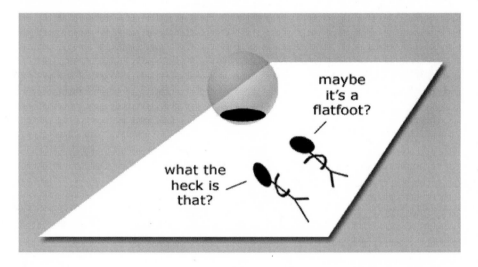

Figure 2-4

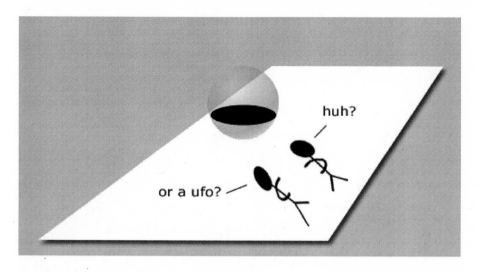

Figure 2-5

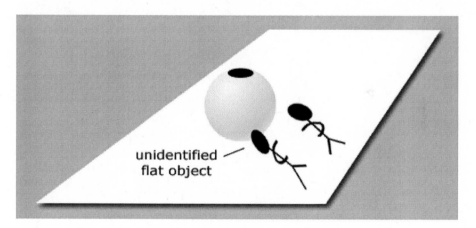

Figure 2-6

Figure 2-7

Just as the flatlanders can be unaware of a larger dimensional universe around them, so might we be unaware of a larger dimensional universe. Neither physics nor mathematics precludes such possibilities. From the example above, one can even see how a higher dimensional world might manifest itself in ours, even if only for a moment. In fact, there are sound theories that the effects of the higher dimensions can impact the physics of our 3D world without actually intersecting it (see "Dark Matter" and "Brane Theory" below).

Finally, the concept of higher dimensions plays an important role in many areas that are critical to the premise of this book, including anomalous events, the "parallel universes" cosmological theories, and string theory, one of the leading theories of the nature of matter and energy.

String Theory and M-theory

"Until like what, 50 years ago, you all thought the atom was the smallest thing, until you split it open, and this like, whole mess of crap came out."
- Phoebe Buffet, character on "Friends", in a dialog with scientist friend (from "The One Where Heckles Dies" (1995))

String theory is the latest in the progression of physicists' ongoing search for the ultimate building blocks of matter. This Russian doll approach to physics is shown in Figure 2-8 below. Atoms, long thought to be the basic constituents of matter, were shown to consist of the three basic subatomic particles (electrons, protons, and neutrons) in the early 1900s. Protons and neutrons, in turn, were shown to be composed of quarks in the early 1960s. There are six flavors of quarks, with such strange names as up, down, bottom, top, charm, and, of course, strange. Other quark-based particles include mesons, and a set of hypothetical exotic particles. Electrons are not composed of quarks but belong to a family of particles called leptons, which also include muons, tauons, and neutrinos.

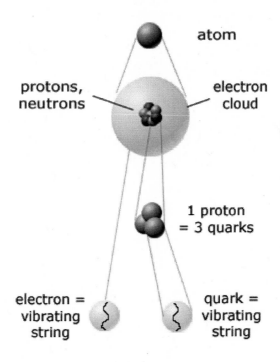

Figure 2-8

There are many other additional particles discovered over the years, including those that carry the fundamental forces (gauge bosons), and anti-particles for each particle. In total, the subatomic particle picture has gotten quite confusing and complex, with no apparent consistency of particle properties like spin, charge, and mass.

String theory essentially says that the ultimate building blocks of matter are tiny vibrating strings. These strings are all identical, which makes the theory very elegant. They manifest themselves as different particles by vibrating at different rates and modes, much like a violin string. Previously, Quantum Mechanics and the theory of gravity collided at Planck distances because "grand unified theories" proposed that particles were an infinitesimally small point (zero dimensional). Because strings are believed to have an actual dimension (although only 1), they allow a solution to Quantum Gravity.[11] Due to these properties, the theory is thought of as a possible TOE, or Theory of Everything. The math all seemed to work out and known particles were incorporated neatly into the theory. So far, so good.

Unfortunately, in order for the physics to work, early string theories (yes, there are several) worked only in 26 dimensions. Yes, you read that right. While we live in a world traditionally considered to have 4 dimensions (3 spatial ones and one temporal one (time)), string theory says that we really live in a world with 26 dimensions – 25 spatial ones plus time. Subsequent string theories improved on the original by incorporating other particles and only requiring 10 dimensions, due to the magic of something called supersymmetry. Hence, this was called Superstring theory. Then, in the 1990's, physicist Edward Witten found that all of the various string theories were really limits of an all-encompassing 11-dimensional theory dubbed M-Theory, which pretty much brings us up to date.

So, if we are to believe the brightest minds in physics, where are the other 7 dimensions? Do we live in flatland? What will this do to property values?

If there are additional unseen dimensions, they could exist in two different forms:

1. Compactified Dimensions – the additional dimensions could be sort of curled up into a space so small that we don't notice them. For example, Figure 2-9 shows how 3-dimensional space could actually be an approximation to 4-dimensional space. In 3D space, point A is identified by its position in 3 different dimensions: width (x axis), height (y axis), and depth (z axis). Arbitrarily, we can define an origin point and say that A is 3 over, 2 up, and 1 deep from the origin. However, an incredibly magnified view of space may show a curled up little ring at every 3D position. Point A could actually be anywhere on that ring at position {x=3, y=2, z=1}. For example, let's say we identify its position on a ring by the angular distance around the ring – in this case, 150°. So, in 4-dimensional space, point A would be at {150°,3,2,1} If the rings are tiny enough, our equipment

could never identify the difference between the various positions on the ring, and so we would never be aware of the 4th spatial dimension. We can easily extend this idea to other dimensional levels. Instead of the ring at each 3D point, for example, a sphere at each point would give us 6-dimensional space. And so on.

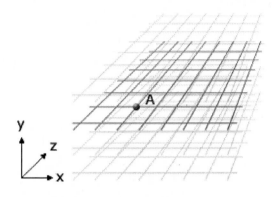

3D Space: Point A = {3,2,1}

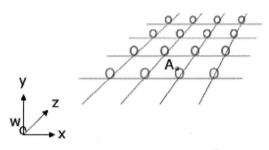

4D Space: Point A = {150°,3,2,1}

Figure 2-9

2. D-Branes – sort of the opposite of the compactified dimensions, D-Branes (the D comes from physicist Johann Dirichlet, who developed the math behind the concept) are self contained spaces of a given

number of dimensions; for example, a D3-brane is a 3D world where the position of any point in the world can be identified by 3 numbers, as shown in the 3D space in Figure 2-9. Figure 2-10 shows 2 D3-branes separated slightly in space. In reality, try to imagine a completely different space, identified by, say, color, or some other attribute. Notice that you can't get from a point on one D3-brane to a point on another D3-brane. This is completely analogous to the flatlanders who can't move off of their 2D world and explore the sphere. Effectively, figure 2-10 portrays a 4-dimensional space. Again, we can easily extend this idea to other dimensional levels.

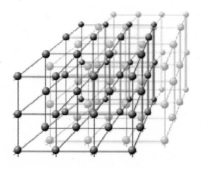

Figure 2-10 – 2 D3-branes

So perhaps, the 10 spatial dimensions of M-Theory are a combination of compactified dimensions and the "full sized" dimensions in Brane-world. These ideas are not only important in comprehending string theory, or the study of the miniscule, but they are also important in comprehending modern theories of cosmology, or the study of the huge, as we are about to see.

Food for thought…

Theories on the Origin of the Universe

Conventional Views

Big Bang

Without delving further into the past beyond the beginning of the 20th century, the theoretical underpinnings of modern cosmology are found in the so-called "Big Bang" theory. The theory has its roots in the 1920's and 1930's when Edwin Hubble noticed that spectral lines of distant galaxies were shifted toward the red end of the visible light spectrum (similar in effect to the Doppler effect of a train whistle changing in tone as it moves away from the observer) and that the further away these galaxies appeared to be, the stronger the red shift, and therefore, the faster they were receding. It seemed as if all galaxies were receding from each other, much like dots on an expanding balloon or raisins in an expanding loaf of bread, to use a couple popular analogies. If one were to assume that the universe had a finite origin and that this expansion began at that origin, then one could project the expansion backward to a point in time when the universe was incredibly dense and hot. In fact, this is where cosmology and relativity meets quantum mechanics and known laws of physics were invoked to predict what must have happened in the first fractions of seconds of the birth of the universe. Physicists speak of the origin of the big bang possibly being a "singularity" – a point of an infinite energy density and gravity – a real theoretical headache, since, assuming that this theory is sound, prior to the Planck time, our known laws of physics fall apart. But setting this little problem aside for a moment, much of the rest of the theory has not only a theoretical basis, but also supporting experimental evidence (see the demise of the Steady State theory below). The expansion rate suggests an origin of the universe 13.7 billion years ago, give or take. The expansion is not really an expansion of stars and galaxies, but rather, an actual expansion of space itself.

Steady State

A competitor to the big bang theory arrived on the scene in the 1940's courtesy of astronomers Fred Hoyle, Thomas Gold, and others. Called the Steady State theory, it proposed that while the universe is actually expanding, matter is continuously being created in such a way that the density and overall cosmic appearance does not change over time. It precluded the need for the universe to have a beginning, and hence the messy singularity. One potential and obvious knock on this theory was its need for matter to be created out of nothing. Then again, the big bang theory requires the same thing on a much larger scale, so it doesn't fare any better on that account. And recall that quantum physics allows pairs of particles to be created from nothing. However, the Steady State theory's prediction that the structure of the universe is unchanging over time was its downfall. The discovery of quasars, extremely distant and intensely energetic objects showed that the universe was very different in its remote past. And the nail in the Steady State coffin was the Big Bang theory's early prediction of cosmic background radiation from the "bang" itself, and the ultimate observation and measurement of cosmic background radiation in 1964 that matched the theory very well.

Problems with the Big Bang Theory

One of the problems with the original Big Bang theory had to do with something called the flatness of the universe. If the universe has enough matter in it (closed universe), the gravity of that matter will cause the expanding universe to slow down and ultimately collapse on itself, creating what is sometimes referred to as the Big Crunch (John Wheeler once proposed the possibility that a closed universe may repeat a cycle of bangs and crunches in a scenario he called the oscillatory universe). If the universe doesn't have enough matter in it (open universe), the universe would fly apart from the impulse of the Big Bang. Just the right amount of matter (flat universe) and the universe would be continuously expanding and never quite reversing direction.

Food for thought...

The average mass density of the universe will also shape the universe at large scales. We don't notice the spherical nature of the earth because we observe the earth at small scales. For example, if we were to measure out a square on the surface of the earth that is 1 meter by 1 meter, we can be sure that the area of the square is 1 square meter, the product of the two adjacent lines. A small equilateral triangle will have angles of approximately 60° each. However, as the distances being measured become large compared to the size of the earth, then flat geometrical formulas no longer hold. Areas are larger that the product of the distances of the two adjacent arcs (the nearest equivalent to a straight line). Angles on equilateral triangles exceed 60°. Ultimately, the area of the earth bordered by two arcs that are each ¼ the distance around the globe exceed the product of the two arcs by more than a factor of 5. And the angles of the maximum sized equilateral triangle drawn on the surface of the earth are 180° rather than 60°. The same rules apply to the universe. The gravity of too much matter can cause the shape of the universe to be bent into a sphere (closed universe), where parallel lines ultimately meet and it is impossible to see past a certain point. Alternately, a universe without enough matter (open universe) will have a hyperbolic geometrical shape (which looks like a saddle), where parallel lines diverge.

All currently observable evidence shows that the universe is just right and very flat. Kind of like a cosmic Goldilocks. The problem is that, for it to be flat today, it had to have exactly the right amount of matter in the first few seconds of the big bang. In fact, it has been calculated that the mass density of the universe at one second after the big bang had to be so perfectly tuned that any deviation of .0000000000001 % would have either caused the universe to have collapsed by now or expanded so quickly that galaxies, stars, and life could never have formed.[12]

48

When astronomers look into space, with telescopes or radio telescopes, in a sense, they are looking back in time. When you look at the sun, you are really seeing the sun as it was 8 minutes ago, because it takes that long for the sun's light to reach the earth. When you look at the Andromeda galaxy, you are looking at the light emitted from that galaxy 2.2 million years ago. Quasars are seen as they were billions of years ago. In 1964, cosmic microwave background (CMB) radiation was discovered by Arno Penzias and Robert Woodrow Wilson upon peering deep into space. Confirming a prediction of the Big Bang theory, it can be thought of as the first emitted radiation from the early universe, occurring about 300,000 years after the big bang. No matter what direction you look in the sky, you will see this radiation and it is uniform in its intensity to 1 part in 100,000 across the entire sky. Unfortunately for the original Big Bang theory, while the discovery of CMB helped confirm the Big Bang theory, its amazing uniformity doesn't make sense in the science of the theory.

Other problems with the Big Bang also surfaced over the years. A relatively new theory, however, modified the Big Bang and offered a theory that explained the anomalies mentioned above. That theory, developed by Alan Guth in 1981, is called the Inflationary theory.

Inflationary Big Bang

The problems mentioned with the original Big Bang theory all go away with Alan Guth's Inflationary Big Bang theory, which proposes that about 10^{-35} seconds after the big bang, the universe underwent a 10^{-32} second period of exponential expansion, where its size increased by a factor of 10^{50}.

Huh?

Fortunately, there is some real science behind this, which involves quantum mechanics and phase transitions at extremely high

Food for thought…

temperatures or energies. The theory not only explains much of what has been observed by galactic surveys and analyses of cosmic background radiation, it also provides an explanation for what the "bang" was after the initial disturbance that initiated it. Essentially, the idea is that the universe at that time got itself into a peculiar state called a false vacuum, which is like a vacuum but with higher energy. Think of it like a roomful of set mousetraps, all precariously touching each other. It is stable in a perfect world (like a false vacuum), but only takes a small perturbation, like the wind blowing through the window, to move a trap that causes one to pop, and then the rest quickly follow suit. The state of the room after all of the mousetraps have popped is like the true vacuum. The period of mousetraps popping is like the inflationary period. Such a false vacuum may be a standard state in high-energy physics, such as would occur during the inception of the big bang. According to the theory, during the inflationary period, small quantum fluctuations became the graininess of the universe that ultimately led to the clumping of matter into galaxies rather than developing into just a huge sea of particles. The Inflationary Big Bang theory is the cosmological theory that perhaps has the highest level of general acceptance today.

The Dark Side – WIMPs, MACHOs, and THE FORCE

Astronomers who have studied the motion of galaxies and clusters of galaxies have noticed that such large astronomical objects rotate too fast for the amount of matter inferred by their size, distance, and luminosity. Further, in order for the universe to be flat, as it is observed, there must be much more matter than is currently visible. In fact, by some estimates, observable matter only accounts for less than 1% of the mass of the universe. The rest, therefore, must be dark – hence the name "dark matter." Many varieties of dark matter have been proposed, including exotic dark matter consisting of various high energy loose particles such as neutrinos and theoretical particles called WIMPs (weakly interacting massive particles). Also in the menu of candidates for dark matter are big chunky masses called MACHOs (massive compact halo objects - don't astronomers have a great sense of humor?), which include brown dwarfs, planets, or black holes. Certain studies of the structure of the early universe, however, have demonstrated that MACHOs can not account for more than a fraction of the total dark matter.

To complicate things further, recent comprehensive studies of the luminosities and red shifts of distant supernovae (massive stellar death explosions) have determined that the expansion of the universe is actually accelerating instead of slowing down. Several subsequent investigations of completely different phenomena corroborate this result. No amount of dark matter can explain this – it is almost as if something from the outside of the universe is pulling it apart. Or, some sort of all pervasive energy is generating a repulsive force, like negative gravity. Scientists have dubbed this force "dark energy."

There are a couple different explanations for dark energy. One is that the energy is inherent in the fabric of space. It turns out that Einstein had proposed a factor in his equations called the cosmological constant. For a period of time, it had been disregarded because the universe appeared to be expanding normally, but now this factor appears to fit in perfectly with the new observational evidence about the accelerated expansion of the universe. Also, recall our discussion on vacuum energy – a ubiquitous energy in the fabric of space. This has been proposed as the source of the dark energy. Unfortunately, the best estimates of the level of this vacuum energy are so huge that they are only off by a factor of 10^{120} (that's a 1 followed by 120 zeros) compared to what is needed to provide the 70% missing mass of the universe in the form of dark energy. If the vacuum energy was really this large, space would expand so rapidly that you wouldn't be able to see your hand in front of your face.[13] Theoreticians to the rescue! Maybe there is some heretofore-unknown factor or physical relationship in space that cancels out most of the vacuum energy effect. But the likelihood that the universal constants would be so finely tuned that they would cancel out 99.999... (115 more 9's) percent of the vacuum energy, leaving just an amount that is comparable to the total matter in the universe is staggeringly small. Another way to look at the problem is that billions of years ago at 10^{-35} seconds after the big bang, vacuum energy came into being but matter was 10^{100} times denser. So why would dark energy wait 10^{50} times its age and then overtake matter in its effect. As physics professors Jeremiah Ostriker and Paul Steinhardt put it "Is it not a coincidence that, just when thinking beings evolved, the universe suddenly shifted into overdrive?"[14] An alternative explanation for dark energy is something called quintessence, which is a proposed quantum field with low energy density and repulsive gravity. Unlike vacuum energy, quintessence is defined in such a way that it may evolve over time, keeping pace with matter density, thereby avoiding the perfectly tuned universe requirement mentioned above.

To summarize the various studies, astronomers more or less agree on the following makeup of the universe:

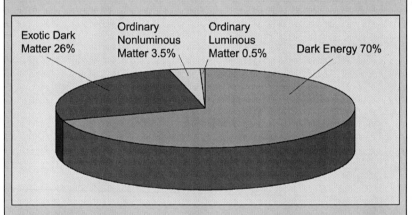

Exotic Dark Matter 26%
Ordinary Nonluminous Matter 3.5%
Ordinary Luminous Matter 0.5%
Dark Energy 70%

Interestingly, this picture of our reality is completely different than it was as recently as 1985. Not only the assumed constituents of the universe, but the entire future of the universe has radically changed, which makes one wonder what the future holds for us, and makes one question the scientific status quo at any point in time.

Alternative Scientific Views

Brane Cosmology, Ekpyrotic & Cyclic Universes

Brane cosmology is the theory that we live on the "wall" of a higher dimensional space, or brane. Superstring- or M-theory makes this possible. Interestingly, the idea may also provide a good explanation for dark matter. The higher dimensions that we live in, or possibly other nearby parallel branes, can theoretically exert an influence on our 3D space in the form of gravity. This may be the explanation for dark matter.[15] Originally, such theories were assumed to be untestable. However, a new generation of accelerators, such as the Cern's LHC (Large Hadron Collider), promise to validate or invalidate such theories within a few years of this writing.

Physicists Justin Khoury, Burt A. Ovrut, Paul J. Steinhardt and Neil Turok have proposed a scenario whereby the big bang was the result of the collision of 2 D4-branes. Prior to the collision, the universe was empty and contracting and the collision began a period of expansion. In fact, Steinhardt and Turok later extended the theory to include the concept of a continuously cycling universe. After the expansion period, dark matter, or the force between the branes, pulls the branes together in a contracting period, which results in the collision of the branes in a "Big Crunch" and the cycle repeats ad infinitum (note: this is similar in concept to John Wheeler's oscillatory universe, mentioned previously). The theory solves some of the same problems as does the inflationary theory and is compatible with M-theory. Clearly a very different theory than the standard inflationary big bang model, it does nonetheless have its adherents in the scientific community.

Parallel Universes, Metaverses, Multiverses, and Songs without Verses

We used to be taught that the universe was everything there is. But, over the past few years, it is beginning to have a new meaning. The universe is now meant to be everything that we can possibly see or experience. Consider Figure 2-11. Here we have Joe Lunchbox happily living in his little universe. His astronomer buddies have used their most advanced equipment to peer into the deepest depths of space and have detected things a few billion light years away in all directions. There could be things beyond that "practical observational horizon", but we are limited by the state of the art of equipment in the year 2005. The letter "a" in Figure 2-11 denotes this observational horizon. There is another horizon beyond "a" which denotes the point at which it would be impossible to see beyond, due to the speed of light. The light from objects at that distance has been traveling toward us since the beginning of the big bang. This is our theoretical horizon, beyond which we can never see or detect anything no matter how advanced our equipment becomes. It should be noted, that this statement presumes that nothing travels faster than the speed of light and even if it did, we would not be able to detect it. Despite a century of hard evidence supporting Einstein's famous assumption regarding the limitations of the speed of light, there are a number of physicists who don't rule out the possibility that this barrier could someday be broken. But that's a topic for another book. Setting such arguments aside, "b" is our "theoretical observational horizon," also known as the Hubble Volume and is generally accepted to be about 42 billion light years in diameter. But that doesn't mean there's nothing beyond "b." In fact, the inflationary theory allows for quite a bit of the material from the big bang to exist beyond "b" because the inflationary period was superluminal. (We were just saying…?) So, "c" could actually denote everything that came from our big bang.

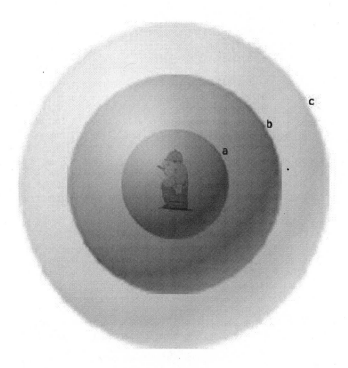

Figure 2-11

So what is the universe? "a", "b", or "c"? Semantics. It doesn't really matter. Look at Figure 2-12. What if there is another universe a few dozen billion light years down the road? If this scenario is possible (and there are a lot of physicists who believe that it is not only possible, but inevitable), then we need a new name for the space that the multiple universes inhabit. The accepted term for this is Multiverse.

Food for thought...

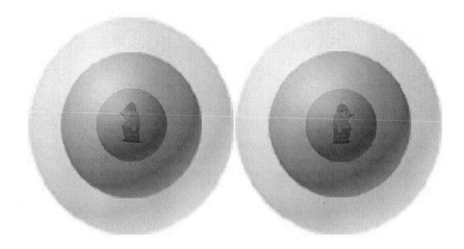

Figure 2-12

The concept of multiple or parallel universes actually has its roots in the Everett interpretation of quantum mechanics, as described in the section on quantum mechanics above. However, big thinkers in cosmology have extended the idea to encompass a variety of types of parallel universes.

Cosmologist Max Tegmark has described some real evidence for parallel universes as well as organized parallel universe theories. Specifically, he notes that recent studies on the distribution of galaxies and the uniformity of background radiation demonstrated that matter in the universe is uniform out to at least 10^{24} meters (roughly 1/400th of the Hubble volume). As a result, it is highly likely that beyond our Hubble lies more of the same. Instead of defining the universe as everything that shot out of the big bang (the "c" horizon, in our example above), he defines the universe as the Hubble volume, or "b." In that context, he identifies 4 levels of multiverse...

Level 1 – People always say that no two snowflakes are alike. However, since a snowflake is just a set of particles in a particular configuration, for a given number of particles (e.g. for a given size of a snowflake) there have to be a finite set of configurations of those particles. Therefore, if you look at enough snowflakes, you will eventually find a duplicate. So it is with ourselves, our planet, and even our Hubble volume. So, a Level 1 multiverse consists of a number of universes that are similar to ours in terms of physical laws, but differed only in terms of initial conditions. Think of them as separate volumes of matter within our big bang expansion bubble, but beyond our observational horizon. Figure 2-13 demonstrates the idea of multiple universes within a larger multiverse. Theoretically, if enough of them exist and if matter density remains constant, some of them will be similar. And since a Hubble volume can be defined by the entire states of the particles that make it up, there has to be a finite set of configurations of matter for any given Hubble volume. Therefore, eventually, you will come across another Hubble volume identical to ours. In fact, it can be estimated mathematically that, on the average, about $10^{10^{118}}$ meters away, there is an identical Hubble volume, e.g. our alter universe (and, of course, Bizarro Universe would have to be about the same distance.) If you want to find the nearest identical copy of you, statistically, it would about $10^{10^{28}}$ meters away. Theoretically, since a Level 1 multiverse is within the same inflation bubble, you could eventually find your twin, given enough time.

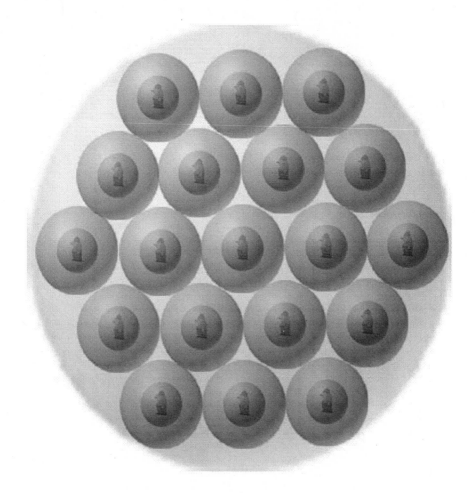

Figure 2-13 – Level 1 Multiverse

Level 2 – A Level 2 multiverse consists of all of the separate inflation bubbles after the big bang. Think of it as consisting of Level 1 multiverses that came from bubbles of matter which expanded independent of each other, much like bubbles in a boiling pot of water. Each bubble has its own Hubble volume and comes with not only its own unique initial conditions, but also its own values for dimensions, forces, particle properties, etc. Even in principle, one could never travel to another Level 1 multiverse because the space between the bubbles expands faster than one can travel. Since the evolution of galaxies and solar systems, let alone life, is heavily dependent on the parameters that define a particular inflation bubble, most of these multiverses would be dead, and hence the concept of a Hubble volume doesn't even make sense. See Figure 2-14.

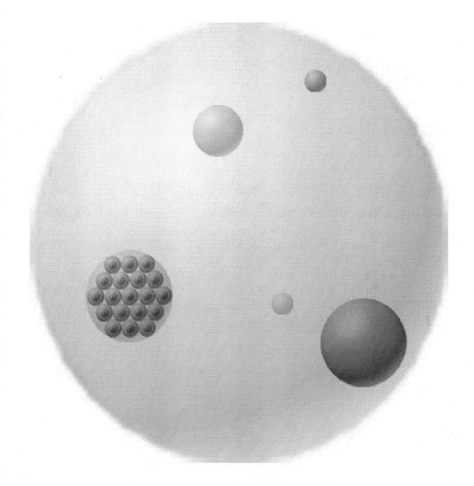

Figure 2-14 – Level 2 Multiverse

Level 3 – A Level 3 multiverse is the good old-fashioned quantum mechanical "many worlds" theory. Every possible configuration of a universe exists at once in Hilbert space, although it is not clear whether it is universes, Level 1 multiverses, or Level 2 multiverses that comprise the set of objects in this Level 3 multiverse. I can't even being to figure out how to draw this one, but Figure 2-15 is my best shot.

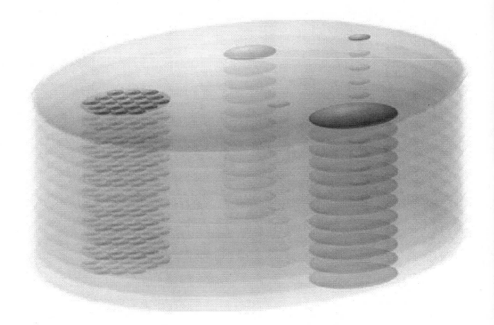

Figure 2-15 - Level 3 Multiverse

Level 4 – A Level 4 multiverse is the ultimate multiverse. Hilbert spaces, different big bangs, Level 1's, 2's, and 3's, alternate mathematical structures, alternate laws of physics, anything that can be.

Self-Reproducing Inflationary – Fractals Gone Wild

Stanford physicist Andre Linde noted that due to the theoretical behavior of quantum fields, the inflationary expansion was chaotic in the sense of proceeding at different rates in different regions. As a result, it was likely that the universe expands in a fractal manner, with bubbles of inflation sprouting other bubbles of inflation, each one being a new "big bang."[16] This theory actually has far reaching implications. If true, the universe, or multiverse, is essentially immortal, continuously evolving and growing as shown in Figure 2-

16. In fact, the question of a starting point to the multiverse is almost irrelevant, as it cannot be verified one way or the other due to the fact that our Hubble volume is just within our local bubble.

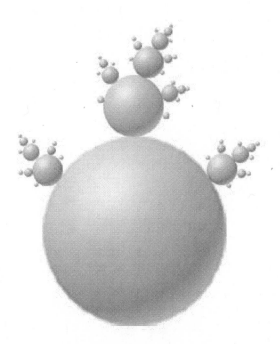

Figure 2-16 – Fractal inflationary multiverse

The Finely-tuned Universe, the Anthropic Principle, and Flexi-laws

Many scientists have noted the manner in which the physical constants of the universe are perfectly tuned for life and even for the formation of matter. We have previously mentioned a couple examples of this, including the way that the universal constants cancel out all of the vacuum energy to an amazing accuracy of 1 part in 10^{115}. In addition, cosmologist and philosopher Ervin Laszlo has identified several more[17]:

- A deviation in the expansion rate of the early universe of 1 part in a billion in either direction would have caused the universe to immediately collapse, or fly apart so fast that stars could never have formed.

- A tiny difference in the ratio of the electric field strength to gravitational field strength would have prevented any kinds of molecules to form.

- If the ratio of the mass of a proton to that of an electron was not precisely what it is, chemical reactions could not take place, rendering life impossible.

Additional examples of fine tuning include:

- The strength of the strong nuclear force could not have differed by more than 2% without either preventing hydrogen from being the only element in the universe, or from being too rare to allow the formation of stars.

- The number of electrons in the universe must equal the number of protons to an accuracy of 1 part in 10^{37} in order for gravity to work.

- A slight difference in the ratio of the number of photons in the universe to the number of baryons would preclude star formation.

- A small deviation in the value of the electromagnetic coupling constant would prevent molecular formation.

Creationists would say "Of course the universe is finely tuned. God created it that way." And they would sleep well at night. Scientists, however, have had to resort to a great deal more thought.

The Anthropic Principle, originally proposed in the 1970's by Brandon Carter, and then significantly developed by John D. Barrow and Frank J. Tipler in the 1980's, goes something like this: "Of course our universe is finely tuned. We wouldn't be here to observe it if it weren't." This idea is a perfect partner to the multiverse theories, for example. Zillions of universes can be formed via your favorite parallel universe theory, all with different physical constants and ratios leading nearly all of them to a matterless lifeless destiny. But, like that lucky guy who won the 200 million dollar lottery by picking the right 6 numbers, somewhere there is that one in a zillion universe that got all of the physical constants and ratios just right. And where else would we live?

And if that concept isn't mind-bending enough, there are always Flexi-laws, a fascinating theory that has evolved as an alternative to the anthropic principle in terms of explaining the finely-tuned universe, or "Goldilocks enigma." Originally proposed by physicist John Wheeler, the concept argues that physical laws are not immutable and may actually have been evolving ever since the big bang. Couple that with our old quantum mechanical friend, the Heisenberg Uncertainty Principle and you get Stephen Hawking's quantum cosmology, which asserts that the past (and therefore the evolution of our physical laws) is influenced by the present state of the universe. Wheeler suggests that "the existence of life and observers in the universe today can help bring about the very circumstances needed for life to emerge by reaching back to the past through acts of quantum observation."[18]

The Big Rip

As mentioned above, the expansion of the universe appears to be accelerating. While most scientists expect that acceleration to remain constant or even reduce over time, there really isn't enough data to predict. Another equally viable alternative is that the acceleration is actually getting stronger, perhaps due to the force of dark matter. If so, that force will ultimately overtake gravity to the point where every molecule in the universe will be ripped apart. Astronomer Robert Caldwell has developed this theory that he called "the big rip" and has projected that the earliest that this can take place would be 22 billion years from now. The good news is that it is a long way off.

Food for thought...

The bad news is that it's a fairly ugly end to the universe, with no good theory to explain what happens afterwards.[19]

Alternative Views – Non-scientific

In the Beginning...

Such a topic couldn't be considered complete, if it didn't at least mention a theory that has billions of advocates, namely creationism. What do various world religions have to say? It helps to understand the breakdown of world religions in terms of adherents. From adherents.com and the Encyclopedia Britannica are the following estimates:

- Christianity – 33% (2.1 billion adherents)
- Islam – 20% (1.3 billion adherents)
- Secular/Nonreligious/Atheistic – 15% (1.1 billion)
- Hinduism – 13% (900 million adherents)
- Primal-indigenous/African traditional – 6% (400 million adherents)
- Chinese traditional religion – 6% (394 million adherents)
- Buddhism – 6% (376 million adherents)
- Other organized religions – 1% (50 million adherents, including Sikhism, Judaism, Baha'ism, Confucianism, Jainism, Scientology, and Shintoism)

The secular/nonreligious/atheistic category probably believe more in the scientific theories that we've presented above, although there are also many people included in the ranks of "adherents" to an organized religion that also believe in such scientific stalwarts as evolution and the big bang theory. For example, while the 2005 Time Almanac reports that 77% of American adults consider themselves Christian, a 2005 Harris Poll (#52, July 6, 2005) shows that 46% believe that "Darwin's theory of evolution is proven by fossil discoveries." At the same time, there are a lot of fundamentalists who believe in a very literal interpretation of the bible. A November 1997 Gallup poll showed that 44% of Americans agreed with the statement "God created human beings pretty much in their present form at one time within the last 10,000 years or so." (interestingly, the identical question posed to people in the UK resulted in only 7% agreement) So, even within a particular religion, the views vary widely. And taking all religions into account, we have some pretty interesting stories. A sampling…

Egypt (Lower Kingdom) – In the beginning there was an ocean. Then Ra (the sun) appeared on the water and brought forth four kids who became the atmosphere (Shu and Tefnut), earth (Geb), and the sky (Nut). Geb and Nut had two sons and two daughters. One son (Osiris) married one daughter (Isis) but he was later killed in a jealous rage by his brother Set. Set cut up Osiris' body and scattered the 14 pieces about. Isis gathered up 13 of them (except the genitals which were eaten by a fish), and brought Osiris back to life with her charm coupled with the amazing embalming skills of another god, the jackal-headed Anubis (whose origins are not entirely clear). Osiris went on to rule the netherworld. Go Osiris!

China – In the beginning, the universe was like a black cosmic egg. After 18000 years, primordial man P'an Gu awoke inside the egg, stretched, grabbed an axe from somewhere, smashed the egg, and spent the next 18000 years building the earth and sky with his egg buddies the Unicorn, the Dragon, the Phoenix, and the Tortoise. When finished with his work, he died, his breath becoming the wind, his eyes the sun and the moon, his voice thunder, etc.

African Boshongo Tribe – In the beginning there was dark, water, and great god Bumba. One day Bumba had a stomach ache and vomited up the sun, which dried up much of the water, leaving oceans and land. Later Bumba, still sick, vomited up the moon, stars, a bunch of animals, and some men. Oddly enough, Bumba was white.

Norse – In the beginning was Ginnungagap (the void), Niflheim (the northern land of fog and ice), and Muspelheinm (the southern land of fire). From a spring in Niflheim, flowed the 11 rivers which merged with the fire (fire and ice) to form primeval giant Ymir and the cow Audhumla. Ymir autoprocreated two frost giants from his armpit sweat, and another from his legs. The great world tree Yggdrasil links the nine Norse worlds.

With all due respect to our ancient friends from around the world, these creation stories are quite entertaining and all very different in some respects. However, there is more in common with many of the great world religions than not. It is well known that Islam, Judaism, and Christianity all have a common "Abrahamic" heritage and history. The Noah flood story is virtually identical to the flood story in the Sumerian Epic of Gilgamesh. In addition to Jesus, the Buddha, the Hindu god Krishna, Zoroaster, and Egyptian god Horus were all the product of virgin births. The Christmas holiday has its roots with Babylonian pagan King Nimrod. His wife Semiramis (known to Greeks as Diana) begat a son Dumuzi (known in Egypt as Osiris, Tammuz in the Bible), who was considered the promised Messiah of his day, and given the name "Mithras" or "Mediator." According to Colgate University professor Joscelyn Godwin, the ancient pagan sun deity Mithras was "the creator and orderer of the universe…His birth on 25 December was witnessed by shepherds. After many deeds he held a last supper with his disciples and returned to heaven. At the end of the world he will come again to judge resurrected mankind and after the last battle, victorious over evil, he will lead the chosen ones through a river of fire to a blessed immortality." The Roman Catholic Church brilliantly chose that story and that day to rewrite history to meet their needs and usurp pagan rituals at the same time. Even the bible implies that Jesus was born in the fall. The birth of Osiris was celebrated on December 25th by placing presents around a Cedar tree. In Sumerian religion, Dumuzi was a shepherd-king who was resurrected from the dead. And so on.

Many take these similarities as evidence that all cultures have a common historical root.

The Holographic Paradigm

One of the most uniquely interesting and promising theories regarding the nature of reality is the so-called "holographic" model.

The late physicist David Bohm, one of the main proponents of this model, believed that the universe behaves like a hologram. A hologram or holographic image distributes the encoding of the information about that image in all parts of the image. So, you can cut a hologram in half and you still see the complete image, although it has lost some resolution (by an amount proportional to the reduction in size). See Figure 2-17, courtesy of my cat, Scully. Each time the hologram of the cat is cut, the resulting image has less resolution. This makes sense if you think about it. The hologram holds a certain amount of information – a specific number of bytes. If you cut out a quadrant as shown in Figure 2-17, then you must only have 25% of the original information. But if there is enough data to render the entire picture, then the loss must come out of the resolution of the image. And it doesn't matter which quadrant – the lower right would yield the same results as the upper left.

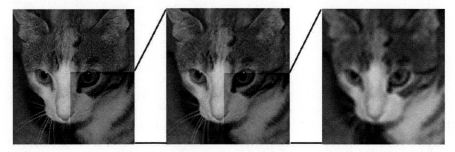

Figure 2-17

Stanford University neurophysiologist Karl Pribham applied the holographic model to the functioning of the brain once he realized that experimental evidence demonstrated a distributed model of brain function. For example, no matter what section of the brain was removed from lab rats, they never forgot how they learned to run through a maze. And it seemed that no human patients who had a significant portion of their brain removed due to necessary surgery ever lost a particular memory. Their overall memory might typically become blurrier, much like the cat hologram in Figure 2-17, but no one specific piece of information was lost. More evidence came from Indiana University biologist Paul Pietsch, who, in an attempt to disprove Pribham's theory, concocted a number of experiments involving learned behavior in a salamander. He found to his dismay that no matter how he sliced, diced, and minced the brains of his unfortunate subjects, they always returned to normal functioning.

It turns out that holographic images have their unique properties due to the nature of their encoding via interference patterns of laser light. Simple patterns of interfering straight lines can produce surprisingly complex "moiré" patterns, as shown in Figure 2-18.

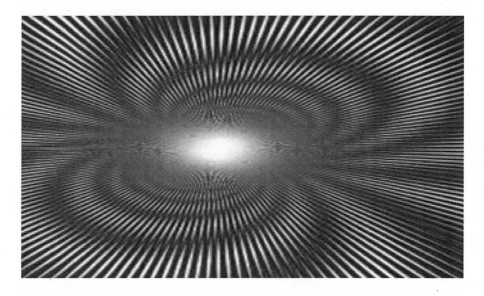

Figure 2-18

Pribham theorized that information might be stored in the brain not in the bit-by-bit manner of the time domain, but perhaps by interference patterns in the frequency domain, which could explain why we are able to learn things in terms of patterns, like facial recognition, or a quick glance at a map.

Fourier Transforms – Time and Frequency Domains

One can describe a musical note in several ways. In the time domain, it is commonly referred to as a waveform and can be viewed on an oscilloscope, or sampled into a computer. But it can also be described by its frequency constituents, or harmonics. For example, in figure A below, we show a pure sinusoidal waveform (dust off those cobwebs and try to remember your high school trigonometry!) in the time domain f(t). As time goes forward, it changes its amplitude according to the sine wave function. In the frequency domain, F(w), where we plot frequency levels instead of waveform levels, you can see that there is only one point, corresponding to the single frequency of the sinusoid. Figure B shows a waveform at twice the frequency and half the amplitude in both domains. If we add the two waveforms in A and B, we get the odd shaped waveform C, which is starting to look something that might come out of a traditional musical instrument instead of a synthesizer. In C's frequency domain, we can see that consists of the fundamental frequency plus its second harmonic at half the amplitude. As waveforms get more complex, it is not so easy to see the relationship between the time domain and the frequency domain. Fortunately, there are mathematical tools to help us do the transformations between the two domains. Those tools are call Fourier Transforms (when going from time to frequency) and Inverse Fourier Transforms (when going from frequency to time). The basic idea is that any periodic signal – that is, one that repeats itself – can be represented by the sum of a number of pure sinusoidal waveforms. In D, for example, the square wave is composed of the fundamental frequency minus 1/3 of the third harmonic plus 1/5 of the fifth harmonic minus 1/7 of the seventh harmonic and so on ad infinitum. The more harmonics that are included in the frequency domain, the closer the waveform gets to a square wave in the time domain. Finally, Figure E shows random noise. Notice that in the frequency domain, noise is the superposition of all frequencies. That is why it is called "white" noise. If you remember your spinning color wheels, white is the superposition of all colors. This makes sense since colors are just frequencies of light.

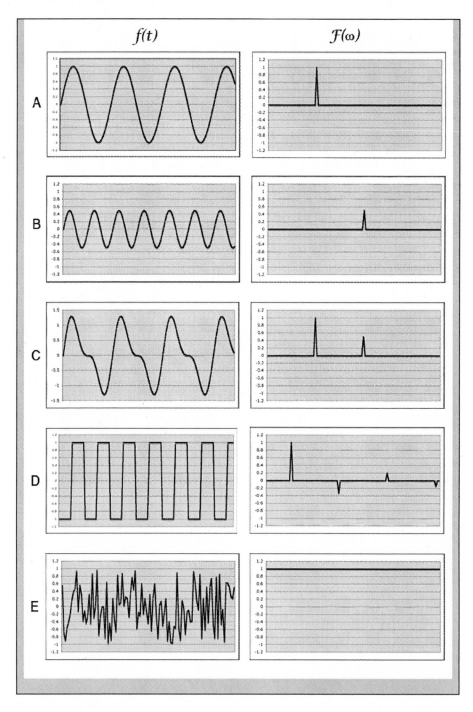

To carry the thought process a step further, in his excellent book "The Holographic Universe," Michael Talbot muses about the possibility that our objective reality – the coffee cups, TVs, cars, and people – may just be "a vast resonating symphony of waveforms, a 'frequency domain' that was transformed into the world as we know it only after it entered our senses"[20]

Physicist David Bohm formalized the ideas of the holographic model of reality and applied them to quantum physics. Just as the interference patterns recorded in a hologram appear disordered or chaotic to the eye, but represent the information needed to encode the image, so might the fabric of space and reality have a hidden or enfolded order, which he calls the "implicate order". Our perceptions are of the "explicate" or unfolded order. To put it another way, everything is a continuum. We are all connected and part of the same fabric of space. Furthermore, all information about the universe – every place and time – is encoded in this fabric at every point of the fabric, just like a hologram. This has profound implications, which Talbot exhaustively explores in the book. In terms of quantum mechanics, for example, such a model provides an excellent explanation for the "action at a distance" paradox mentioned earlier in this chapter (which, in my humble opinion, is the source of a lot of hand waving on the part of most physicists, who otherwise have no real solid explanation for the effect). Basically, it is not hard to imagine two particles acting in synchronicity even though separated by a distance precluded by the speed of light limitation. If those particles were simply two parts of the same underlying construct, they must behave synchronously. Chemist Ilya Prigogine won a Nobel Prize for his analysis of chemical structures that seem to violate the 2nd Law of Thermodynamics by progressing into more ordered structures. If the underlying fabric of space is more structured than previously thought, such anomalies could easily be explained.[21] Photographic memory, phantom limb sensations, and the power of belief are all well studied phenomena that find a perfect explanation in the holographic paradigm.

The idea that there is an imprint of events past, present, and future at every point of the fabric of space is a consequence of the holographic paradigm. It also resonates perfectly with the concept of the Akashic Record, a similar idea that came out of the Theosophical movement in the 19th century. Talbot also uses this concept as a possible explanation for all sorts of anomalous events described in the paranormal literature. Clairvoyance? Simply the ability to detect the encoding of a remote scene in the local holographic space. Out of Body Experiences (OBEs)? Same thing, except you travel virtually through the encoding. Precognition? Accessing the time dimension in the hologram. Past life regressions? Quieting the mind enough to be able to detect the subtle energies that encoded previous incarnations into the Akashic Record.

How can such an incredible amount of information be stored in such small volumes of space? Recall the vacuum energy discussion from earlier in this chapter. According to some quantum physicists, the vacuum is literally filled with quantum energy fields, at such an extreme level that the energy contained in the vacuum of a light bulb is enough to boil the worlds oceans. In the metaphysical community, much has been made of this concept of the "zero point field," which has become the metaphysicist's answer to everything from solving the world's energy crisis, to explaining all paranormal phenomena. In this context, Bohm's holographic field, the Akashic Record, and the zero point field are all one and the same and explain the fields ability to store such a huge volume of data. David Bohm is one of the physicists who believe that this is the case and has formalized his argument in his book "Wholeness and the Implicate Order." Other scientists who have either accepted or agreed with some aspects of his theories include Nobel Prize nominee Ervin Laszlo, famous Oxford cosmologist Roger Penrose, and Nobel Prize winning physicist Brian Josephson.[22]

Along a very similar line, Geoffrey Chew, Dean of Physics at the University of California, Berkeley, has developed an approach to reality referred to as the "Bootstrap Hypothesis" which asserts that all physical particles, laws, and equations are nothing more than a web of interrelations, that are ultimately just properties of the collective human mind.[23]

The Nature of Time

> "Time flies like an arrow; fruit flies like a banana."
> - Groucho Marx

Before leaving the somewhat grounded worlds of physics and philosophy for the slightly less grounded world of entertainment, a few things need to be said about the nature of time. The concept of time might seem like a simple idea until you try and describe it without circular arguments. Scientists have historically treated it as either a real measurable entity or a conceptual convenience for making temporal measurements. Conveniently, time was represented as an arrow, continuously flowing in one direction. German philosopher Friedrich Nietzsche considered the possibility that time was circular and that all events in the past would ultimately occur again. Which is probably the reason that the music inspired by his book "Also Sprach Zarathustra" was played during the opening (dawn of civilization) and final (circular rebirth) scenes of "Stanley Kubrick's 2001: A Space Odyssey" (Why the Boston Red Sox chose to play it at the opening ceremonies following their 2004 World Series victory is a little harder to figure out.)

Einstein, as usual, turned the whole concept of time on its head, by showing via his General Theory of Relativity, that time is not an absolute property, but, along with space, a part of the space-time continuum. Like spatial dimensions, time is fluid, in that observers in different reference frames will measure time differently. Thus, it becomes difficult to identify concepts like simultaneity, and even the order of events. Again, as with Zen and Quantum Mechanics, the observer becomes an integral part of the measurement and even existence of time.

Rethinking Relativity?

Poor Albert Einstein. Here it is, exactly 100 years after he published a set of papers that shook the foundations of science, and every scientist and would-be scientist seems to be taking pot shots at his theory of relativity. The genesis of this book was actually my short-lived attempt to prove that the speed of light is not a fundamental limit to the propagation of information. While I studied and understood relativity in school and did very well on the exams, something about it always bothered me. The theory was presented using space-time diagrams and mathematical calculations based on simultaneity and light pulses, which was fine except that the constancy of the speed of light always seemed to be a foregone conclusion. Intuitively, it seems to me that just as it would be very difficult for a blind race to demonstrate that something could travel faster that the limitations of their remaining senses (e.g. the speed of sound), so would it be difficult for us, whose "fastest" sense appears to be sight, to be able to perceive anything beyond that speed. Einstein started his revolutionary theory with the intuitive *assumption* that the speed of light is constant in all reference frames and everything else was derived from there. But where did the derivation of the speed of light come from? According to Maxwell's equations, c, the speed of light, is a function of the permeability and permittivity of a vacuum, and can therefore be considered a property of space. This also implies that nothing can propagate through a vacuum at a speed other than c. But, if space is nothing more than information (see Loop Quantum Gravity below), can that information propagate relative to some other region of space? If so, what would be the limit of its propagation?

It turns out that there are a lot of dissenting views on the constancy of c, some of which are clearly misunderstandings, and some which are thought provoking. Here are a few:

- Although relativity forbids the acceleration of a mass

to a speed faster than light, it does not forbid particles that begin their life traveling faster than c. Such particles, called tachyons, are a theoretic possibility with an "imaginary" mass (in the sense of the square of the mass being negative), but are very experimentally elusive, having the conceptual difficulty of disappearing before they exist. Still, in 1973, Philip Crough and Roger Clay identified such a particle in a cosmic ray shower, although the results have not been repeated.

- In 2000, physicists in Princeton, NJ created a pulse of light (aka the "group" velocity) that traveled faster than the speed of light, but it was done in a cesium chamber rather than a vacuum. Still, it proved that faster than light travel is possible.[24]

- Tom Van Flandern wrote a paper in 2000 that presents evidence that the speed of gravity may be much faster than c, and one experiment determined its speed to be at least 20,000,000,000 times c.[25]

- The constancy of c has also been hotly debated over the years, with some experimental evidence showing that it has been slowing down on a cosmic time scale, and is therefore not a universal constant. Russian cosmologist, Dr. VS Troitskii published a paper in 1987 postulating that the speed of light was originally 10^{10} times faster than it is now.[26] Along the same lines, a number of websites have reported that Dr. Van Flandern, who, for 20 years, was Research Astronomer and Chief of the Celestial Mechanics Branch at the U.S. Naval Observatory in Washington D.C., released some tests that demonstrated that the rate of atomics clocks are slowing.

- Dr. Florentin Smarandache from the University of New Mexico has proposed that there is no real speed barrier in the universe. His argument seems to be mostly based on the quantum entanglement phenomenon.[27]

The bottom line is that no one has yet disproved Einstein's light speed limitation. But it still seems that the speed of light is only about the electromagnetic propagation in a vacuum and there are as many questions that remain unanswered as there are loopholes to c being the ultimate limit. What is the propagation speed of the strong nuclear force? Or gravity? What is the underlying reason for entanglement? Can space itself propagate? At what speed (the definition of a vacuum is immaterial to such an argument)? Could exotic forms of matter (dark matter, dark energy) play by different rules? Does the limit of c apply when traversing parallel universes? What about in the extended dimensions of string theory? If telepathic communication is a real mechanism that does not make use of electromagnetism, what is its propagation speed? If the world is a program, how fast do back-channel messages propagate and is there any reason why we might not be shown a little bit of it at some point? Like, maybe when we think we have it all figured out. Remember that Newtonian physics is valid only at low speeds. Non-quantum physics is valid only at large scales. Those theories held ground through hundreds of years and thousands of the world's brightest minds. Why would we be so arrogant as to think that relativity will not someday just be valid only in 4-dimensional non-exotic electromagnetic space-time, an approximation to a grander theory?

"The hardest thing in the world to understand is the income tax."
- Albert Einstein

Quantum mechanics and relativity don't peacefully coexist at the extremes, e.g. the singularity inside a black hole. So physicists came up with a new theory, called Loop Quantum Gravity, which takes over in those realms. Essentially, it undoes what Einstein did to unify space and time, splitting them apart, rending time non-existent, and space just probabilistic foam.[28] Loop Quantum Gravity is a rigorous modeling of quantized space and time, where space is represented as a network of states called a spin network. Matter and energy are simply properties of each node in the network. Therefore, in this model, reality is nothing but data, and matter and energy are data "disturbances" that propagate through the network.[29]

At least one physicist, Julian Barbour, believes that even outside of the realm of Loop Quantum Gravity, time doesn't really exist and is just an illusion of our minds. In his book "The End of Time," he argues that time is nothing more than a set of quantum states. It is our sequencing of these states that leads to the illusion of time, much like stills in a movie reel. Furthermore, removing time from equations of physics has a nice unifying side effect. Such a theory is interesting, but begs the question "why does time seem to move in one direction only?" It turns out that there is nothing in the laws of physics that precludes the movement of time from present to past – all such equations are self-consistent. So why does time only seem to move forward? I submit that it is because of the reality program again. Julian Barbour is right. There is no time. I will present my argument in Chapter 7.

This isn't your father's time travel...

And then there is the concept of time travel. Long thought to be only a product of the minds of science fiction writers, many reputable scientists are giving time travel a serious thought. First of all, time travel into the future is well established as a scientific probability, due to general relativity. A person or object that travels at near the speed of light in one direction, turns around and travels at near the speed of light back to the original position will have less time elapse than the people or objects that remained stationary. Therefore, that person or object has effectively traveled into the future. What about the past? It turns out that there is nothing in the laws of physics that preclude the possibility of time travel into the past either. In fact, in Cal Tech theoretical physicist Kip Thorne's excellent book "Black Holes and Time Warps," he identifies methods of time travel in both directions that are perfectly consistent with today's laws of physics. All that is required is the existence of something called "exotic matter," which has negative energy density. Although not yet proven to exist, there is already observable evidence for it in the forms of behavior at the horizon of a black hole and experimental evidence for it in the form of the Casimir effect, a known attractive effect between uncharged metal plates. Thorne's time machine is essentially a wormhole created from this exotic matter that not only allows time travel but "faster than light" travel[30]. Figure 2-19 shows the model:

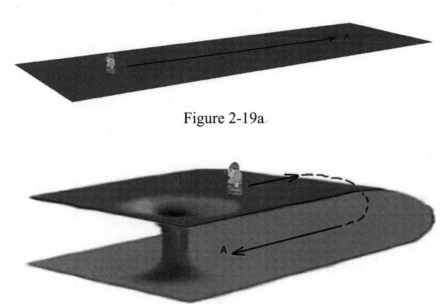

Figure 2-19a

Figure 2-19b

Our old friend, Joe Lunchbox is standing on the "surface" of his flatland universe in Figure 2-19a. To travel to point A, he would follow the old maxim "the shortest distance between two points is a straight line." If A is a light year away, and Joe travels at the speed of light, he gets to A in a year. However, recalling our discussion about multiple dimensions, lets warp Joe's universe as shown in Figure 2-19b and create a wormhole between him and point A. Now, he can travel through the wormhole and get to A faster than light, thereby traveling back in time. Although it is hard to draw, imagine the same effect applied to our own three dimensional universe. The wormhole connects two points through a higher dimension, allowing forward and reverse time travel.

Physicist Amos Ori has even gotten around the exotic matter restriction and come up with a more "approachable" time machine model that is "topologically trivial."[31]

All this is cool, but what about the philosophical implications, such as the well known "grandfather paradox," whereby you go back in time and kill your grandfather, negating your own existence, all Back-to-the-Future-like? It turns out that the big brains have already thought this one through as well, using techniques like parallel universes and the Everett interpretation of quantum mechanics to leave you a way out of the paradox. As soon as you kill grandpa, reality forks a new universe, in which he is dead and you are never born. Who is the guy who killed him? Somebody from another universe. Entirely self-consistent.

Nanotechnology

Time to say a little something about the direction we are headed in terms of technology. Nanotechnology is the technology of working with objects on the scale of nanometers, or 10^{-9} meters. At this level, individual molecules can be manipulated to create materials and structures with properties (strength, conductivity) that were previously impossible. Eric Drexler's excellent book "Engines of Creation" outlined much of the potential of nanotech as well as some of its inherent dangers.

Nanotechnology is being utilized today in many fields. Clothing, cosmetics, sports equipment, water filtration, and new inks are all products that have benefited from it. Quantum dot crystals are used in the blue laser technology that we are now seeing in the Sony PlayStation 3 and high density DVDs.

Some of the far reaching envisioned applications of nanotech include spectacular ideas like the development of nanobots (nano-sized robots) that can be injected into the body to seek out and destroy cancer cells, or to reverse human aging. The ability to synthesize new molecules will allow for the possibility of creating designer drugs and chemicals for all sorts of medical and industrial applications, including the ability to destroy the AIDS virus[32]. Molecular assemblers will be able to create any desired material or object, such as nuclear fuel, diamonds, or rocket engines, which will have significant impacts on the distribution of the workforce (mining and factory workers will become obsolete) and global economies (countries that depend on income from rare natural resources will need to find another way to survive). Genetic engineering may create a new division of "haves" and "have nots." Improved food production has the potential to conquer world hunger and nanobots may be programmed to clean up environmental pollution and disasters.

Computer Scientist J. Storrs Hall developed the incredibly cool concept of a "Utility Fog." Imagine a "nanoscopic" object called a Foglet, which is an intelligent nanobot, capable of communicating with its peers and having arms that can hook together to form larger structures. Trillions of these Foglets could conceivably fill a room and not be at all noticeable as long as they were in "invisible mode." But at any point, they could conspire to form a structure – an impenetrable wall, a sofa, a full sensory experience of a different reality – the possibilities are endless.[33]

On the other hand, like all technologies that came before it, nanotech has the potential to be weaponized. Swarms of virus-carrying or flesh-eating nanobots could be tomorrow's nuclear deterrent, creating a "nano gap" between the "nano club" and the "non-nano club." Even more insidious is the spectre of "grey goo," the theoretical catastrophe that results from the creation of a nano-device with two instructions: self-replication and consumption of everything in its path, ultimately gobbling up the earth.

Artificial Intelligence

It is no secret that computers are getting faster and faster, software is getting more and more sophisticated, and the modeling of human intelligence is getting frighteningly complete. Hollywood and science fiction writers have thoroughly explored the idea of machines taking over the world with movies like "Terminator 2", "The Matrix", "I Robot", and "AI". So, how likely is this and when might it happen?

Ray Kurzweil, in his book "The Singularity is Near," identifies the principles of the technological singularity, which include the following blueprint of what is to come[34]:

- *The rate of technical innovation is doubling every 10 years.*

- *Computer power is doubling every year.*

- *Exponential growth in information technologies is growing exponentially (e.g. the rate of acceleration is increasing)*

- *By the mid-2020s, the human brain will be completely modeled and we will be able to model human intelligence to the point of passing the Turing test (named after mathematician Alan Turing, this is a conceptual test that consists of a human asking an unknown entity a sufficient set of questions to determine if that entity is human.) Once an artificially intelligent machine passes the test, humanity will no longer be able to claim the position at the top of the intelligence ladder and machines will be able to combine human intelligence and the strengths of machine processing in a very powerful manner.*

- *Knowledge sharing amongst nonbiological intelligences (aka "machines") will be nearly instantaneous (as opposed to our slow cumbersome learning process).*

- *Machines will be able to switch and process signals 3 million times faster than humans.*

- *Machines will absorb all human-generated knowledge from the Internet.*

- *Machines will be able to create their own software and systems at a much faster rate than humans have been able to, and without the limitations that our biological structure and evolutionary processes impose on us. Pure humans will simply not be able to keep up.*

The rest of the elements of the envisioned singularity will be presented in Chapter 5, once we have had a chance to digest virtual reality. But first, how about a little fun in fantasy land…

CHAPTER 3

Alternate Realities

The Matrix, Past Lives, Mushrooms, and Everquest

The purpose of this section is to introduce the reader to the possibilities of alternate realities. Such experiences can occur in many forms and, in fact, it is the rare person who has not experienced many of them.

Definition

By definition, a reality is an experiential environment – a world experienced through your senses and mental faculties. At the center of this concept is the reality that you experience every day - the orange juice you drink in the morning, the drive to work or school, the people with whom you interact; in short, your life. By convention, we can refer to this as "reality," although it is far from clear that it is more "real" than anything else. But, given that convention, an alternate reality would be anything that you might experience outside of that reality.

There are various ways to characterize the experiences of alternate realities, so we'll identify some terms that can be used to describe them...

Immersion - Some experiences may only partially immerse you into the environment, such that you are clearly aware of your "real" surroundings at the same time. Other, total immersion experiences, such as dreams, make it difficult to determine what is "real."

Realism - There are different levels of "realism" that can be achieved. Typically, one might consider color imagery to be more "real" than grayscale. A different characteristic than immersion, one can imagine a virtual reality experience with total sensory immersion but with very unrealistic sounds and imagery. Conversely, the now ubiquitous technology of CGI (computer generated imagery) in the movies provides high levels of realism in a partial immersion (sight and sound only) environment.

Spillover – Certain experiences can be so effective in emulating reality that the effects spill over into the "real" world.

Movies and other Media

People refer to the concept of "escaping" through the movies. When you watch a movie, there is more happening than simply observing the activity on the screen. You can become involved with the movie and, sometimes, actually feel like you are there. Why else would people jump out of their seat when a shark suddenly jumps out of the water on the screen? Why do we cry when the heroine dies or the mama tiger loses her cubs? Have you ever felt drained by a psychological drama? Or wired after a high-paced action thriller? In effect, becoming engrossed in a movie is a form of alternate reality. Movie makers use various techniques to enhance the effect, such as 3D glasses, surround sound, wide screen, or filming from the 1st person view. Note that each of these effects serves to more accurately create a "real" sensory experience. Wide screen, dome, or 360° theaters increase the field of the imagery on the screen to extend into the region of peripheral vision, more accurately modeling how our eyes perceive reality. Surround sound does the same for the sense of sound, and 3D emulated the stereophonic vision that we don't otherwise experience with traditional flat movie screens. Popular theme parks (e.g. Disney's "Honey I Shrunk the Audience") take the experience a step further and add to the interactive experience the sense of touch by squirting water at the audience during a scene with a sneezing dog.

Other forms of media can cause the same escapism effect to occur. Depending on the title and the imagination of the reader, books can be excellent vehicles to a partial immersion alternate reality. Who hasn't been so engrossed in a book that they don't even hear the phone ring? Television, due to its inherently small screen, would typically have a lower immersion effect than the movies, but home theater technology is certainly blurring the distinction.

In short, various media, and especially movies, have the capacity to provide a partial immersion and moderately realistic alternate reality. Technology only promises to increase these effects.

Sleep and Dreams

> "In sleep we are all equal."
> - Spanish Proverb

Why do we sleep?

Many scientific sources will admit that we really don't know what the function of sleep is. Academic reports are filled with phrases like "it is possible that…" and "we think that perhaps…" when referring to the purpose of sleep. This is most certainly strange, considering that the average person spends a full third of her life in that state. Some of the commonly held views, many of which are supported by results of academic studies, include ideas that sleep helps to restore energy levels, strengthen immune systems, and repair tissues and cells. Some theories subscribe to the notion that sleep simply had an evolutionary origin, as mammals that moved about at night were much more at risk to accidents and nocturnal predators. The need for sleep also appears to decrease, as one gets older. On average, infants sleep 16 hours per day, children about 9 hours, adults 8 hours, and elderly people 6-7 hours.

Even more curious, perhaps, is the need for dreaming. There are two types of sleep: Slow wave sleep (SWS) and rapid eye movement (REM) sleep. SWS accounts for 4 of the 5 stages of sleep, while REM sleep is the fifth stage, during which dreaming occurs. Infants experience 8 hours/day of REM sleep and 8 hours/day of SWS sleep. By one year of age, REM sleep only accounts for 4 hours/day, while elderly people typically only experience 1 hour/day of REM sleep.[1] So, one might conclude from this that sleep, and particularly dream sleep, is associated with the development of the body, mind, or spirit, or all three.

> "I do not know whether I was then a man dreaming I was a butterfly, or whether I am now a butterfly, dreaming I am a man."
> - Chinese philosopher Chuang Tzu
>
> "Perhaps even dreams will be able one day to lay claim to reality."
> - German Philosopher, Gottfried Leibniz

There is no shortage of theories behind dreaming, and not surprisingly, no consensus. Physiological theories typically assert that dreaming maintains the exercising of synapses and brain functions, although this is sort of opposite to the physiological need for sleep – to rest and rejuvenate. Why bother to REM sleep at all if you can just stay awake and exercise those synapses instead? On the psychological front, Freud said that dreaming was unconscious wish fulfillment. Others believe that dreaming addresses problems that are better solved without the usual waking sensory stimuli. Francis Crick and G. Mitchinson theorized that dreaming was a way for the brain to remove unnecessary data accumulated during the day, perhaps to avoid information overload. Psychologist Joseph Griffin says that dreaming is a way for the brain to flush out "emotional arousal" – emotions that were suppressed during the day. However, this seems to run counter to the notion that as we get older and our lives more complex, we would typically need more, not less, emotional "flushing," while our periods of dream sleep are instead decreasing.

Some of the metaphysical approaches to dreaming can be thought provoking, especially when considering the following studies and anecdotes:

Between 1966 and 1972, psi dream studies were conducted at the Maimonides Medical Center in New York whereby "senders" in one room attempted to psychically influence the content of the dreams of "receivers" in REM state in another isolated, soundproof, and electromagnetically shielded room. The distance between the senders and receivers was varied between 32 feet and 45 miles.[2] The results of those studies indicated that psi effects occurred more during a dream state than a waking state.[3] Dean Radin has done an exhaustive "meta analysis" of 450 dream-telepathy experiments across 25 different studies conducted during this time period. The overall "hit rate" is 63% (vs. 50% if purely due to chance) with a 95% confidence interval of +/- 5%. Statistically, the likelihood that such a result would occur by chance is 75 million to one.[4]

According to Stanford University lucid dream researcher Stephen LaBerge, "accounts of "mutual dreaming," (dreams apparently shared by two or more people) raise the possibility that the dream world may be in some cases just as objectively real as the physical world."[5] One such example is the set of dreams by dream researchers Ed Kellogg and Harvey Grady, each of whom, on December 20, 1994, at approximately the same time, had a dream about an excavation in the desert for ancient artifacts by a small but organized group of men in which each appeared in the other's dream. Further similarities included dealing with multiple levels of awareness and the realization that the dream was a "rehearsal for a physical event."[6] If this and other reports of mutual dreams are not simply a coincidence, there appear to be only two explanations for it. Either there is a common field of information that both parties are tapping into, or both parties have left conventional reality and traveled to a common alternate one.

Cases of apparent clairvoyance or precognition in dreams are very common. Bernard Gittelson reports such a case: "A woman on an Oregon farm was jolted awake one morning at 3:40 by the sound of people screaming. The sound quickly vanished, but she felt a smoky, unpleasant taste in her mouth. She woke her husband, and together they scoured the farm but found nothing irregular. That evening on a television newscast, they heard about a plant explosion that started a huge chemical fire, which killed six people. The explosion had occurred at 3:40 AM."[7]

On June 28, 1914, Hungarian Bishop Lanyi dreamt that he received a letter from Archduke Franz Ferdinand of Austria informing him that he and his wife were going to be assassinated in Sarajevo. He wrote down the dream, had it witnessed, and watched history unfold later that day in nearly the same manner as his dream.[8] Abraham Lincoln was said to have dreamed of his assassination a couple weeks before the event. In the dream, he witnessed people surrounding his coffin in the white house, in exactly the same room that the situation ultimately occurred. For her doctoral dissertation, Mary S. Stowell carried out a study of 51 precognitive dreams, of which 37 were confirmed to be accurate.[9]

As usual, it is the methodical scientific western world that has reduced dreaming to mere brain activity. In other cultures, the view of dreaming has been much less reductionist. In the Yogacara school of Buddhism, for example, the external world (aka our "reality") is considered to be an illusory projection of our minds. Dreaming, therefore, is just another state of mind in which reality is an illusion. The Chinese believed that dreaming was the soul traveling to another world. Various Native American cultures have similar views of dreams and also believe that ancestors can live in the dream world and can therefore be visited during the dream state. Dream researcher Robert Moss notes that the Iroquios people believe that dreams are ways to access the departed, other dimensions, space and time outside of our common experience. Dreams help us to "reclaim the knowledge that belonged to us…before we entered our present life experiences."[10] Ancient Greek and Egyptian civilizations interpreted dreams as messages from the gods and so treated the dream dimension as much more than an imagined experience.

There is a growing school of research that suggests that dreams can be therapeutic. Robert Moss has described many anecdotal cases where a patient stricken with a serious illness such as cancer, may become aware of their ailment in a dream. Further, "imagery for healing" is often experienced in the dream state, which helps the patient identify successful methods of healing and even eradication of the illness. Where do these images come from? Jung would say the collective unconscious. Edgar Cayce would identify the Akashic Record as the source of such information. Whatever the truth, dreams have often been shown to be very therapeutic.

So, if one were to believe that all of these extraordinary dream experiences and studies are more than sheer coincidence, as the evidence and cultural record appears to show, one has to conclude that dreaming is more than a random pattern of meandering consciousness explained solely by the physical nature of the brain. Rather, it appears to be a total immersion and sometimes extremely real alternate reality.

Altered States

By definition, an altered state can be considered any state of consciousness that deviates from the norm. Being awake and not under the influence of any artificial drugs, there are still many ways that a person can enter an altered state of consciousness as well as a variety of categories of experience. Some intentional, some accidental, we explore a variety of altered states in this section.

Meditation, Yoga, and Trance

The point of meditation is to quiet the mind. Typically achieved through concentration on a single element, such as breathing, a word (mantra), geometric shape (yantra), or sound, it brings the subject to the present, eliminating the stresses of future plans and recounting past events. Research indicates a wide variety of benefits including deep relaxation, increased creative abilities, heightened awareness, decreased susceptibility to illness, reduction of pain, and effective treatment for drug addiction, heart disease, cancer, depression, and pretty much everything else. Physiological effects observed of Yogis engaged in Transcendental Meditation (TM) include reduction of blood pressure, slowing of heart rate and respiratory rate, alpha brain waves, and increased resistance to electric stimulation.[11] The effects of practicing yoga are similar to those of meditation since meditation is generally a critical component to the particular practice. The goals of yoga, similar to martial arts, are typically to attain mastery over the mind and body, and to attain enlightenment and transcendence of earthly desires. Ultimately, to the adept, yoga and meditation are said to lead to the true knowledge of reality. Eastern philosophies claim that the state of nirvana ends the cycle of birth, suffering, death and rebirth and places the practitioner into a new state of being, at one with the universe, and free from the negative trappings of the concept of "self." In fact, advanced practitioners of yoga and meditation are reported to have performed some amazing and gravity-defying feats, such as levitation and yogic flying. The website www.amazingabilities.com documents Indian yogi Subbayah Pullavar, who supposedly levitated himself in 1936 for five minutes in front of 150 witnesses, including The "Illustrated London News," who photographed the event. Paranormal investigator Vincent J. Daczynski claims to have experienced yogic flying at a TM-Sidhi program in Switzerland and shows the photographic evidence on the the same website.

The renowned American psychic, Edgar Cayce, had a vision at the age of 13. He saw what appeared to be a beautiful woman or an angel, and he told her that he wanted to help people. She said "Thy prayers are heard. You will have your wish. Remain faithful. Be true to yourself. Help the sick, the afflicted." Thereafter, he began to display inexplicable talents, such as the ability to have a photographic memory of the contents of books and papers, merely by sleeping on them. Later on, he realized his ability to lay down and fall into a deep trance, at which point he received knowledge and instructions consisting of remedies for ailments that had previously stumped traditional doctors, sometimes involving unique osteopathic or surgical treatments, and often consisting of natural remedies involving herbs, roots, tree bark and instructions for preparation and application. He would speak these instructions back in a very different voice. When applied to the patient, in most cases, the result was completely successful and there were many documented cases of full recovery from ailments considered "uncurable" by traditional medicine. An example was his wife Gertrude, who, in 1911 was diagnosed with incurable tuberculosis. Medical experts said there was nothing they could do and that she would die by the end of the year. Edgar's trance-produced reading called for a set of drugs and the inhalation of apple brandy fumes from a charred oak keg. She was fully recovered within months. Another case involved a local little girl, who, by the age of 5 was in convulsions on her deathbed, having suffered for 3 years from the effects of the flu and getting progressively worse. In Cayce's trance, he determined that her ailment really stemmed from an infection in her spine resulting from a fall she had shortly before being diagnosed with the flu (called "the grippe" at the time). Edgar prescribed osteopathic adjustments to her spine, and, after being carried out on the girl, she fully recovered within months. But most readings were conducted on behalf of sick people previously unknown to Edgar, and often residing in various locations around the country. It has been estimated that the accuracy of such readings exceeded 85%. Over 14,000 of his readings have been efficiently recorded and cataloged, effectively comprising an encyclopedia of homeopathic remedies. He also gave readings during the World War I, on behalf of people seeking the status of their loved ones overseas. In one case, Cayce was contacted by a wealthy woman in Sicily. His reading turned out to be in Italian, a language he had no way of knowing. Even stranger, after his son went to a nearby town to find a fruit vendor who could translate Italian, the vendor was amazed that Cayce's language was in a dialect that he had a little trouble fully understanding, but that he recognized as being native Sicilian.[12]

As most of his readings were clearly were beyond Edgar's capacity and knowledge level, it was a certain indication of something mysterious going on. So, later in life, Edgar began to probe the mechanism behind the readings by having a script of questions presented to him while in a trance. In these readings he connected with an entity that he referred to as "The Source." In a nutshell, he was told the following by the Source:

- *Souls may reside on different planets or in different dimensions.*

- *Souls inhabit a physical form in order to experience senses and feelings that can't be experienced in their realm.*

- *When you die, your soul meets with a spiritual guide, who helps you design your next life.*

- *The goal of each life is to learn universal lessons and improve the quality of your soul.*

- *The life force is manifested in terms of vibrations, similar to electromagnetic theories of physics. In the material realm, knowledge of the full scale of these vibrations is limited by the senses. This theory is very similar to quantum mechanics, which considers all of matter to be a wave function.*

- *The people that you select to play a role in each life are some of the same people with whom you have been involved in past lives. Genders may change (previous life as a man, next one as a woman), roles may change (your wife in the past life may be your son, or best friend in the next one), but the collection of soul mates remains the same.*

- *Positive and negative thoughts are like energies that affect health. Quiet meditation can bring balance to your life and to the energies in your body*

Note that the concepts of positive suggestion and meditation are very current in the west, indicating that Cayce, or his readings at least, were way ahead of their time. The positive and negative energy forces are strongly reminiscent of eastern philosophies (Zen) of balance, and again are only now slowly accepted and successfully practiced in the west in fields like "touch healing" and "Nambudripad's Allergy Elimination Technique."

Much like the body of homeopathic knowledge that resulted from his trance readings, these so-called "life readings" form the basis for much metaphysical thought today (you will see very many similarities to the concepts encountered by hypnotherapist Brian Weiss later in this chapter). Cayce himself was a devout Christian, whose beliefs were in some conflict with the reincarnation and metaphysical aspects of the trance readings. However, he maintained a separation of his personal beliefs and those resulting from his trance-induced state as he recognized that those speaking through him were clearly not he himself. This and the man's reputed character are strong evidence that there is more to the universe than our traditional reality.

Hypnosis

Hypnosis is often described as guided meditation. The mental states are effectively the same except that there is another party present (the "hypnotist") to guide, direct, suggest, or influence you. Hypnosis has long since been an accepted therapeutic practice by the American Psychiatric Association. Practitioners often refer to hypnosis as a state of deep relaxation, accompanied by heightened awareness. Researchers identify specific brain wave patterns, namely Alpha waves, which are associated with hypnosis. Some have categorized levels of "trance," and, although such categorization is somewhat arbitrary, the evidence does reflect that the deeper you go, the more interesting things become.

Level of Hypnosis	Characteristics
Consciousness	Waking State
Light Trance	Daydreaming
Somnambulism	Subject to suggestions, improvements Able to access suppressed memories Stage hypnotic state

Esdaile State	Hypnotic anesthesia Able to undergo surgery without anesthesia
Sichort State (deepest)	Consciousness gone, completely susceptible to suggestion

In addition to the more traditional aspects, however, hypnosis is also the home to stage acts, past life regressions, and some incredible claims of strength and paranormal phenomena.

Author Michael Talbot recounts an event that he witnessed in the 1970's. On that evening, his father had hired a hypnotist to entertain some friends at a social gathering. The hypnotist selected a subject named Tom, whom he had never met before, and put him into a trance, telling him that when he came out of it, his daughter, Laura, would be completely invisible to him. He placed Laura in front of Tom and took him out of his hypnotic state. He stood behind Laura, and held a watch against her back so that no one could see the inscription on it. He then asked Tom to read the inscription. Tom leaned forward and squinted as if Laura were not even there, and successfully read the inscription.[13] We can think about several possible explanations for this event, but all of them take us beyond normal reality. One possibility is that the hypnotist knew the inscription and Tom received it, along with the image of the watch, telepathically during the session. This would require a large assumption on the part of the hypnotist, however, who neither knew Tom nor his capacity for telepathy prior to the session. Another possibility is that Tom tapped into the "Akashic Record," the Jungian "Collective Consciousness," or the Bohmian "Holographic Universe." Or perhaps, his daughter really was never there in the first place and we only sense what we are instructed to sense subconsciously. The hypnotist helped Tom to bypass his subconscious instructions for recognizing his daughter, leaving him only with the instructions for recognizing the watch and everyone else in the room. We'll come back to this example in Chapter 7.

Dr. Brian Weiss is a graduate of Columbia University and Yale Medical School. Trained in traditional psychotherapy, he was surprised one day when a patient under hypnosis began to recount experiences from past lives. Remaining skeptical, yet open-minded, he investigated the case literature on reincarnations. He found that, in the cases of his own patients, the recollection of events from past lives seemed to be very therapeutic (note the therapeutic similarities to the dream therapies described above) and so he continued the technique, ascribing the effect to some sort of Jungian subconscious connection. However, when people began describing things that only he would know (such as the specifics of his infant son's death) and things about past lives and places that were corroborated upon investigation, he became a believer in reincarnation. Similar to Edgar Cayce in his self-induced trance, some of his patients began to channel messages from the "space between lives" in a completely different voice. The net of these messages includes the following concepts, carefully recording in these sessions:[14]

- *Our souls are immortal. Upon death, we meet with spirit guides (aka "The Masters") who help us design our next life.*

- *Our soul's task is to learn and become "God-like through knowledge" (charity, hope, faith, love).*

- *There are many dimensions, or planes of consciousness, seven to be exact. The one that we go to after death depends upon the level of progression of our soul.*

- *Bad habits that are not cured in a particular life are carried over into the next, until the soul learns to rid itself of the habit. (This is nearly identical to the Hindu and Buddhist concept of karmic debt)*

- *When you die, your soul meets with a spiritual guide, who helps you design your next life.*

- *The people that you select to play a role in each life are some of the same people with whom you have been involved in past*

> *lives. Genders and relationships between people may change from life to life, but the collection of soul mates remains the same.*

- *People may cross over into other planes of existence via the use of drugs, but in so doing, they don't understand what they have experienced.*

Sound familiar? It should, if you recall the Edgar Cayce section earlier in this chapter. It is important to note that the patients who "channeled" these masters under hypnosis often had no background in metaphysics and completely different beliefs from the ideas that were verbalized. For this reason, and due to the corroborating past life evidence, it appears to be unlikely that these many cases are hoaxes.

OBEs, Remote Viewing, NDEs

Michael Talbot recounts the story of Maria, a patient in a Seattle hospital, who suffered a cardiac arrest while in her room. While she was being revived, she had an out of body experience (OBE) where she floated up out of her body and watched from above as doctors and nurses assisted her. She allowed herself to go out the hospital window, up a couple floors and observed a sneaker on the ledge. After coming to, she described the experience and the sneaker to a social worker at the hospital. Deciding to investigate, the social worker went up to the third floor, opened the window, and retrieved the sneaker. It was in exactly the condition and position as Maria had described and could only have been observed by floating outside the window.

Hundreds of anecdotal cases like this prompted Michael Sabom, a professor of medicine at Emory University, to conduct his own research with a set of cardiac patients who had experienced OBEs and a control group who had not. Of the OBE group, when asked to describe what they saw, 97% gave at least correct general descriptions, a quarter of which were highly detailed and accurate. Of the control group, when asked to describe what they think happened, only 12% gave correct general descriptions while the rest either had major flaws in their stories, or had no idea what had transpired.[15]

Furthermore, lab experiments conducted at the American Society for Psychical Research in New York revealed several subject who were able to "OBE" around the country at will and describe specific objects and images.

Author William Buhlman has conducted an extensive survey and determined that an estimated 50 million people have experienced an out of body experience. Based on research by English psychology and skeptic Susan Blackmore, a wide variety of other surveys show that typically 10% of those surveyed have reported experiencing an OBE at some point in their lives. Typical characteristics of the OBE include:

- *Often occurs either in the middle of the night, or during a very high stress situation (e.g., a violent attack)*

- *The "middle of the night" variety often begins with a buzzing sound and a feeling of sleep paralysis*

- *Feeling of floating and ability to travel by thinking*

- *Ability to observe things that the "grounded" person should not be able to observe (aka "veridicality")*

Although many people experience OBE involuntarily, many others have learned to self-induce the experience through a variety of techniques.

The sun shines, but the ice is slippery...

In 1972, the CIA initiated and funded a program at Stanford Research Institute, to investigate remote viewing, a methodology for collecting intelligence via observing remote objects through psychic clairvoyance. The program was in response to intelligence concerns about Soviet parapsychological (aka "psi") investigations. The documents describing this program and its sponsorship were declassified by the Clinton administration in 1995. The program was carried out and the methodologies formulated by Dr. Hal Puthoff, physicist Russel Targ, and artist Ingo Swann in the 1970s.[16] All of these individuals, in addition to practitioners in the program such as Joseph McMoneagle and Lyn Buchanan from the U.S. military, have, since the declassification, had plenty to say about remote viewing. Some have gone on to develop training courses, most have written books about it, and they all have fascinating evidence that the practice is real and accurate. Targ, for example, has described how he, Hal Puthoff and Pat Price were called in to work with the Berkeley Police to find Patty Hearst in the famous Manson kidnapping case. He recalled that Price picked out a kidnapper from the mug shot book and identified the correct location of that person's car. He also describes an "architecturally accurate drawing of a gantry crane located at a Soviet weapons laboratory, and verified by satellite photography."[17] McMoneagle was used to help find Brig. Gen. James Dozier, who was being held captive by the Italian Red Brigade in 1981. According to the Washington Post, "Joe McMoneagle, was particularly successful. He zeroed in on the room where Dozier was held, chained to a wall heater. He described it, but couldn't get the house number. Yet he did get the location, the Italian city of Padua."[18] In a more enterprising application, Mary and Cherise Rivera, remote viewing students of Ed Dames, claim to have used remote viewing to win the Texas pick three lottery twice.

In 1995, Jessica Utts, professor of statistics at the University of California, Davis, completed a report on the analysis of remote viewing at SRI, which shows a statistical significance of 10^{20} to 1 against chance, and concludes that remote viewing is a real ability:

"Using the standards applied to any other area of science, it is concluded that psychic functioning has been well established. The statistical results of the studies examined are far beyond what is expected by chance. Arguments that these results could be due to methodological flaws in the experiments are soundly refuted. Effects of similar magnitude to those found in government-sponsored research at SRI and SAIC have been replicated at a number of laboratories across the world. Such consistency cannot be readily explained by claims of flaws or fraud."[19]

Going into the light...

According to a 1991 Gallup poll, more than 13 million Americans have had near death experiences, or NDEs. Based on various studies, people of all religious beliefs or non-beliefs are just as likely to have one. NDEs have been recorded as far back as ancient Greece, Egypt, and India and appear to be very similar to those recorded today.[20] The classic NDE occurs when the person experiences a near death situation and includes the following characteristics:

- *Out of body experience; viewing your body from above*

- *Traveling at high speed through a tunnel toward a light*

- *Entering a region of bright light and warmth*

- *Greeted by deceased relatives and/or friends*

- *Overwhelming feeling of joy and peace*

- *Meeting of spiritual guides, or "light beings"*

- *A life review (quick review of all life events)*

- *Either making a decision to go back (to earth) or being told your time is not yet "up"*

"Don't go to the light. It's a trick."
- John Lear paraphrasing Whitley Strieber, author of "Communion"[21]

Typical after effects of the NDE includes a newfound spirituality and belief in the afterlife. Oddly, many people have reported physical changes after experiencing an NDE, such as ripples on the fingernails.

Skeptics have attributed the NDE phenomenon to the physiology of a dying brain, much as they have attributed OBEs to a deprivation of sensory input. However, this explanation does not account for the many cases of experiential details that the person would have no way of knowing, such as observing someone's clothes who had not previously been seen by the patient. Or, consider the cases of completely blind patients who have seen accurate details of objects around them during the NDE. Finally, there are many cases of NDEs occurring while the patient has a flat EEG, which conflicts with the normal high level hallucinatory EEG activities.[22] Like physician and researcher Dr. Melvin Morse and psychiatrist and researcher Raymond Moody, many scientists who have studied the phenomenon for years have arrived at the same conclusion; namely that NDEs represent the real traveling of the soul. What about the skeptics? According to Maurice Rawlings, author of "Beyond Death's Door", he hasn't met a single atheist or agnostic who didn't become a believer in life after death upon having an NDE.[23]

Dr. Bruce Lipton has an interesting take on "the light." Remember the Fourier transforms from Chapter 2? Well, in Lipton's model, every soul is effectively a vibrating frequency. And from Fourier analysis, the sum of all frequencies is white light. So the white light that you see when you die may be the collection of all souls or spirit energy, also known as God.

> "I have been born more times than anybody except Krishna."
> - Mark Twain

Hallucinogens or Entheogens?

Drugs that affect perception and induce altered states of
consciousness have historically been termed hallucinogenic drugs.
Experimentation prior to 1970 yielded controversial opinions as to
what was actually going on during a "trip." Some believed that the
induced experiences were purely due to physiological changes in the
brain, while others believed that the drugs might open gateways to
other levels of reality. In the 1970's, the war on drugs commenced,
and scientific experimentation ended, along with mainstream belief in
the possible spiritual aspects of the experiences. Psychedelics, it was
generally thought, simply interfered with the balance of chemicals in
the brain, impacting neurotransmitters, thereby altering perception.
However, recently there has been a resurgence of inquiry about what
really happens while under the influence and a growing school of
thought that certain drugs may actually "tune" the brain to a different,
but no less real, reality. Some are using the term "entheogen"
(meaning "God inspired") for a certain class of drugs.

> "There are two major products that came out of
> Berkeley: LSD and UNIX. We don't believe this to be a
> coincidence."
> - Jeremy S. Anderson

Perhaps the most notorious of the psychedelics, LSD (D-lysergic acid
diethylamide) is a semisynthetic (created from the ergot fungus) drug
that produces psychedelic symptoms when ingested. It is similar in
chemical structure to serotonin, a naturally occurring neurotransmitter
in the brain. Early research into the effects of the drug by Stanislav
Grof, assistant professor of psychiatry at Johns Hopkins, revealed
cases of individuals who experienced things under the influence that
could not be accounted for by simple hallucinations, such as detailed
descriptions of prehistoric reptiles, events and objects from centuries
ago, ancient tribal and cultural rituals, teachings, and clothing.[24]

Santa was a mushroom…

Psilocybin (4-phosphoryloxy-N, N-dimethyltryptamine) is a psychedelic drug in the tryptamine family that occurs naturally in Psilocybe mushrooms. Mescaline (3,4,5-trimethoxyphenethylamine) is a psychedelic drug in the phenethylamine family that can be extracted from a variety of cacti, including Peyote, San Pedro, and the Peruvian Torch cactus. Evidence of the use of psychotropic flora date back 9000 years. Shamanic rituals utilizing these compounds to aid in attaining ecstatic and spiritual trance states have been an integral part of aboriginal religions throughout the world for millennia.[25] Both Psilocybin and Mescaline have been used for centuries in shamanic Native American rituals in North, Central, and South America. In a famous hallucinogen experiment carried out under the supervision of Dr. Timothy Leary, called "The Good Friday Marsh Chapel Experiment," 10 subjects were given a high dose of psilocybin and another 10 given a placebo. They all then participated in a Good Friday religious service. According to psychology student Rick Doblin, who conducted a 25-year follow up study, "everyone I talked to who had the psilocybin felt after 25 years of reflection that the experience was a genuine mystical experience…It was a clear viewing of some ultimate level of reality that had a long-term positive impact on their lives."[26] In a more contemporary setting, the Peyote Way Church of God describes their beliefs about Peyote on their website: "We believe that the Holy sacrament Peyote, when taken according to our sacramental procedure and combined with a holistic lifestyle … can lead an individual toward a more spiritual life." It seems that, while certain cultures attain enlightenment through many years of meditation and purification, other cultures see nothing wrong with achieving similar results via the shortcut of hallucinogenic drugs. The late James Arthur (ethnomycologist and ordained Priest) made a career of studying the symbiotic relationship between plants and humanity. He notes that all indigenous cultures had spiritual leaders who made use of the native psychotropic plants to attain spiritual and mystical states. As previously noted, most historical and religious scholars acknowledge that Christmas as we know it today is a holiday that has its roots in ancient Pagan rituals celebrating the winter solstice. The Roman Catholic church has a long history of usurping pagan sites and practices and replacing them or incorporating them into Christian ones. This was a doubly useful practice, since it both replaced pagan sites and rites, thereby rendering them useless to their former adherents, as well as incorporating them into the new religion, thereby making it easier for the masses to accept the new religious dogma. James Arthur took the concept a step further, believing that the ancient roots of most Christmas traditions are found in pagan shamanic practices involving the Amanita muscaria mushroom. Examples on his website include the following:[27]

- *Saint Nicholas is the patron Saint of children in Siberia (Russia), a supplanter to the indigenous Shaman.*

- *The Amanita muscaria mushrooms grow nearly exclusively under the Christmas (Coniferous) Trees.*

- *The Reindeer eat these mushrooms, hence the presumed flight.*

- *Santa brings presents in his white bag/sack. Mushrooms are gathered in bags, and Amanita muscaria sprouts out of a white vulvae sack.*

- *The mushrooms are red and white and grow under a green tree. Christmas colors are red, white and green.*

- *Typically, the red and white mushrooms are dried by stringing them on the hearth of the fireplace. Christmas stockings are red and white, hung in the same way, and shaped similarly.*

- *The Virgin Birth is symbolic for the "seedless" growth/germination pattern of the mushroom. To the ancient mind, with no microscope to see the spores, its appearance was thought to be miraculous.*

- *The very name, "Christmas" is a holiday name composed of the words, "Christ" (meaning "one who is anointed with the Magical Substance") and "Mass" (a special religious*

> *service/ceremony of the sacramental ingestion of the Eucharist, the "Body of Christ"). In the Catholic tradition, this substance (Body/Soma) has been replaced by the doctrine of "Trans-substantiation", whereby in a magical ceremony the Priests claim the ability to transform a "cracker/round-wafer" into the literal "Body of Christ"; ie, a substitute or placebo.*

Incidentally, he is not the only adherent of this belief, or to the belief that Jesus was also symbolic of the mushroom. A recent Google search of "mushroom", "Santa", and "Jesus" yielded 373,000 results.

The Spirit Molecule...

DMT (N,N-dimethyltryptamine) is to LSD what the New York Yankees are to the Mudville Nine. Not in the sense of potency or intensity of the resulting experience, but in the sense of the perceived reality and far reaching implications of the experience. Chemically, DMT is a tryptamine, like seratonin, the neurotransmitter common in our brains that appears to regulate or impact depression, sexuality, and appetite. DMT is also present in our brains and, in fact, our brains appear to crave it. The blood-brain barrier is a shield that protects the brain from most all compounds carried in the blood, with only a few exceptions such as glucose (the brains fuel), amino acids (critical for protein maintenance), and, for some unknown reason, DMT. Dr. Rick Strassman, Clinical Associate Professor of Psychiatry at the University of New Mexico School of Medicine, one of the foremost authorities on DMT, refers to it as the "spirit molecule," a name which has caught on. In the early 1990's he conducted the first new American research into the effects of psychedelic drugs on humans in over 20 years, and selected DMT as his drug of choice. He believes that DMT is created in the pineal gland, a mysterious little endocrine gland in the middle of the brain that philosopher Rene Descartes called the "seat of the soul." Some call it the "third eye," or Anja, the Tantric chakra responsible for intuition and extra-sensory perception (ESP). It turns out that there is some scientific basis for such a description, as the layout of the cells are similar to photoreceptor cells in the retina. According to researcher K.W. Min, "it is reasonable to conclude that human pineal glands exhibit transient cellular features reminiscent of developing photoreceptor cells as shown in other mammals."[28] Edgar Cayce associated the pineal gland with the "silver cord", that supposedly connected him to the collective subconscious during his trances. He referred to the energy associated with it as "life force" or "kundalini," which is a well known concept in Eastern religions, such as Hinduism. Kundalini "awakening" or "arousal" is the enlightening experience of a sudden spiritual awakening, which, in the West, we might call a religious experience (see below). Dr. Strassman noted the interesting correlation of the Tibetan Buddhist teaching that the soul reincarnates 49 days after leaving its previous body, with the 49 days that it takes for the pineal gland to form in a human fetus, and the 49 day point of fetal development where it differentiates itself into a male or female body. He believes that the pineal gland is the seat of the soul and proposes that the sudden surge of "pineal DMT release at 49 days after conception marks the entrance of the spirit into the fetus."[29] Esoteric thought is that the human capabilities that are under control of the pineal gland are lying dormant and may be activated at some point when we have attained the cultural maturity needed to handle such capabilities. Of course, this flies in the face of Darwinism and smacks of creationism, but we certainly can't prove either side of *that* battle.

Lifting the veil...

> "Smoking DMT is like being shot from a cannon into another dimension and returning to this world in less than ten minutes"
> - Daniel Pinchbeck, from "Breaking Open the Head"

[Authors Note: This section is not meant to be an endorsement of the use of DMT]

DMT has been experienced in a variety of different ways. Strassman's DMT subjects received DMT injections under clinical conditions. Some recreational users smoke it or inhale it. The onset of the experience via these methods occurs within a minute and the effects are over within 10-30 minutes. When taken orally, DMT is broken down quickly by a stomach enzyme, called monoamine oxidase. However, if taken in conjunction with a monoamine oxidase inhibitor, the experience can last for hours. This is the secret of Ayahuasca, a tea brewed in Brazil from a combination of a psychotropic plant such as chakruna (the source of the DMT) and a giant Yage vine (aka Banisteriopsis caapi, the source of the monoamine oxidase inhibitor) native to the rainforest. Historically, it has been used in religious contexts during shamanic healing rituals and may even date back to the earliest known inhabitants of the Amazonian jungles. How these tribes discovered the secret of brewing a combination of just the right two plants out of millions of tropical species is unknown, but dozens of widely separated tribes in what is today Peru, Ecuador, Colombia, Bolivia, and Brazil, all developed different concoctions of Ayahuasca. Nowadays there are a number of churches in Brazil who use it in their practices. So, naturally, it wasn't long before modern pleasure seekers discovered its magic and made the pilgrimage to Brazil to partake of the experience. In Sting's autobiography, "Broken Music," he spends the first 60 pages describing his experience. An excerpt:

> *"Now all is swamped in this tidal wave of energy which grounds the skies to the earth so that every particle of matter in and around me is vibrant with significance. Everything around me seems in a state of grace and eternal. And strangest of all is that such grandiose philosophizing seems perfectly appropriate in this context, as if the spectacular visions have opened a doorway to another world of frankly cosmic possibilities."[30]*

Benny Shanon, professor of psychology at the Hebrew University of Jerusalem, has documented his study of the effects of Ayahuasca on a variety of subjects including himself. The results are quite interesting in that the experiences that people have contain some consistent and similar themes, despite their wide variety of backgrounds and cultures (e.g., from Amazionian tribe members to cultural sophisticates from New York City). Between his results, Strassman's studies, and other researchers and authors, such as Daniel Pinchbeck and Clifford Pickover, here are some of the common themes to a DMT experience:[31]

- *Intricate landscapes and ornate cityscapes*

- *Precision design, reflective of a deep mathematical fabric*

- *Gilded, sparkling, fairytale, cities of light with gold and jeweled palaces and temples*

- *The feeling of the "lifting of the veil," i.e. removing the curtain that normally prevents the viewing of the true reality*

- *Realization of the certainty of life after death*

- *The superposition of the DMT world with the "normal" world*

- *Serpents and wild cats, especially black pumas*

- *Other beings tend to be elflike, alien, angelic, and insectoid*

- *The visions are not distorted and changing as with dreams and other hallucinatory experiences, but rather appear complete and intact as the veil is lifted. Once the drug wears off, they similarly just disappear as the veil falls.*

The most significant result of these studies is that a great majority of subjects feel that the DMT experience is not simply a hallucination, but rather, a separate reality that is even more real than the "normal" one. The fact that common themes occur in so many user experiences, despite their background and culture, plus the fact that these themes in many cases make no sense from a psychological subconscious standpoint (who dreams about black pumas and machine elves?) actually lends a lot of support to the idea. Perhaps there is something else out there – something completely different than what we are programmed to think. Some liken the concept to the tuning of a radio. Signals from thousands of broadcast stations saturate the air at all times. But your radio can only tune to one signal. Your brain is analogous to the radio in the sense that tuning in reality is a matter of processing sensory input. What if the chemicals and neurotransmitters in your brain, perhaps specifically, DMT generated by the pineal gland, are responsible for tuning in "normal" reality when present in just the right amounts. If the chemicals are out of balance, e.g. the level of DMT is sufficiently higher than normal, the brain tunes to an alternate reality. Could the alternate reality be a "truer" reality with our brains intentionally tuned to the bogus reality that we consider normal? As we've seen, there is some evidence for this. We'll come back to this later in the book in a great deal more detail, and explore the probabilities of alternate realities as well as the question of who might be in control of our tuning system.

Psychoses

The old adage "there is a fine line between madness and genius" has its roots in a quote by Seneca, the Roman philosopher, 2000 years ago: "There is no great genius without some touch of madness." Lord Byron, Samuel Taylor Coleridge, Paul Gauguin, Jackson Pollock, Pyotr Tchaikovsky, Winston Churchill, John Keats, Rudyard Kipling, Edgar Allan Poe, T. S. Eliot, and Virginia Woolf are all considered by some to have had bipolar syndrome. Brilliant mathematician and Nobel Prize winner John Nash had Schizophrenia, as did Pink Floyd founder Syd Barrett, and artist Vincent Van Gogh. Benjamin Franklin, Albert Einstein, Thomas Jefferson, Wolfgang Amadeus Mozart, Leonardo da Vinci, Mark Twain, Leo Tolstoy, and Charles Dickens lead the list of famous Autistics. The experience of those who have any of these disorders can certainly be considered an alternate reality in the sense that their perception of reality is quite different from that of the rest of us. After all, that's really what defines them as disorders or diseases – a departure from the norm. If 99% of people were Schizophrenic, it would be we "normal" ones that would have the strange Greek name for our condition.

In fact, mental disorders are very common, especially among gifted or talented people. It is estimated that 1 in 100 may have Schizophrenia, the big Daddy of mental disorders. Symptoms of this disorder are almost identical to symptoms of users of hallucinogens – inability to determine what is real, hallucinations, altered perception. It almost seems as if Schizophrenia may be a natural state of the alternate consciousness that so many researchers, Shamans, and experimenters seek through psychedelics or religious rituals. Perhaps the Schizophrenics are the lucky ones?

"The schizophrenic is drowning in the same waters in which the mystic swims with delight"
- Joseph Campbell

It is noteworthy that there is no specific lab test that can determine Schizophrenia and no know organic cause. Perhaps madness, like the DMT experience, is simply an imbalance of neurotransmitters and general brain chemistry – a departure from the balance that is meant to keep us in *reality*. Again, we have to wonder, which is the true reality?

Uh oh, fifteen minutes to Wapner...

Autistic savants are people who exhibit incredible cognitive abilities in specific areas, such as photographic memory, the ability to perform lightning fast arithmetic or memorize facts and statistics. Often the "disorder" results from the individual receiving a head injury. Edgar Cayce supposedly traced his extraordinary mental capabilities to a head injury that he suffered as a boy. Is it possible that humans have an effective regulator or "higher level function" governor in their brain that limits brain function to that 10-20% of its total capacity of which we often hear? And that this regulator can be impaired with a head injury, thereby releasing certain aspects of a fuller brain function?

Some experts in psychological disorders place Albert Einstein and Sir Isaac Newton among the ranks of famous autistics.

Shamanism and Religious Experiences

We've mentioned the consistency of Shamanic rituals and practices across millennia of time and around the world. But the alternate reality religious experience does not need to come from artificial stimulants. In many cases, the experience is brought about through ritual dance and tribal drumming, such as with various Native American tribes as well as halfway around the globe with the African Basarwa bushmen. The modern day equivalent may be the Rave, where hundreds or thousands of people dance in synchronicity to the repetitive rhythms of Trance music.

The Wikipedia article on Kundalini notes:

> *"Kundalini as a spiritual experience is thought to have parallels in many of the mystical and gnostic traditions of the world's great religions. Many factors point to the universality of the phenomenon. The early Christians might have referred to the concept as 'pneuma', and there are some recent parallels in contemporary Christian charismatic 'Holy Ghost' phenomena. Religious studies also note parallels in Quakerism, Shakerism, Judaic davening (torso-rocking prayer), the swaying zikr and whirling dervish of Islam, the quiverings of the Eastern Orthodox hesychast, the flowing movements of tai chi, the ecstatic shamanic dance, the ntum trance dance of the Bushman, Tibetan Buddhist tummo heat as practised by Milarepa, and the Indically-derived Andalusian flamenco."[32]*

Author and researcher Graham Hancock believes that for 40,000 years, human cultures around the world have been having the same basic spiritual experience, only slightly filtered perhaps by the specifics of their cultural beliefs. For example, he maintains that the prehistoric art from ancient Africa, Europe, and Australia that depict entities known to the shamans of those cultures as "gods" and "spirits" are astonishingly similar to entities known in the European Middle Ages as "elves" and "goblins," and to today's "Grey Aliens." The behaviors and abduction experiences, he says, are similar, only the names and cultural context have changed. It is also interesting that the figure of 1% of the population having Schizophrenia is also consistent with his assertion that 2% of the human population has always been able to have other worldly experiences without needing artificial stimulation. In some cultures, he says, these people are revered as Shamans. In our culture, they are ridiculed. In his book, "Supernatural", he muses that perhaps today's UFO abductees are the new Shamans.

To summarize these sections on entheogens, psychoses, and spiritual experiences, they all have quite a bit in common. They are all associated with some changes in the balance of chemicals in the brain. They all produce similar experiences and perceptions of alternate realities. Again, think of the brain as a radio receiver. The radio can be tuned to any particular channel by adjusting the balance of inductance and capacitance in the tuned circuit. Perhaps the brain works in a similar manner and is typically locked on to what Rick Strassman calls "Channel Normal." But under certain circumstances, we are able to defeat the "channel lock" and retune the brain to "Channel Alternate Reality."

Simulators

There are two categories of simulations discussed in this book. One consists of flight simulators and similar enclosed systems that simulate motion in all directions, with the accompaniment of visual and auditory cues. The other type of simulation is a virtual reality simulation, which involves less bulky equipment and more neural stimulation. The distinction between the two gets very blurry at some point, but for the purpose of this section, we will only consider the big bulky "analog" simulators. An entire chapter will be devoted to the other type in a few pages.

Flight simulators have long been developed for airlines to train their pilots and crews. They are ideal for inexperienced pilots, experienced pilots practicing on new aircraft, and for the practicing of maneuvers that would normally be too dangerous to attempt on a real flight. Simulators typically cost millions of dollars and consist of an enclosed cabin with motors and hydraulics to generate motion in all directions. Inside, there are large screens driven by computer systems simulating the visual aspect of a flight; what the pilot sees from the cockpit. Audio systems also emulate a true flight experience. Instrumentation is also identical to the aircraft being simulated. The net result is that the 3 of the 5 most important senses to flying in a plane (visual, auditory, and tactile) are fooled into thinking that you are actually flying. In addition, the effects of motion are replicated so that it feels like you are flying. Note that although we've all learned in grade school that we have five senses, that's really just a matter of convenient categorization thanks to Aristotle, and the "five senses" idea is now stuck in our scientific status quo. Some sources consider as many as 20 different senses, including sensing heat, pain, and balance. And certainly, the ability to detect orientation in a gravitational field doesn't fall neatly into any of the big five. Anyway, even more complicated simulators were of course developed for astronaut training; as such simulation was the only way to get a feel for weightlessness and other aspects of space flight.

Theme park simulators like Universal's "Back to the Future" and Disney's "Soarin' Over California" bring the simulation experience to the laymen, or rather, the thrill seeker. Another category of simulators are the programs like Microsoft's Flight Simulator, which sacrifices the motion sensations for a very high degree of visual realism for under $100. Every few years, the company puts out a new and improved version that ratchets up the level on realism. In fact, some have complained that the program is a little too realistic and speculated that it could have been used to train the September 11, 2001 hijackers to fly airliners. Fooling the brain is what these alternate realities are all about. The simulators described provide a high level of reality and immersion.

Games

[*Warning*: The gaming community seems to develop more acronyms than the Telecommunications industry… *<soapbox>* although nobody can beat the bloated and bureaucratic European International Organization for Standardization (ISO) for acronym hell. *</soapbox>*]

Gaming provides a very rich genre of alternate realities. Even a board game, like Monopoly, puts the player into an alternate role – that of a real estate wheeler-dealer. Very small level of immersion, and very light realism (how many of us live in a world that consists of a single block?), but an alternate reality nonetheless. Also in the category of "low tech alternate realities" is Dungeons & Dragons, the quintessential role playing game, or RPG. In D&D, players create their own characters and play out a very open-ended adventure or fantasy, which is created by the DM (Dungeon Master). Activities include traveling, fighting, and social interactions but all of the action is played out with paper and pencil and the roll of the 20-sided die. Players advance to various levels as they gain experience, kill monsters, etc. Taking the genre a step further are so-called Live Action RPGs, or LARPs. Instead of a tabletop or a BBS (bulletin board system, from the early community-enabling system allowing multiple computer users with dial up connections to play games with each other), LARPs are played out in real life, with players totally immersed in their character playing out a role in their home town. Observers of a LARP character in action might see somebody dressed up as a wizard looking for a hidden key, or a group of medieval-dressed peasants involved in a beanbag battle in a field. For example, a group called the Lorien Trust conducts an annual event in Derbyshire, England, called "The Gathering," where, according to their website…

> *"events take place in the game world of Erdreja, an egg shaped fantasy world floating in the Cosmic Void. This fantasy world was created by the Lorien Trust, over the last decade it has expanded and been given a greater depth by the*

> *people who have attended and played with in the system. The
> world of Erdreja is still developing and attending the events is
> your chance to influence it's future. The heart of Erdreja and
> the campaign world is the region known as the Heartlands, an
> area of the world mainly inhabited by humans. This is also
> home to dozens of fantasy races, from the classic known races
> of Elves and Dwarves above land, to Frithen dwelling in the
> seas and Dark Elves who inhabit the deeper reaches of
> Erdreja. Travelers from other related fantasy worlds and the
> far reaches of the game world visit the Heartlands to add even
> more excitement and adventure.* "[33]

As a player, you can be a Human, Werewolf, Elf Goblin, Dwarf, or
Halfing. Depending on your character type, you may join an
Alchemist, Archer, Armourer, Bank, Bard, Healer, Incantor, Mage,
Militia, or Scout guild and be a member of a player group such as
Defenders of Adelena, The Knights Templar, and Primal Urge. The
Defenders of Adelena website describes character Miss Celestria
Worthington (played by "Elly") as a 20 year old Halfling, a diplomat
in the Unicorn faction who "wears long dresses, big cloaks and a
signature Silver Circlet round her head, with white flowers in her
hair… She was brought to the Gathering of Nations after leaving
Treseryn, the town where she grew up. Once she joined the Unicorns
Faction she applied for a diplomat position, which she got. Celestria
now lives on Adelena Isle after Molly and Grendal kindly took her in
where she helps care for Molly's children and waits for her beloved
Valten Dredd Knight of Ancalime and Acting General of the 3rd
Armies to come home to her from battle. Celestria joined the
Defenders of Adelena so she may protect the warriors and heros who
fight for her beautiful home."[34]

Computer and console gaming ushered in a whole new era of RPGs,
including such notables as Final Fantasy VII (Playstation), Star Wars:
Knights of the Old Republic (PC and X-Box), and Diablo (PC and
Macintosh). The graphics and sound added an exciting level or
realism and intrigue to the games. Another category of computer
gaming is First Person Shooter, or FPS. In these, the player exists in
a simulated environment, usually dark dungeons, or misty spy

settings, and has a basic goal to attain and an arsenal of weapons that would impress the Mossad. Highly violent and controversial, these games are damn fun to play. Early FPSs were in 2D, but in the early 1990's, a number of 3D versions hit the market, such as the infamous Doom, and Duke Nukem 3D. Some of them allowed a limited set of multiple players connected via a LAN (local area network) or serial port. Quake ushered in the truly multiplayer FPS experience over the internet, where a 16 year old kid in Thailand can band together with a 60 year old lawyer in the UK and a 35 year old housewife in Toledo, Ohio to kill a bunch of monster goons in cooperative mode. Alternatively, players from around the world can participate in a deathmatch where the player with the most frags (aka kills) in a given period of time wins. Quake was licensed under the GNU General Public License (GPL) in 1999, which allowed its source code to be modified by the player community. New scenarios, textures, weapons, rules, and restrictions have all been developed as "add ons" to the original game. Another well-known FPS, Sierra Entertainment's Half-life is known to have a very complex storyline and has a setting reminiscent of the infamous Area 51.

Since then RPGs and FPSs have evolved considerably as PC power follows Moore's Law, doubling in speed every 18 months or less. The dramatic increase in CPU speed has allowed incredible realism such as advanced real time calculation of shadows and lighting, physics engines that emulate gravity real time (as opposed to building these things into canned movements of the players). The parallel increase in disk sizes allows much more involved and lengthier games, with extremely complex settings containing many more rooms and areas to explore.

Enter the genre of the massively multiplayer online role-playing game (MMORPG), sometimes simplified as MMOGs, also known as the massive money making games (MMMGs – *OK, that's my acronym*).

115

> ## The Economics of the Online Gaming Business
>
> As an interesting aside, I thought I would make some notes about the financial success of the online gaming business. Industry analyst DFC Intelligence estimates that the "online game industry in 2003 was US$1.9 billion...By 2006, they predict revenue growing to $5.2 billion."[35] Blizzard Entertainment's "World of Warcraft" boasts over 1,000,000 subscribers. At $15/month to play, this represents annual revenue of $180 million, not even counting the $50 million that those subscribers had to lay out initially to buy the game. According to another analyst, Jupiter Research, it costs $10 million per year to run such a game.[36] That means that the profit margin for "World of Warcraft" is roughly 1000%. Try to find another industry with numbers like that! Of course, there are MMORPGs that aren't as successful, so, like anything, the magic is in the product. But, with the right combination of game and marketing strategy, this can certainly be a very lucrative market niche.

Anyway, MMOGs are online games that are designed to support a very large base of simultaneous users, often in the thousands per server. What this means is that a very important aspect of the game environment is the player community. Rather than the dozen or so players that made up some of the early FPSs, thousands of players can make up a small town or society. And so these games are designed to be much more open-ended. There is often very little plot to the game. Rather, it is all about being part of an alternative community – one in which nobody really knows who you are.

> "On the Internet, nobody knows you're a dog."
> - from a famous cartoon by Peter Steiner that appeared in the July 5, 1993 issue of "The New Yorker", showing a dog at the keyboard telling another dog about one of the beauties of the Internet

The original Everquest (there is now an Everquest II), for example, is basically a 3D virtual world in a Tolkeinesque fantasy setting. You, the player, have an avatar, a graphical representation of yourself, that wanders through the land fighting monsters and evil critters, socializing, carrying out quests and adventures, and building up trade skills related to your character. The virtual world, Norrath, consists of a number of continents, each with its own flavor and geography. Misty forests, rivers, deserts, lowlands, mountains, and oceans are all part of the experience. To accomplish most tasks, you need to band together in groups. The general object is to continually improve your level by accomplishing progressively difficult tasks and killing progressively difficult monsters. Higher levels open up new hunting grounds, new weaponry, and new spells. For example, Rangers can't cast spells until they reach level 9. The other characters that you encounter in the game may be other player's avatars or a non-player character (NPC), such as Mrysila, the nice gypsy (good) and Zarchoomi, the Ogre Shaman (bad). Sony Entertainment has released a large number of updates to the game, such as expansion kits The Ruins of Kunark, The Scars of Velious, Legacy of Ykesha, and Lost Dungeons of Norrath. Each of these expansions provides new continents, hunting zones, races, items, and quests. In a couple cases, the number of possible levels was increased from 50 to 60 and then from 60 to 70, ostensibly to keep the power users playing and paying.

Everquest has spawned an entirely new vocabulary amongst its users. For example, the "butt-scratch brigade" is a large group of Trolls or Ogres, who have a tendency to… well, you get the idea. "Buff hunting" is the act of seeking someone who can cast enhancement spells on you. "Slum looting" is looting corpses that have been left unlooted by the original killers. And so on. The game does have its detractors. There are clearly plenty of obsessed fans that play until they lose their hygiene, friends, and/or wives, and psychologists warn of its addicting qualities, spawning such names as "NeverRest" and "EverCrack." Online support groups, such as the Yahoo group "EverQuest Widows," have popped up to provide support for neglected loved ones.

But that's not the half of it.

In November 2001, Shawn Woolley, 21, Everquest aficionado, shot himself at his computer while playing EverQuest. According to his mother, Liz Woolley, he was completely addicted to the game. "He couldn't stay off it. That's how strong that game is. You can't just get up and walk away" she said, "He shot himself because of the game." Rumors circulated about the reasons for his action, and the general consensus is that his player character was killed and it's body "looted," before he had a chance to recover it and regain its life. CBS News reported that "in the end, the game became his life."[37]

Possibly even stranger, on August 3, 2005, a 28-year old man started to play a game called Starcraft at an internet café in South Korea (a country where online gaming is huge, with 30% of the population registered for at least one MMOPRG, and where the Annual World Cyber Games are hosted). After 50 hours straight of game play, with only minor breaks for sleep or toilet use, the man collapsed and died from exhaustion. A local police official noted that the man had recently been fired from his job for skipping work to play computer games.[38]

Spillover into Reality

An entire economy of virtual gaming artifacts has sprung from MMORPGs. An item such as a weapon acquired by a player's character in a game can actually be sold to another character. In 2003, eBay alone saw over $9 million worth of transactions of virtual gaming artifacts. According to Bob Kiblinger of UOTreasures, the second-party MMORPG loot market grossed about $500 million in 2004. Writer Julian Dibbell demonstrated that you can actually make a living trading virtual goods when he earned a profit of $3917 in one month simply by buying and selling virtual artifacts.[39] If you think he takes virtual objects seriously, consider the case of Chinese gamer Qiu Chengwei, who lent a virtual sword to another gamer, Zhu Cauyuan in 2005. When Mr. Zhu sold the other mans sword, an incensed Mr. Qiu stabbed and killed him.[40] At the time of the writing of this book, the rise in virtual crime is exploding, at least in countries who have passed laws against certain activities. In August 2005, a man was arrested in Japan for conducting virtual "mugging sprees" with software "bots" in the online game Lineage II. The cybercriminals stole other players possessions and then sold them on the virtual artifact market for real cash.[41] And then there are the gold farm sweatshops in China where people spend 12 hours a day monitoring automated macro programs that control online agents who kill, heal, and steal gold on Lineage II. Employees earn $150/month for work that can earn the employer as much as $60,000/month.[42] Now, gaming companies are fighting back and applying patches to the games that discourage or prevent gold farming. That is, at least until the hackers figure out ways around them. Blizzard Entertainment has shut down over 1000 accounts due to gold farming in World of Warcraft.[43] Economist Edward Castronova estimated that, based on the wealth created by all players inside the game, Everquest's Gross National Product (GNP) was $2216 per capita, making it equivalent to the 77th richest country in the world. [44]

None of this is any surprise to Neal Stephenson, author of the landmark virtual reality cyberpunk novel *Snow Crash* (and, by the way, one of Time Magazine's All-Time 100 Best Novels). Written in 1992, prior to the World Wide Web, his concept of "The Metaverse" was a virtual society which people "goggled" into by donning a pair of Virtual Reality goggles and plugging into a terminal. In the Metaverse was "The Street," a place with virtual property - clubs, stores, apartments, Laundromats, restaurants – basically mirroring most everything that exists in real life. The Metaverse had currency, with which you could buy goods, weapons, and rent your flat (which cost more the closer you got to the epicenter of The Street, not unlike uptown Manhattan.) You could be a pizza delivery guy in the *real* world and a sword-slinging hero in the Metaverse. The VR experience described is one of total immersion and total realism and the dangers of the Street spilled over dramatically into the *real* world. The book introduced the concept of the avatar, the graphical representation of a person in a virtual world. It may also have inspired the invention of VRML – the Virtual Reality Modeling Language, which makes browser-based 3D worlds possible. It was certainly the genesis for the formation of the company "Black Sun

Interactive" which created VRML browser plugins and virtual worlds similar to the Metaverse. Other Metaverse wannabies included Cybertown, a 3D VR browser-based community, and the Active Worlds 3D browser.

But the web-world that most closely resembles the Metaverse is Linden Labs' "Second Life." Inspired by "Snow Crash," Second Life (aka SL) is a free form community with over seven million registered accounts, as of July 2007. Players are represented as usual by their avatars and the world has its own economy (as of this writing the exchage rate is 270 Linden per dollar), but unlike MMORPGs, SL is much more free-form. Players work, have relationships, travel, buy and sell property, and actually create their own environment. Universities such as Harvard, Rice, University College Dublin, New York University, and Stanford are using SL as virtual classrooms.[45] Businesses are getting in on the SL action as well. Fully in-world businesses have sprung up within the virtual world; casinos, design studios, real estate, stores, and marketing agencies.[46] Traditional companies, like International Business Machines (IBM) have launched products, given presentations, and conducted conferences and collaboration events, all within Second Life.[47]

In chapter 5 we will take a much deeper ride into the world of Virtual Reality and consider whether these gaming trends will ultimately lead to a full-immersion virtual reality. In Chapter 7, we will consider whether or not they already have.

CHAPTER 4

A Brief History of Coding

Don't be scared. This is not a book on programming in the 21st century, nor an attempt to get your eyes to glaze over. I'm only introducing some basic programming concepts here because, well, they are sort of key to the whole premise of the book, as we'll see. So, for those of you who are machine-computationally-challenged, bear with me, this won't last too long, I promise! And for those hackers among you, you can probably skip this entire chapter.

Hopefully, the last section on MMORPGs whetted your appetite a bit in terms of discovering a little about how these spectacular games are developed. Unfortunately, we aren't going to get that far. We'll just cover the basics of hierarchical programming. But for the initiated, there are lots of books in the computer section of your local bookstore on game programming.

Language levels

Machine Code – Level 1

German engineer Konrad Zuse developed the Z1, the world's first programmable electronic computing machine back in the late 1930's.[1] Computers in the 40s consisted of rooms full of vacuum tubes and relays and were programmed via the setting of switches. The combined state of the switches, each being on (1) or off (0) constituted the binary program. Such a program, written in binary (1s and 0s), is referred to as machine language. Ultimately, all of today's processors understand only machine language as they are devices that function on a logical binary level. Higher level languages, such as Java or C++ must be converted to machine language through steps called compilation, interpretation, or assembly. Machine language is therefore the lowest level of languages, referred to as a "Level 1 language." In binary, it looks like this:

```
1 0 0 1 0 0 1 1 1 0 1 0 1 1 ...
```

A computer processor has a set of instructions that it can execute – things like "move this bit of data into that memory location." The actual binary digits represent either instruction codes, parameters for those instructions, or data. "Disassembled" code is usually written in hexadecimal format, or base 16, where 4 binary digits are combined into each hexadecimal digit. Hexadecimal is the same as decimal from 0 through 9 and then uses the letters A, B, C, D, E, and F for 10, 11, 12, 13, 14, and 15 respectively. Hexadecimal code, or "hex" for short, looks something like this:

```
F601 AA78 7FFF C10D ...
```

Hex is easier to read and someone who really knows the instruction set of a particular processor can actually figure out what the program is doing by looking at it.

Assembly Code – Level 2

Clearly, writing in and reading machine code (aka "hex" or "binary") is extremely difficult and tedious. Wouldn't it be better if you could write your instructions in English instead of numbers? So, in 1948, the UNIVAC Company invented assembly language.[2] Assembly language uses English language-type words to replace the hex instruction codes and data. So, for example, the following assembly code adds two numbers together and stores them in a register (one of the processor's internal memory locations):

```
        mov    ax,2        ; Set register ax to 2
        mov    bx,1        ; Set register bx to 1
        add    bx,ax       ; Add ax to bx and store the sum
in bx
```

The syntax, or grammer, of an assembly language is generally tied to the actual processor that it will run on since each assembly language command corresponds to the processor's instruction code. So there are roughly as many assembly languages as there are processor types. A program called an "assembler" will convert the list of assembly instructions to machine code, which the computer can then read and execute. Because Assembly language is a higher level than machine code, it is considered a "Level 2 language."

High Level Languages – Level 3

One of the problems with assembly language is that it is unique for the computer on which it runs. So, let's say that you create an assembly program for a Pentium processor that finds the square root of a number. If you want that program to run on a PowerPC processor, you have to start all over and rewrite it in a different assembly language. Wouldn't it be cool if the program you wrote could be run on any computer? Well, that's exactly what a Level 3 language, or "High Level Language (HLL)" is for. The first of these, called FORTRAN (for FORmula TRANslation) was developed by IBM in 1957. A program could be written in the FORTRAN language and then compiled into any assembly language via a program called a "Compiler." A high-level language program is therefore "portable" to different computers. HLL programs also had the advantage of taking fewer instructions to get the same result. There is generally a small performance impact to using HLLs instead of assembly because the compiler can't always create the most ideal implementation of assembly from the input program, but for all but the most performance-sensitive applications, this effect is swamped by the estimated 500% improvement in the speed of writing software.[3] By some estimates, there are more than 2500 different high level languages today. C++ and Java are two of the most popular.

The following is a snippet of Java code that writes "Hello World" to the computer screen:

```
public class HelloWorld {
    public static void main (String[] args) {
       System.out.println("Hello World!");
     }
}
```

Hierarchical code

It doesn't make sense to reinvent the wheel every time you write a program. Let's say you write interactive business applications. Do you want to write a program that presents a pulldown menu every time you create a new software product? Of course not. Instead, you take that program you wrote the **first** time you had to present a pulldown menu and reuse it for your next program. It helps to structure, or package, the piece of software in such a way that it can be reused easily. Such packaging can be in many forms. At the most basic form (and the nomenclature depends on the actual language being used), it will be a standalone program called a function, subroutine, method, or object. For simplicity, let's just call it a function. This pulldown menu function can be reused as a building block in your future applications. It can also be freely sold on the web to little hacker-wannabes all over the world for use in their programs.

When you build a house, you don't start with raw materials, like piles of wood, metal, and plastic. Instead, you have building blocks – windows, 2x4s, pieces of plywood, concrete, tiles, wallboard, shingles, nails, etc. So it is with programming. It is much easier to use, write, and understand a program that consists of building blocks than a "linear" program that has, for example, 42,000 sequential lines of code. In the building blocks for the house, some components, such as a sink, are themselves composed of other building blocks (bowl, plumbing, faucet). Similarly, software may consist of building blocks which are composed of smaller building blocks. Such programming is called hierarchical programming.

The advantages to hierarchical programming are numerous:

- *Easier to Maintain or Modify – if you make an improvement to or fix a bug in a line drawing algorithm, instead of fixing every instance of the algorithm (there may be hundreds in a non-hierarchical, or linear, program), you only have to fix it in one place with the hierarchical method.*

- *Easier to Share – hierarchical components can be easily "exported" or "imported", making software development much faster and cheaper.*

- *Easier to Scale – creating larger scope programs may be as simple as increasing the number of iterations in the code, as opposed to writing lots more code.*

- *Easier to Understand – see below*

Let's say that you are writing a program called `CreateVirtualDoors` that creates all of the doors for a house in a virtual world (of course, this is not the way such programs are written, but it serves to illustrate the point). Each instance of a door requires some of the following operations to render it:

```
CreateHinges
CreateDoorKnob
SetDoorPosition
DrawDoorOutline
ApplyDoorTextures
ApplyDoorShading
ApplyDoorShadows
```

Each of these operations would also be a function that may contain other functions, such as `DrawLine` or `DrawPoint`.

And `CreateDoorKnob` requires the following operations:

```
DrawDoorKnobOutline
ApplyDoorKnobTextures
ApplyDoorKnobReflections
```

So there are a couple basic ways to write the program that creates the doors to a house…

Option 1 - The brute force "linear programming" method of writing the program `CreateVirtualDoors` follows:

```
{
DrawDoorOutline(Door 1)
ApplyDoorTextures(Door 1)
ApplyDoorShading(Door 1)
ApplyDoorShadows(Door 1)
CreateHinges(Door 1)
DrawDoorKnobOutline(Door 1)
ApplyDoorKnobTextures(Door 1)
ApplyDoorKnobReflections(Door 1)
SetDoorPosition(Door 1)
DrawDoorOutline(Door 2)
ApplyDoorTextures(Door 2)
ApplyDoorShading(Door 2)
ApplyDoorShadows(Door 2)
CreateHinges(Door 2)
DrawDoorKnobOutline(Door 2)
ApplyDoorKnobTextures(Door 2)
ApplyDoorKnobReflections(Door 2)
SetDoorPosition(Door 2)
DrawDoorOutline(Door 3)
ApplyDoorTextures(Door 3)
ApplyDoorShading(Door 3)
ApplyDoorShadows(Door 3)
CreateHinges(Door 3)
DrawDoorKnobOutline(Door 3)
ApplyDoorKnobTextures(Door 3)
ApplyDoorKnobReflections(Door 3)
SetDoorPosition(Door 3)
DrawDoorOutline(Door 4)
ApplyDoorTextures(Door 4)
ApplyDoorShading(Door 4)
ApplyDoorShadows(Door 4)
```

```
CreateHinges(Door 4)
DrawDoorKnobOutline(Door 4)
ApplyDoorKnobTextures(Door 4)
ApplyDoorKnobReflections(Door 4)
SetDoorPosition(Door 4)
DrawDoorOutline(Door 5)
ApplyDoorTextures(Door 5)
ApplyDoorShading(Door 5)
ApplyDoorShadows(Door 5)
CreateHinges(Door 5)
DrawDoorKnobOutline(Door 5)
ApplyDoorKnobTextures(Door 5)
ApplyDoorKnobReflections(Door 5)
SetDoorPosition(Door 5)
}
```

Option 2 – The Hierarchical method would be implemented by executing the instruction `CreateVirtualDoors(5)`, as implemented by the following building blocks:

```
CreateVirtualDoors(n)
{
For i = 1 to n {
     CreateDoor(i)
     CreateHinges(i)
     CreateDoorKnob(i)
     SetDoorPosition(i)
     next i }
}


CreateDoor(i)
{
DrawDoorOutline(i)
ApplyDoorTextures(i)
ApplyDoorShading(i)
ApplyDoorShadows(i)
}


CreateDoorKnob(i)
{
DrawDoorKnobOutline(i)
ApplyDoorKnobTextures(i)
ApplyDoorKnobReflections(i)
}
```

A graphical representation of the hierarchy of this program is shown in Figure 4-1. I took the liberty of adding lower layer (or level) functions that would make sense for this example.

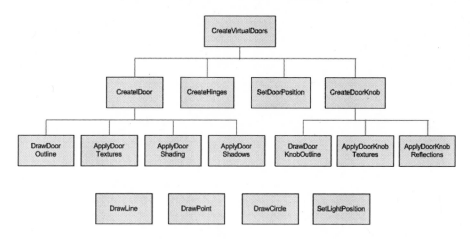

Figure 4-1

The actual details of this hierarchical graph are somewhat flexible, but the basic rules are that the lower the layer (toward the bottom of the chart), the more fundamental the operation. The bottom layer of the chart would typically be "atomic" operations that any higher layer function can use. For convention, let's refer to this lowest layer of functions as Level 1. The higher you go on the chart, the more "sophisticated" the operation is. Creating a set of virtual doors, for example, is a much more sophisticated and higher layer function than drawing a point. Also note that no function on any layer calls, or makes use of, another function on that layer; rather, they use lower layer functions to build up their capabilities. Outlining a good hierarchy would consist of ensuring that each function at a particular layer is roughly comparable in terms of sophistication. `AddTree` should be at the same layer as `AddCloud`, for example, while `AddForest` and `CreateSky` would each be at the next layer up.

This would be very analogous to any large-scale project – creating a skyscraper for example. The highest layer function is creating the skyscraper. The low layer functions are riveting, cutting, measuring, positioning, etc. Mid layer functions would be adding an elevator shaft, installing plumbing, etc. You get the idea.

One final note on this section is that the example above was created for illustrative purposes only. In reality, a good piece of software would not make distinctions between different object types, like the drawing of doors and doorknobs. For example, any object would be defined by its position and points, and the same function `ApplyTextures` could be applied to all objects. Creating flexible functions and flexible data structures that fully model the objects allow higher level programming to be very organized and concise.

Application programming and API's

Once such a set of well-defined and flexible objects, data structures, and functions are created, the programmer no longer has to worry about details like the fact that a door knob is round and shiny and reflects light differently than a flat wooden door. It is all taken care of by the lower layer functions. At this point, the programmer is free to write at a very high layer, or application level, and can write functions like "CreateForest" (density = .52), or "CreateEarthquake" (Richter=7.2, epicenter=Middletown). The set of functions that the programmer has at his/her disposal is called the API, or Application Programming Interface.

Let's imagine that someone has already created an API for a Virtual Reality Program and this API is at Layer 14. One could then add an additional layer of sophistication on top of it and refer to that layer as Layer 15. In this way, the complexity and sophistication of the program can be built up over time. This means that, for the same number of "lines of code", a program can be written that appears to do a lot more and be much more sophisticated than one written at an API a few layers down from the top. There might be no end to the number of layers that can be added to certain types of programs, especially for virtual reality programs; software that models reality.

Back to our example, let's say that you use your
`CreateVirtualDoors` function as part of a program called
`CreateHouse`, which also includes functions like `CreateYard`,
`CreateWindow`, `CreateChimney`, and `CreateTree`. You can give
your `CreateHouse` function some parameters that tell it what kind of
house to create; for example,
`CreateHouse(type=Colonial,age=50,color=white,lotsize=1ac`
`re,woodiness=50%,hilliness=20%)` and the program will create an
entire house, based on the functions already developed at the API
later beneath it. What happens when you want to create a
neighborhood of houses? Each statement
`CreateHouse(type=Colonial,age=50,color=white,lotsize=1.1`
`a,woodiness=50%,hilliness=20%)` would result in exactly the
same house, making your neighborhood pretty boring. To make them
interesting, you would have to specify specific parameters for every
single house that you want. Ah, but there's a better way! Using a
programming construct called a random number generator, each
house can look a little different. You can create a table of house
types and parameters for a particular region, like this:

```
HouseTypeTable={Colonial(55%),Cape(25%),Split(10%),Ranch
(10%)}
HouseAgeTable={5(40%),10(15%),15(15%),25(10%),50(10%),75
(10%)}
HouseColorTable={White(30%),Yellow(20%),Country
Grey(20%),Beige(15%),Blue(15%)}
```

Then your program statements to create houses in the neighborhood
might look like this:

```
CreateHouse(type=HouseTypeTable(RND),HouseAgeTable(RND),
HouseColorTable(RND))
```

Each house uses the same statement, which greatly simplifies the
process of creating a neighborhood. RND is what tells the program to
pick a parameter from the corresponding table based on the
probabilities in that table. The result is a nice distribution of houses
of various types, ages, colors, lot types, etc. You can make your
parameter tables as complex as you want, or even use distribution

functions to model a typical distribution of, for example, woodiness in a lot.

In fact, you can now move up a level in the API and create a function called `CreateNeighborhood(houses=50,location=x.y,averageage=10, woodiness=50%,socioeconomicclass=middleupper).` Go to town again with your parameter distribution tables and random numbers, and pretty soon you are writing `CreateTown` and then, `CreateWorld`.

I think I can actually hear a chorus of "Aha, now I see where he's going" out there.

CHAPTER 5

Virtual Reality and Mind Melding with our Future Silicon Masters

History

Virtual Reality (VR) is a term that was coined in 1989 by Jaron Lanier, a pioneer in the field. It is generally considered to be a computer-generated simulation of an alternative reality that is experienced with the aid of devices that fool the senses. Temporarily ignoring the senses of smell and taste that are less critical to simulating an alternate reality, VR deals mostly with emulating the senses of sight, sound, and touch.

Sound is easily obtained with a set of unobtrusive headphones. For sight, stereoscopic displays, also known as head-mounted displays, VR goggles or visors, can be worn that have small computer screens in front of each eye. So far, this would be little more than watching a 3D movie on a wraparound screen with surround sound headphones. But, in addition, tactile sensations can be provided by special gloves worn by the experiencer. However, this would still be a one-way experience, like a dream. A final critical element is needed for a good immersive experience and that is the ability of the subject to interact with their environment and for the computer to sense that interaction. The gloves can provide part of this via sensors on the fingertips that are bi-directional. That is, not only do they provide the tactile sensations to the fingers of the wearer, they also detect his finger and hand movements and can therefore position the hands properly in the field of vision, emulated grabbing items, etc. Also, the headset typically contains a head tracker that senses the orientation of the person's head. Overall, this is a little bit of a cumbersome set of gear, but suffices to create the effect of being in and interacting with a computer-generate alternate world. Figure 5-1 below shows an astronaut training in Johnson Space Center's virtual reality lab. Commercial visors are currently a little less cumbersome and typically provide 800x600 resolution.

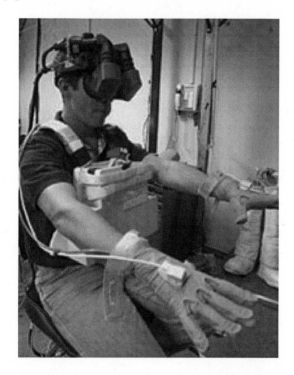

Figure 5-1 (image courtesy of NASA)

Virtual Reality had tremendous promise back in the early 1990s, when the fledgling industry was hyped as the next big thing. Slow computers, slow networks, unrealistic expectations, poor glove and goggle resolutions and expensive components all share some of the blame for the failure of the fulfillment of that promise, at least in the entertainment field. However, VR has found a home in pilot and astronaut training, medical and surgical training, dangerous equipment operational training, automotive design, and other scientific and industrial venues. Many futurists believe that it is just a matter of time before the concept takes off again. We are already seeing a plethora of gaming devices that provide haptic feedback – rumble seats, rumble vests, rumble packs, vibrating steering wheels, etc. And then there is teledildonics, the marriage of virtual reality and pornography. Although Vivid Entertainment's Cyber Sex Suit, launched in 1999, failed FTC testing and never made it to market, the pleasure industry has not given up. At the 2004 Erotica trade show in Los Angeles, sex toy maker Doc Johnson demonstrated their products that enable two people to have virtual sex over the internet by controlling the "speed and rhythm" of the device that their remote partner is wearing.[1]

Senses

Conventional wisdom is that we receive all of our sensory input through the 5 senses – sight, hearing, smell, touch, and taste. It is how we perceive our reality. In all cases, we have specific sensory receptors that gather environmental data. Each of these sensors transmit data to the brain, which processes it into a sensory experience. Retinal sensors in the eyes collect light and color, which is collectively interpreted, by the brain as an image. Hair fibers in the inner ear sense pressure vibrations in the air that are collectively interpreted by the brain as a sound. Taste receptors on the tongue send data to the brain, which interprets taste. Pressure sensors in the skin deliver data to the brain, which interprets touch. And molecular sensors in the nose send signals to the brain, which produces the sensation of smell. So, in all cases, there are two major components to sensing – the actual sensors themselves, and the processing unit known as the brain. In the Virtual Reality World described above, the senses are fooled by injecting an alternate reality into their associated receptors. What would happen if the brain was fooled by sending it alternate data?

Consider the following thought experiment. A device, that we shall call *the Interceptor*, is placed between the sensory nerve endings and the pathways to the brain of our subject, who we shall call Jessica (see Figure 5-2).

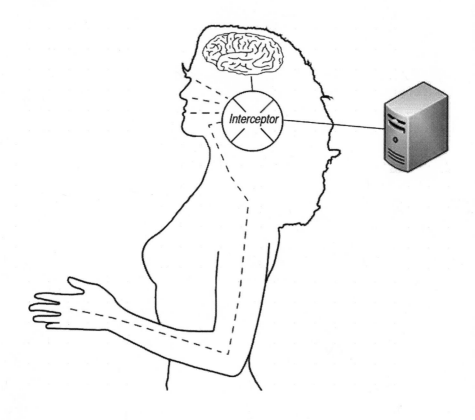

Figure 5-2

A switch controls the pathway that the sensory signals would take. Initially, we shall set this switch to "passthrough" mode, whereby, all of the signals from each sensory organ pass directly to her brain (see Figure 5-3). This makes it completely transparent to Jessica – she should have no idea that the Interceptor is there.

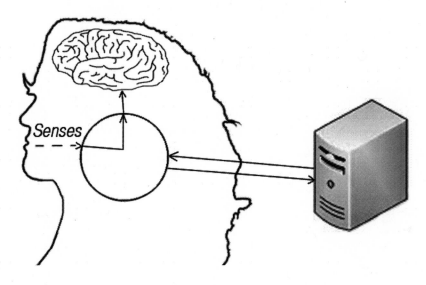

Figure 5-3

The Interceptor also has a connection to a sophisticated remote computer, which is fully capable of emulating the human brain, at least to the level of processing sensory stimuli. When we set the switch to "remote control" mode, all sensory signals are transferred to the remote computer, which can then respond by sending another set of sensory signals back to Jessica's brain (see Figure 5-4).

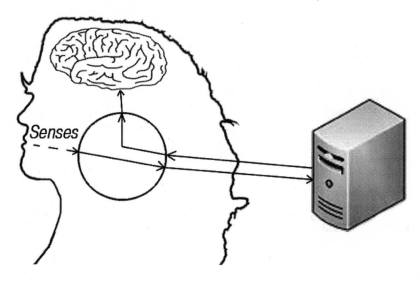

Figure 5-4

If the signals that the remote computer sends to Jessica are identical to the signals coming from her eyes, ears, nose, tongue, and nerve endings, then she will still not know the difference (unless, of course, the remote computer has introduced a delay into the whole signal path, in which case, she may just feel a little slow, or drunk). However, if the remote computer sends different signals back to Jessica, then she will think she is experiencing something completely different. Let's say, for example, that Jessica opens a can of tuna fish and takes a bite. The remote computer intercepts the "this tastes like tuna fish" signal being sent from her tongue and replaces it with a "this tastes like chicken" signal. If Jessica didn't actually look at or smell the tuna fish, she may fully believe that she is eating chicken. If she did look at it, the remote computer need only add the "this looks like chicken" signal to the mix.

Now, we load the "turn Jessica's self image into a chimp" program and ask her to step in front of a mirror. Visual signals of Jessica's reflection are reprocessed by the computer in order to make her believe that she is looking at a chimp in front of the mirror. Her brain says "this can't be" and commands her to raise her arm and touch the hair on her face. As she raised her arm, the signals are again replaced by equivalent signals of a chimp raising its arm. Puzzled, she attempts to touch her face to reassure herself that there really isn't any strange Simian hair there. Although her fingers actually touch her smooth face, the computer is smart enough to realize that when her fingers get close to her face, it must generate "this feels like body hair" signals that are perfectly in synch with her motions. For all intents and purposes, Jessica can be completely fooled into thinking that she has turned into a chimp. Every sensory stimulus can be reprocessed to make her believe anything that the programmer of the computer desires. The feeling of gravity can be modified to make her feel heavier or lighter. She can be made to feel like she is standing up, even when she is lying down, and vice versa. In short, the computer program can give Jessica a full virtual reality experience by simply manipulating her sensory signals.

Jessica's memory, however, retains the knowledge that she was once human. For this reason, she will most certainly be traumatized, especially if this is not a consensual experiment. However, as time goes by, she may become accustomed to being a chimp. And if her life as a chimp is made to be pleasant, her memories of being human may slowly fade. If this Interceptor process is done from birth, she will actually never know anything different from being a chimp. From her perspective, she has always been a chimp and fully thinks she knows what it is like to be a chimp.

Let's take it one step further. Let's say that the Interceptor switch has a third position. In that position, it has fully transferred control to the remote computer, essentially replacing all of the sensory stimuli from Jessica's sense organs with stimuli generated by the remote computer (figure 5-5).

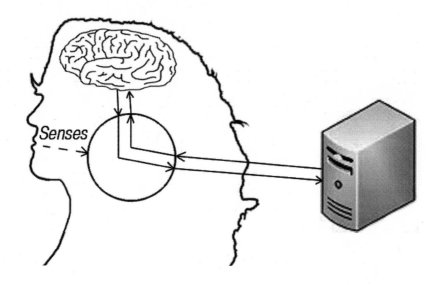

Figure 5-5

Further, let us assume that the remote computer has access to all of the electrochemical bits in Jessica's brain and is able to modify them at will. This is not so unrealistic as we shall see. Essentially, Jessica's senses have now become the remote computer and her brain is fully under its control. Now, it is even possible for the remote computer to completely erase all memories that Jessica had of her pre-Simian existence and replace them with a full set of typical Simian experiences. In such a case, then, Jessica can instantly become somebody else. She doesn't have to wait for memory to fade and this process doesn't have to be done from birth.

Question – how do you know you are who you think you are?

Is it possible that you have been fooled by an Interceptor? From a strict logical point of view, you would have to admit that such a scenario may be possible. For those who have seen the movie "The Matrix," this thought experiment will be familiar. Furthermore, it doesn't even have to be a clunky implant with wires sticking out of it as depicted in Figure 5-2. It could be a little nano-transceiver implanted in your head, which communicates wirelessly with a remote system. Why is that so hard to believe? Everything is wireless today – TV, phones, computers, tracking devices, RFID. It is certainly not a stretch to imagine a world where everyone's brain is linked to the "mother computer" somewhere. Or, if we want to get biochemical and metaphysical, perhaps the culprit is a gland in your head (such as, for example, our friend the pineal gland) that takes the sensory signals, transmits them through an unknown field (the "A-field", the "ether"), to the cosmic consciousness, which processes them and sends the control signals, encoded memories, etc. back down through the ether into your brain, via the same or a similar gland. Why not? Have you ever been in a wireless videoconference (laptop to laptop)? All of the functional components described in this thought experiment are present in the videoconference – sensory receivers, transmitters, receivers, network switching, computer processing. It's just a matter of scalability.

For one final note in this section, in the final phase of the thought experiment above, we said that Jessica could instantly become somebody else. This is not quite true, however. More accurately, her self-image can instantly change. We haven't really addressed the question of who Jessica really is. If she is nothing more than the state of her brain, then she can become someone else at the flick of a switch. But, if Jessica is defined by her soul, then this scenario doesn't change who she is, just her self-image.

Implants

Modern medicine has brought us hip replacements, knee replacements, breast implants, artificial heart valves, artificial limbs, teeth implants, synthetic arteries, cochlear implants, and penis implants and pumps. The near future promises more sophisticated artificial organs like the liver and pancreas, artificial retinas, and eventually less crude methods of synthetic replacement parts via nanotech assemblers. Ultimately, our bodies may be largely synthetic, at least in today's terminology. However, it seems as if the process of creating bionic humans will have to stop with the nervous system and brain.

Or will it?

We seem to be heading in the direction of transplantable or artificial brain parts. In 1984, a frontal cortex transplant was conducted between lab rats, with the transplantee surviving the operation.[2] While that only proved the ability of an animal to survive the operation, in 1987, Lehman et al replaced the nucleus of the hypothalamus (responsible for the sleep cycle) of one hamster with that of another. The sleep rhythm of hamster with the new nucleus was restored after the operation, demonstrating that brain parts can be transplanted with functional recovery in the recipient.[3] The first brain prosthesis (an artificial hippocampus) was developed and tested on rat brains in 2003.[4] Higher mammals and then humans will not be far behind.

Mind Melding with our Future Silicon Masters

> "You're suffering from a Vulcan mind-meld, Doctor."
> - Kirk (from "Star Trek III: The Search for Spock" (1984))
>
> "That green-blooded sonofabitch. It's his revenge for all those arguments he lost."
> - McCoy (from "Star Trek III: The Search for Spock" (1984))

Ray Kurzweil outlines a future scientifically feasible method of storing the brain state of a human into an artificial device and restoring it at some point, essentially providing the ability to download and upload memories. For those who believe that "our essence" is simply our memories, this allows the possibilities of full organic body replacement or replacement of the organic body with a synthetic body, and therefore, immortality![5]

But for those who believe that our essence is something more (aka, a "soul"), what would be the consequences of this direction? There seem to be two possibilities, depending on the location of the soul. It may be in the brain, because it is the one organ that seems to be irreplaceable by an artificial replica. There is a traditional view, with a somewhat religious foundation, which holds that the soul or spirit comes from "out there" and enters the body at some point during fetal development. Although the Catholic Church has no official position on when this occurs, it is central to the Pro-Life/Pro-Choice debate. And recall that Dr. Strassman's belief that the spirit enters the fetus on day 49 is based on Buddhist teachings. If this is so, could it be possible to store our brain state, including the soul, onto silicon? It seems to me that if the soul is this mysterious energy force, it can't be tied to something physical, in which case it may simply cease to follow the transplanted memories, or it may follow them and take up residence in the new artificial vessel. There is certainly no conclusive answer.

On the other hand, perhaps the function of the brain is simply to act as a cache – a local data store of information and processing function that is frequently required. Recall Dr. Bruce Lipton's view (Chapter 2) that mind and consciousness are not in the brain, but "somewhere out there." He is by no means alone in his thinking, but accompanied by an eclectic set of scientists, metaphysicists, philosophers, theologians, and new age researchers. In this case, the spirit remains elsewhere and may make the same choice of what to control after the transplant – the old organic entity or the new silicon clone. So, in either case, the human evolutionary move from the organic to inorganic vessel could occur without a hitch. Kurzweil's last few elements of his singularity are: [6]

- *Nanotech will enable the "manipulation of physical reality," and nanobots will "interact with biological neurons to…[create] virtual reality from within the nervous system." Swarms of nanobots in the brain will "vastly extend human intelligence".*

- *Foglets will have the ability to create alternate physical realities at the push of a button.*

- *The distinction between virtual and physical realities will blur and we will tend to select the virtual realities as the stage for our experiences, allowing us the freedom to exist in different forms.*

At the risk of making this book seem like just a collection of my favorite theories, I must include just one more, which I always found fascinating, and, as it turns out, highly relevant to the topic of this book. [Don't worry, it all comes together in Chapter 7.] Professor of Mathematical Physics at Tulane University, Dr. Frank Tipler, wrote a book in 1995 called "The Physics of Immortality: Modern Cosmology, God and the Resurrection of the Dead." In this book, written 10 years before Kurzweil's singularity, he posits that humans will ultimately merge with silicon AI (Artificial Intelligence) and the resulting intelligent life will be able to populate the universe at a rate exceeding its entropy decay. When this expansion reaches its ultimate point, we will discover, or rather, create, the Omega Point, an intelligence that encompasses all quantum mechanical life-paths, aka God. Compare this to Kurzweil's Singularity, whereby "intelligence, derived from its biological origins in human brains and its technological origins in human ingenuity, will begin to saturate the matter and energy in its midst. It will achieve this by reorganizing matter and energy to provide an optimal level of computation to spread out from its origin on Earth...superluminally...[and, ultimately] our civilization infuses the rest of the universe with its creativity and intelligence."[7]

So where does that leave us? It seems that no matter what you believe, we are in for quite a ride in the 21st century. We'll pick up this topic again in Chapter 7. But first, what about all those funny little topics that make us question everything we thought we knew...

CHAPTER 6

Life's Little Anomalies – Green Men and Black Gold

This chapter presents a set of strange anomalies from our everyday experience. I propose that these anomalies are actually evidence for an underlying planned structure to the Universe. For those of you that are trained in logical thinking and the scientific method (as I was), you will have a tendency to laugh at some of the topics in this section. For this reason, we start the chapter with an exercise in open mindedness, which can be taken as a warning to not be too sure of your belief system. If, after digesting this exercise, you still find yourself having a hard time with some of the anomalous topics later on, try to treat them as not necessarily real, but just phenomena with no satisfactory explanations. You may not ever believe in UFOs, for example, but you have to admit that millions of people are convinced beyond a shadow of a doubt that they have seen them. And that itself is a bona fide phenomenon.

Be Careful Out There

We have all learned that "you can't believe everything you read." Absolutely true, a point that the Internet has driven home exceptionally well. But, in addition to fringe ideas, this also applies perfectly to the ideas that we commonly consider to be factual and proven. Today's conventional wisdom or "scientific fact" may be tomorrow's humorous anecdote. Consider the following:

In 1964, when physicist George Zweig proposed the existence of what is now termed 'quarks', he was rejected for a position at a major university and considered a "charlatan." Today, quarks are an accepted part of the standard nuclear model.[1,2]

In the 1800s, the scientific community considered reports of rocks falling from the sky (aka meteors) in the same way that the scientific community views UFO reports today.[3]

"I think there's a world market for maybe five computers."
Thomas Watson, chairman of IBM (1943)

"There is no reason for any individual to have a computer in his home."
Ken Olsen, the founder and CEO of Digital Equipment Corporation (1977)

In 1879, an amateur archaeologist from Spain named Marcelino Sanz de Sautuola discovered prehistoric cave art in a cave in Spain. He believed it to be from the same pre-ice age period to which other regional cave artifacts had been dated and published a document to that effect in 1880. For the rest of his life he was brutally ridiculed, shunned, and his reputation smeared by the French-influenced scientific orthodoxy of the time. Only after his death did the scientific community slowly come to realize that he was correct and had actually initiated the study of Paleolithic cave art that is active to this day.[4]

"In a few years, all great physical constants will have been approximately estimated, and that the only occupation which will be left to men of science will be to carry these measurements to another place of decimals."
- James Clerk Maxwell (1871)

"This 'telephone' has too many shortcomings to be seriously considered as a means of communication. The device is inherently of no value to us. "
- Western Union internal memo (1876)

"I see no good reasons why the views given in this volume should shock the religious sensibilities of anyone."
- Charles Darwin, The Origin Of Species, 1869.

"There is not the slightest indication that nuclear energy will ever be obtainable. It would mean that the atom would have to be shattered at will."
- Albert Einstein, 1932.

"The bomb will never go off. I speak as an expert in explosives."
- Admiral William Leahy, U.S. Atomic Bomb Project.

"The demonstration that no possible combination of known substances, known forms of machinery and known forms of force, can be united in a practical machine by which men shall fly along distances through the air, seems to the writer as complete as it is possible for the demonstration to be."
- Simon Newcomb, former American Math Society President, 1900

"The aeroplane will never fly."
- Lord Haldane, Minister of War, Britain, 1907 (statement made four years after Kitty Hawk.)

"Louis Pasteur's theory of germs is ridiculous fiction."
- Pierre Pachet, Professor of Physiology at Toulouse, 1872.

Unfortunately, there are countless more examples of "Pathological Skepticism" that has occurred throughout history. In fact, it actually seems that new ideas are far more often rebuked than accepted by the scientific and medical communities. There is often good reason for this. Professors lose tenure if they stray into fields that their university considers "inappropriate research." Funding suddenly dries up and the scientific community often shuns the brave individual who dares to investigate topics beyond the accepted norm. As an example, consider what happened to electrochemists Stanley Pons and Martin Fleischmann from the University of Utah, when they announced their results of "cold fusion" experiments in 1989. When subsequent experiments initially failed to reproduce their results, they were ridiculed by the scientific community, even to the point of driving them to leave their jobs and their country, and continuing their research in France. Since then, nearly 15,000 similar experiments have been conducted, scientists from Oak Ridge National Laboratory and the Russian Academy of Science have replicated cold fusion experiments, and the US Department of Energy has given the green light for related research. According to a 50-page report on the current state of cold fusion by Steven Krivit and Nadine Winocur, the effect has been reproduced at a rate of 83%. "Experimenters in Japan, Romania, the United States, and Russia have reported a reproducibility rate of 100 percent."[5] So, while fringe research can be career suicide, that doesn't at all mean that such investigations are invalid.

It seems as if it is human nature to resist change and fear the ideas that can topple existing foundations of belief. I include this section at this point in the book to encourage people to keep an open mind as they read. Some ideas that you may think are proven beyond a doubt, will crumble as the years pass. Some ideas that now seem fringe will become orthodox. How do you determine which will be which? You can't. All you can do is keep an open mind – open to new ideas, and open to the possibility that orthodox views may not necessarily be right. If you can do that, you're ready to head down the rabbit hole.

The Truman Show

> "We believe the reality we are presented with"
> - The character Christof, from "The Truman Show",
> 1998

Many critics viewed the movie "The Truman Show" as a metaphor for the way that the media manipulates our view of reality. I viewed it as a metaphor for reality itself.

To revisit our introductory questions, did you ever feel like there is something about reality that isn't quite random, as it should be? Something a little too organized, a little too planned, a little too programmed? Obviously I can't speak for other people and other lives, but I've always had the feeling that there is something watching over me, keeping the world in check, and keeping my life and the collective world experience in a narrow band of quality. What I mean is this: You have some good days and some bad days, right? The world has some good days (Fall of the Berlin Wall) and bad days (September 11, 2001) as well. Let's quantify "good" and "bad." 100 is really really good. -100 is really really bad. 0 is average. Let's further assume that, to a large extent, your mood at the beginning of the day pretty much equals your mood at the end of yesterday. This might not be true for everyone. Some people feel better after a good nights sleep. But others are at their best late at night and are NOT morning people. So it evens out. Given this, your mood at the end of the day will be your mood at the beginning of that day plus the cumulative effect of all of the positive and negative impacts that hit you during the day. Maybe you start the day at a 10, feeling a little above average. Then the boss insults your work, your pet pees on the bed, and you find a nasty virus on your laptop. Maybe that represents -30 worth of negative "mood points." So you end the day at -20. If you had started the day off at -10, these things would leave you at -40, because you were starting off in a negative mood and the negative experiences only made things worse. On the flip side, the next day, you get a great job offer, your pet just wants to give you love, and you win new laptop in a raffle. And then you're pretty much back to where you started.

If life were truly random, there would be an equal probability of having positive or negative experiences at any point in time, no matter what your current mood is. I programmed this model into a spreadsheet, using what felt like a typical deviation of 20 mood swing point in a given day (representing the fact that on a given day it might be reasonable to move 20% closer to a really really bad day or a really really good day. I could scale back the daily deviation and the result would end up being the same, only spread out more in time. In any case, I ran the model four times with random numbers. The results are shown in the four charts in Figure 6-1. Notice that in all cases, life's mood index crosses over the positive or negative limits at least once in 50 days. In fact, the nature of this model is that it doesn't matter what your mood is, it always has an equal probability of getting worse or better, depending on life's events. And if no one is overseeing life's events, as the atheists and reductionists would have us believe, such a model should represent how life works.

But it doesn't.

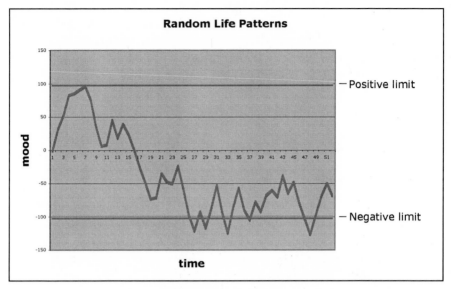

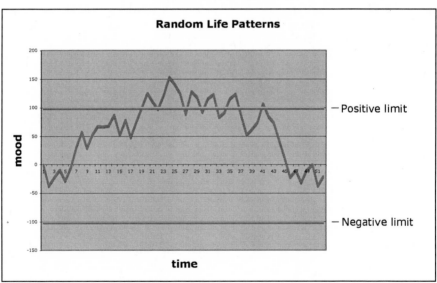

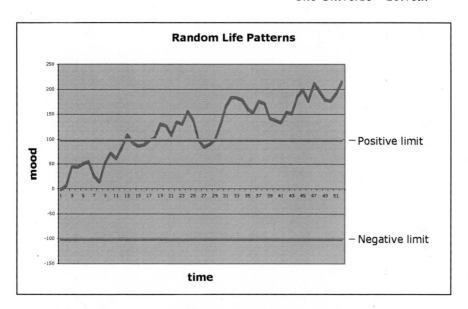

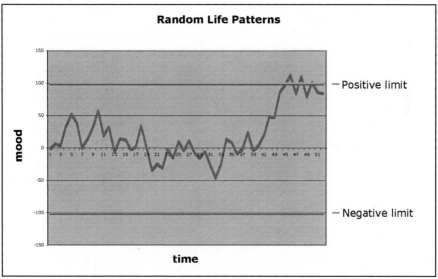

Figure 6-1

I submit that there is an "evening out" effect to life. That when you are feeling your lowest, something brings you up. When you are feeling your highest, something tends to bring you down. So it is with the world. The high flying 20's got corrected by the stock market crash of 1929. The doom and gloom 70's predicted nuclear

151

Armageddon, imminent overpopulation, and financial disasters. But the 80's and 90's corrected it with the end of the cold war, reduction in population growth, and stability of the world's economy. Why?

With my own life, I never feel like I break the negative or positive mood limits. There always seems to be something that keeps it in a narrow range. I'm not talking about psychology or physiology. I'm talking about actual events. At work in the high tech industry, whenever I felt most frustrated and at an impasse, I would suddenly be presented with solutions out of nowhere. When I felt most confident, I would suddenly be presented with a confidence-shaking experience. In life, when I feel most down, something positive always happens. When I feel most ecstatic, something will always occur to bring me back down to earth.

So I added a stabilizing factor to my spreadsheet program which had the effect to pulling life's mood toward zero, especially the further it gets from zero. I ran the model and got the following results, that seem to reflect reality much more than the random model does (Figures 6-2).

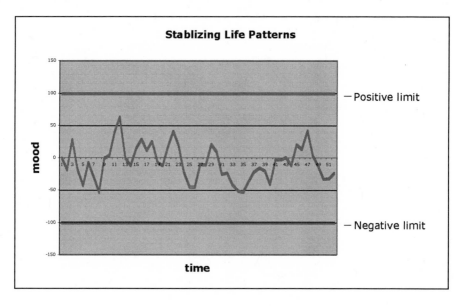

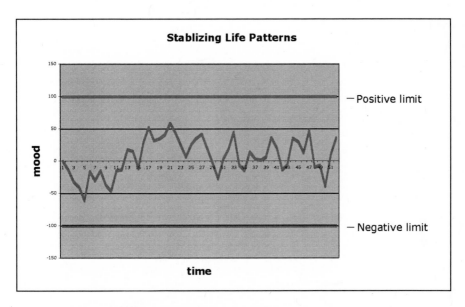

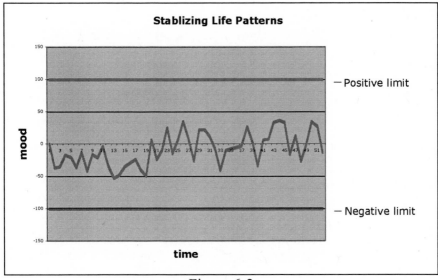

Figure 6-2

There is something that seems to maintain a narrow window of mood and experience. I am not aware of any studies that have applied the scientific process to this phenomenon, but the results would certainly be interesting.

Coincidences

"A woman in Berkeley, California, is locked out of her house; the postman walks up, holding a letter from her brother... inside is a spare key."
- Incredible Coincidence: The Baffling World of Synchronicity, by Alan Vaughan, 1979

"Laura Buxton, aged ten, releases a balloon from her garden in Staffordshire. It lands 140 miles away in Wiltshire, in the garden of another Laura Buxton, aged ten."
- Beyond Coincidence, by Martin Plimmer and Brian King, 2004

What we are talking about in the above examples are "meaningful coincidences", also known to followers of famous Swiss psychiatrist Carl Jung as *synchronicity*. In his 1979 book "Incredible Coincidence: The Baffling World of Synchronicity," Alan Vaughan methodically documented 150 cases of sets of coincidental events that defy explanation in the standard clockwork universe that scientific orthodoxy believes represents reality. In the 2004 book "Beyond Coincidence", authors Martin Plimmer and Brian King bring the topic up to date with even more startling stories.

Mathematicians might argue that statistically, rare and special coincidences are bound to occur simply due to random probabilities. For example, one morning you are thinking about a song you haven't heard in a long time and later, while you are listening to the radio, the song comes on. Seemingly improbable at first glance, how many times do you think of a song and then *don't* hear it that day on the radio? Because most of those non-coincidental examples go straight into your subconscious untagged as a special experience, while the coincidental ones by their very nature are tagged as special, you tend to remember many more of the "meaningful coincidences" than non-coincidental events. However, this doesn't prove that there isn't significance to synchronistic experiences. To do that, one would have to properly calculate all of the probabilities relating to the events, which is impossible to do for real life anecdotal data. Therefore, science can neither prove nor disprove synchronicity.

There have been some attempts, however. Carl Jung himself conducted an experiment to determine whether there is any significance in planetary alignments and astrology to suitability of marriage partners. The results of his experiment concluded that there was statistical significance to some underlying "synchronistic phenomenon." Responding to Dr. Richard Dawkin's mathematical analysis of the likelihood of people experiencing a stopped watch during a Uri Geller-type media appearance (a true synchronistic experience to the watch holder), Mr. Geller claimed that he typically experiences 2000 reports of started watches (a much more significant event than a stopped watch – all watches stop when the battery runs out, how many spontaneously start after being dead for a while?) through the TV station switchboard vs. the 6 estimated cases of stopped watches calculated by Dr. Dawkins. If we are to believe his numbers, and even if we allow that the likelihood of a newly rejuvenated watch is the same as a dying watch battery, the odds of 2000 occurrences against 6 projected by a probabilistic normal distribution are astronomical. For example, with a standard deviation of 4 (meaning that 68% of the time, the number of people experiencing a started watch would range between 2 and 10), the odds that even 40 people would experience the same thing during the show are over 10,000,000,000,000,000 to 1.

Anecdotal evidence should not be ignored just because it doesn't fit with the scientific method. And the sheer volume of synchronistic anecdotal evidence is staggering. Most of us have had several such experiences that just don't seem to be explainable by chance. For my part, I recall an event that occurred when I was a teenager. I was reading, in a quiet house. Suddenly, something compelled me to walk over to the phone, pick it up, and say "Hi Bill." When I did, my friend, Bill, was on the line. He was dumbfounded because the connection had just been made and there hadn't been time for any ringtone feedback. From my perspective, the phone had not rung. In fact, given that the amount of time that elapsed from the point that my friend had finished dialing and he heard me answer was less than the amount of time it took me to walk across the room, it could not have been explained by even a brief subliminal sound of the phone connecting. It was also not like I had attempted this before. This was the one and only time in my life that I was ever compelled to pick up the phone in this manner. The odds? Given that he probably called me once every 2 days or so, during the 6 hours between arriving home from school and going to bed, and that the timeframe during which the coincidence would seem remarkable had to be less than 1 second, the odds of this occurring at any point that I would consciously attempt it would be 43200 to 1. However, to that figure, one must multiply the odds that I would even be struck with a thought to do that, which is a figure much harder to determine. Given that there are about 10,000 2-day periods in the average person's typical phone-calling lifetime, the odds that I would pick that specific two day period are 10,000 to 1. And how many people do you know who have ever been struck by a thought to do such a thing? Maybe 1 in 100? That would give a total probability of over 4 billion to 1 that such an event would occur by chance. If we've all had a few similar experiences in our lives, that accounts for billions of anecdotal cases of highly improbable events.

The Acceleration

"There is more to life than increasing its speed."
- Mahatma Gandhi

Does it seem to you that everything is moving at an increasingly fast pace? The media speaks of the population explosion, the technology explosion, the information explosion. People reminisce about the good old days, when life was slower. One wonders how much of this is an effect of getting older, and how much is due to an objective fact that world events are indeed accelerating.

Mayan Calendar

Mayan scholar Ian Xel Lungold believes that, in reality, "consciousness is speeding up."[6] He has observed a 15 billion year long string of coincidences between cosmological events, human evolution and development and the Mayan calendar. To summarize, the Mayan calendar has 9 stages, beginning at the beginning of time. Each stage has a definitive end point (such as the appearance of the cell, or a mammal). Each stage has a duration that is 20 times shorter than the previous stage. And, the final stage will end on 10/28 2011 (note: many scholars count the dates differently and have the final stage ending on December 21, 2012). If we were to plot these stages on a timeline, they would look something like Figure 6-1.

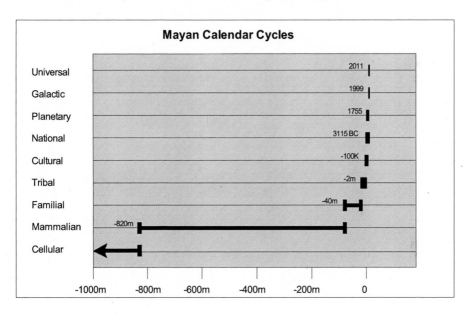

Figure 6-1

Population

The following graph shows the estimated population of the earth over the past 2000 years. This can also be viewed as a temporal acceleration effect if you consider the question "How long does it take to increase the world population by a given amount." It doesn't matter – it's the shape of the graph that jumps out at you. It appears that the graph is approaching some sort of asymptote in the coming century. One wonders, how many humans can the earth sustain? Gaia Watch has done a very thorough and fascinating analysis of the "carrying capacity" of the earth with respect to human population (food, energy, breathable gases, etc.) Their study determined that at a world population of 6 billion, we are currently at about 50% of the earth's capacity to indefinitely sustain that mass of humanity.[7] A quick glance at Figure 6-2 reveals that unless something causes the growth trend to reverse, we will run out of space in the next 100 years.

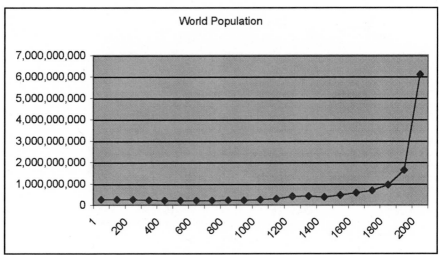

Figure 6-2

The Singularity

The Acceleration Studies Foundation (ASF) is a nonprofit organization based in California that "explores the accelerating development of special domains in science and technology, and examines their impact on business and society." They have developed a paradigm of human development in terms of various societal evolutionary ages or stages. Each successive stage appears to be equally advanced relative to the previous stage, so one might think that each stage should take as long to get through as all of the others. But, because of the fact that we build on all of the tools and knowledge acquired from the previous stages, each stage takes considerably less time than the previous one. In fact, these stages asymptotically are approaching a date this century that the ASF refers to as a "technological singularity", around the year 2060. A variety of well known futurists, including Vernor Vinge, Ray Kurzweil, Marvin Minsky, Richard Coren, James Wesley, Damien Broderick, Robin Hansen, Eliezer Yudkowsky, and Nick Bostrom have come to the same conclusion, although their predictions for the year in which the singularity occurs typically varies between 2020 and 2060.

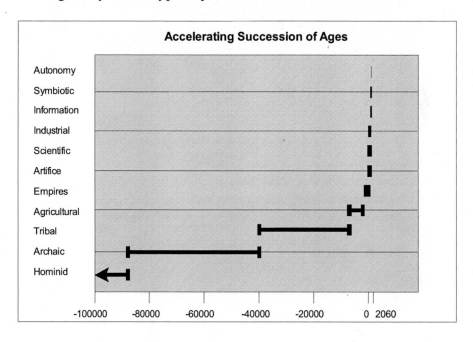

Figure 6-3

Recall Ray Kurzweil's projections of AI outpacing human intelligence, the merge of humans and computers, and the ability of nanotechnology to blur the distinction between reality and fantasy. It all seems kind of unavoidable, doesn't it? What does the singularity mean? Time ends? Everything happens at once? Maybe not. Perhaps we will simply wake up.

Little Green Men

> "Mulder: They're notorious for their extraction of terrestrial human livers, due to iron depletion in the Reticulan galaxy.
> Cultin: You can't be serious.
> Mulder: Do you have any idea what liver and onions go for in Reticula?"
> - The characters Mulder and Cultin, from "The X-Files", Season 1, Episode 2 ("Squeeze")

A CNN/Time Magazine poll released in June 1997 reports that 80 percent of Americans think the "government is hiding knowledge of the existence of extraterrestrial life forms." In that poll, 64% believed that aliens have contacted humans and half believe that humans have been abducted. (note: sampling error reported as +/-3%)[8] In the UK, in a telephone poll conducted 3 days after the ITV airing of a UFO debate, 87% of the respondents said they believed in the extraterrestrial hypothesis.

Still, skeptics will argue that UFOlogy is bunk and no one with a right mind would ever believe in it.

So let's examine some of the evidence and the skeptics' viewpoint and the possible theories to the anomaly.

The Evidence

The case for UFOs consists of sightings and various forms of physical and non-physical evidence. The sheer number of sightings is staggering. The ufoevidence.org website claims that "according to the United Nations, since 1947, approximately 150 million people have been witnesses to UFO sightings throughout the world."[10] More formally, they cite about 120,000 documented UFO sightings in the modern age and refer to various surveys and polls conducted over the past 50 years reporting that 5%-10% of the US population believes

they have seen a UFO. According to the late Harvard University
Professor of Psychiatry, Dr. John Mack, "UFO abductions are not a
rare phenomenon and have been estimated to have occurred to three-
million Americans [note: this figure was based on a 1991 Roper
poll].[11] There is a remarkably precise correspondence to the reports."
Researcher Brad Sparks' "Comprehensive Catalog of 1,500 Project
Bluebook UFO Unknowns" identifies, out of 12,000 cases
investigated by the US Air Force in "Project Blue Book," 1500
(12.5%) that have remained unidentified after investigation.[12]

Physical evidence includes photographs, videos, radar imagery, and
actual physical effects resulting from the craft themselves. Roy
Craig's "The Condon Report: Direct Physical Evidence" identifies
cases of markings, material residues, recovered parts of UFO's, and
strange metals with unearthly compositions. The Condon Report also
reviews indirect evidence such as radiation levels, magnetic
disturbances, engine malfunctions, and electric power interruptions.
The French GEPAN/SEPRA Project has cataloged 489 cases of radar
evidence, including 101 that involve both radar and visual
confirmation.[13]

It is hard to make the case that 150 million people are crackpots, or
that 120,000 documented observations were all hoaxes. Nor is the
phenomenon limited to recent times. The UFO phenomenon, and its
"fringier" corollary, the abduction phenomenon, have been with us
for thousands of years. They didn't start with the Roswell incident in
1947 (note: I use the word "incident" not to assert an opinion on the
truth of the story, but more to ascribe the nature of today's view of
Roswell). Jim Marrs researched many accounts of ancient UFO
sightings in his book "Alien Agenda." For example[14]...

- *The Hindu texts Bhagavata-Purana, Mahabharata, and
  Ramayana all speak of flying machines called vimanas that
  travel to other worlds.*

- *The Tibetan book Kantyua speaks of "transparent spheres
  containing gods who come to visit men."*

- *Stone plates were found in graves in China in 1962, which described a group of beings who "crash landed on the 3rd planet of this star system 12,000 years ago".*

- *Roman writer Julius Obsequens reported that "things like ships were seen in the sky" in the year 212 BC.*

- *In 1254, in Saint Albans, England, it was recorded that "there suddenly appeared in the sky a kind of large ship elegantly shaped."*

- *There were reports in Nuremberg, Germany in 1561 that various objects emerged from two cylindrical craft in the sky and carried out a battle.*

And more recently, here are just a few cases and reports by seemingly credible witnesses...

- *In Los Angeles in 1942, thousands of witnesses observed flying objects that "zigzagged", "hovered", and/or moved at high rates of speed, which prompted air raid sirens, 1430 rounds of antiaircraft fire, and ultimately an official explanation of "jittery nerves."[15]*

- *In an interview conducted by Bruce Roger Anderson, retired Sergeant-Major Robert Dean working for Supreme Headquarters Allied Powers Europe (military arm of NATO) in the early 1960s, with a top level NATO clearance, described a document that he was given called "A Possible Military Threat To The Allied Forces In Europe." The report documented a study of the UFO sightings by the military, and was complete with "photographs, the autopsy reports, the detailed analysis of experts all over Europe." Dean described several incidents where unknown aircraft cause high alert levels both within NATO as well as the Soviet Union, due to which "we almost went to war."[16] In addition, in their book "Clear Intent," Larry Fawcett and Barry Greenwood present actual Department of Defense documents that report multiple cases of UFOs penetrating secure nuclear missile bases.*

• *Colonel Philip Corso was a decorated World War II and Korean War veteran, a member of the National Security Council under President Eisenhower, and was Chief of the Army's Foreign Technology Division in the early 60s. In his book "The Day After Roswell," he claims that the US Army retrieved a crashed UFO in Roswell and that he analyzed some of the wreckage and related documents.*

• *Mercury and Gemini astronaut Colonel L. Gordon Cooper has publicly addressed a United Nations Panel Discussion on UFOs and ETs in New York in 1985 and declared that he has encountered UFOs and that there are thousands of supporting reports, documents, and radar evidence. In other interviews he has alleged that there has been a large government cover-up of the phenomenon, and that there are other astronauts who agree with him.*

• *Lt. Walter Haut was the public information officer at the Roswell AAF base during the 1947 Roswell UFO "incident." He filed a sealed affidavit in 2002, only to be opened after his death (it was opened in 2007, more than a year after his passing), in which he described examination of the wreckage, observation of the recovered bodies, and stated "I am convinced that what I personally observed was some type of craft and its crew from outer space."* [17]

These reports barely scratch the surface of UFOlogy. Believe them or not, there seems to be something unexplained going on.

There is also a fairly established, yet unorthodox view among some scientists and writers that alien civilizations visited our planet in the distant past, perhaps to passively observe, perhaps to modify our DNA, perhaps to start the civilization that we know and love today.

"I don't laugh at people any more when they say they've seen UFOs. I've seen one myself. "
- President James Earl Carter (as Governor of Georgia at a Southern Governors' Conference)

"I believe it is a reasonable time to take the UFO problem seriously as a reality"
- Toshiki Kaifu, former Prime Minister of Japan

"More than 10,000 sightings have been reported, the majority of which cannot be accounted for by any 'scientific' explanation .... I am convinced that these objects do exist and that they are not manufactured by any nation on Earth." "I can therefore see no alternative to accepting the theory that they come from some extraterrestrial source."
- Air Chief Marshal Lord Dowding, Commander-in-Chief of the Royal Air Force Fighter Command during the Battle of Britain

"I certainly believe in aliens in space. They may not look like us, but I have very strong feelings that they have advanced beyond our mental capabilities."
- Major General (U. S. Air Force Reserves) and Senator Barry Goldwater, (the Republican Party's 1964 nominee for U. S. President)

"We all know UFOs are real. All we need to ask is where are they from."
- Dr. Edgar Mitchell, Apollo 14 astronaut and the sixth man on the moon

(All quotes)[18]

The Theories

Today's view of the UFO phenomenon varies widely and includes the following schools of thought:

1. *The Skeptic Theory* - There is no real evidence of UFO's, they are all either explainable by natural phenomena, or they are delusions in the part of the observer.

2. *The Jungian Theory* - It is a mass consciousness psychological phenomenon, which has nothing to do with real extraterrestrials, but rather with mass psychic projections, due to the nature of our society.

3. *The DMT Theory* - UFO abduction experiences and some sightings are due to high levels of DMT in the brain, which occurs naturally in the middle of the night, or may be triggered by physiological mechanisms at other times.[19]

4. *"They're Ours" Theory* – Top secret military facilities, such as Area 51, may be the source of experimental aircraft which fly, move, and appear so strange as to be considered anomalous.

5. *The ETH (Extraterrestrial Hypothosis) Theory* - Aliens have been visiting the planet for thousands of years and are either conducting genetic experiments on humans for their own ends, slowly modifying our species to help us avoid a catastrophic end to our civilization, or have various other motivations.

6. *Interdimensional Theory* – Rather that real ET's, the UFO sightings are examples of entities from other dimensions or universes, and may be modern day examples of demons, pixies, elves, and other historical mythological creatures.

7. *Time Travelers* - Extraterrestrials are really humans from the future trying to correct the course of the evolution of our society and/or species, a la "Back to the Future."

Let's examine the likelihood of each of these ideas in turn.

The Skeptic Theory

The evidence alone (150 million witnesses to sightings, 1500 unsolved US Air Force sightings, 100s of combined radar and visual sightings, etc.) should discount this theory.

The Jungian Theory

This theory has a great deal of momentum and many researchers consider the UFO abduction phenomenon, in particular, to be an effect of deeply rooted cultural memories, perhaps even written into our DNA.

Note that it is a curious feature of the UFO phenomenon that sightings are often of craft that are just beyond the reach of our technology, but not entirely beyond imagination. In the late 1800's, it was cigar shaped airships. In the 1950's, it was discs. Today, it is black triangles and balls of light. It is almost as if there was a deliberate attempt to dazzle us with something that is sufficiently futuristic, but not impossible to comprehend. This is very consistent with the idea of the common cultural spiritual experiences (shaped by cultural context) that we explored in Chapter 3.

I consider this to be the leading logical existing explanation, at least in terms of our standard existing reality paradigm. However, Chapter 7 will present a more compelling explanation.

The DMT Theory

This seems reasonable for abduction-in-the-middle-of-the-night scenarios, but it falls flat when considering mass sightings, mass abduction experiences (all that is needed to reject this theory is a mass experience of even two people, who describe the same thing), and abductions in the middle of the day.

They're Ours Theory

While some sightings certainly appear to be ours, others appear to be of objects and technology that are well beyond the typical 10 year advance that experimental aircraft have over released products (for example, balls of light that defy gravity, accelerate at rates exceeding that which the human body can handle, and appear to have intelligence). A simple dialog illustrates the level to which ascribing all sightings to experimental aircraft strains credulity:

Q: If they are ours, why are there many reported cases of scrambled air force jets chasing after them? (e.g. Waldorf Maryland siting on July 26, 2002, jets scrambled from Andrews Air Force base, reported on WTOP, CNN, FOX News)

A: Our black ops programs are so compartmentalized that the Air Force is simply unaware.

Q: Then what would explain the sightings in other countries?

A: They have experimental aircraft programs too.

Q: Then what would explain sightings in other countries that do not have advanced aircraft development programs, such as Iceland, Belize, or Nigeria? And why are the sightings sometimes similar or identical around the world.

A: Perhaps our experimental aircraft are allowed to roam freely throughout the world.

Q: Then what would explain sighting that occurred long before anyone even had experimental aircraft programs.

A: Hmmmm

The ETH Theory

For this one, we would need to consider the likelihood that aliens are really visiting our planet. Let's take a brief diversion into transhumanism and cosmism…

The Drake Equation

The standard for estimating the number of extraterrestrial civilizations in our galaxy with which we might expect to be able to communicate is the so-called Drake Equation, developed by Dr. Frank Drake in 1961:

$N = R^* \cdot f_p \cdot n_e \cdot f_l \cdot f_i \cdot f_c \cdot L$, where

- N is the number of extraterrestrial civilizations in our galaxy with which we might expect to be able to communicate
- R^* is the rate of star formation in our galaxy (or, number of stars per age of the galaxy)
- f_p is the fraction of those stars which have planets
- n_e is average number of planets which can potentially support life per star that has planets
- f_l is the fraction of the above which actually go on to develop life
- f_i is the fraction of the above which actually go on to develop intelligent life
- f_c is the fraction of the above which are willing and able to communicate
- L is the expected lifetime of such a civilization

In 1961, Drake and colleagues settled on the following values for the parameters:

- R^* = 10/year
- f_p = 0.5
- n_e = 2
- f_l = 1
- f_i = 0.01
- f_c = 0.01

> - L = 10 years
>
> This results in an estimate of N=.01, which would imply that the odds of contacting an extraterrestrial civilizations is 1 in 100.

Different researchers, of course, have wildly different estimates of the Drake parameters. Some of the differences over the years reflect new knowledge that we have about the likelihood of the formation of life and planets. Because of recent advances in the detection of planets in remote solar systems, the parameter f_p can be assumed to be nearly 1. As it turns out, various bacteria are found to thrive in environments that are devoid of sunlight, oxygen, normal temperatures, and water. In his book "The Fifth Miracle," Paul Davies identifies a variety of bizarre microorganisms whose environment defy explanation. For example, there is the Thiobacillus concretivoris, which consumes concrete and lives in sulfuric acid. Then there is the Micrococcus radiophilus, which eats uranium, plutonium, and other radioactive elements and waste products. Streptococcus mitis are known to have survived 2 years of living in a vacuum. Pyrolobus fumarii grows at 113° C.[20] It seems that life is able to form in almost any environment.

> ### Life on Mars
>
> Percival Lowell's theory in the late 1800's that Martian civilization built canals on the red planet turned on the human imagination to the possibility of life on Mars. As late as the 1960's, the seasonally changing patterns of color on the planet were attributed to plant life.[21] Various probes have since photographed and mapped the surface and the prevailing scientific opinion over the past 40 years has been that Mars is a desolate planet with no life supporting conditions. Despite that orthodox view, an entire subculture of Martian civilization enthusiasts evolved in the 1990s due to some interesting satellite photographs of objects resembling glass tubes, and of a region called Cydonia, that include a large surface feature resembling a face

and others resembling large pyramid-like constructions. Such ideas, of course, have been dismissed by NASA as fantasy, accompanied by plausible explanations.

In August 1996, a team of scientists led by David McKay of NASA's Johnson Space Center, published in Science magazine, evidence of bacterial life embedded in Martian meteorite ALH84001. Strongly debated over the years, there has been no definitive conclusion to the story.

In February 2005, Vittorio Formisano, head of research at Italy's Institute of Physics and Interplanetary Space, presented evidence at the Mars Express Science Conference at Noordwijk in the Netherlands of the presence of high levels of formaldehyde in the atmosphere of Mars. Based on this and the fact that there is no other known source for the compound, he said "I believe there is extremely high probability that microbial subsurface life exists on Mars."[22]

In February 2005, according to "Space News," NASA scientists Carol Stoker and Larry Lemke told a group of Washington, DC space officials that they found evidence by way of their Rio Tinto river research that might indicate that life could exist on Mars. The scientists and NASA quickly retracted and denied the statements.

In April 2005, writer Leonard David reported that Michael Mumma, a lead investigator at the Center for Astrobiology and Solar System Exploration Division at the NASA Goddard Space Flight Center in Greenbelt, Maryland, presented findings at the University of Colorado, Boulder, that indicated the presence of "pronounced enhancements" of methane on Mars that are consistent with "enhanced local release"   and could be the result of biological processes.[23]

In short, the trend of evidence and contemporary scientific thought is leaning toward the idea of microbial life on Mars. I predict a definitive announcement by the end of the decade.

The foregoing evidence tends to increase the parameter f_l to nearly 1. The jury is still out on f_i and f_c. We tend to assign attributes of our own civilization and our own values to other potential civilizations. But there is really no reason to assume that once life forms on a particular planet that it will evolve into a life form that is eager to communicate. One could argue that the intelligence of dolphins, elephants, and humans are roughly equivalent (turn the clock back 50,000 years and look at what we assume about the behavior of each species; is there much difference?) We don't see dolphins building SETI dishes. The estimate for L can vary widely. When used as the duration of a civilization communicating with electromagnetic radiation in the radio spectrum, one can make the assumption that it might be similar to ours and in the range of 50-100 years. But this is a big assumption. Maybe ET modulates magnetic fields, or seismic waves, maybe they got fully wired for broadband internet before discovering radio wave propagation, maybe they communicate via telepathy, or some form of communication that is completely unknown to us. Expecting them to have a period of radio wave technology that just happens to overlap ours is probably quite unlikely. I prefer to factor this likelihood into f_c, and leave L as the typical duration for radio wave communication if and only if such a civilization uses that mode. For these reasons, I set each of f_i and f_c to .01, and L to 50, which results in .08 overlapping radio wave civilizations per galaxy, making it unlikely that SETI will find anything before funding dries up.

The purpose for this exercise was to determine the likelihood of ET visitation of our planet. However, the Drake equation has to do with estimating the likelihood of contacting another civilization and is really a tool for estimating the chances for success of SETI. It can be modified to estimate the likelihood of ET visitation if we make the following adjustments:

1. Replace f_c with f_t, the fraction of intelligent life forms that are willing and able to travel across the galaxy to visit us. We have to assume an average travel distance of half the diameter of the galaxy

(50,000 light years), because the Drake equation applies across the entire galaxy.

2. Modify L to be the typical duration of a civilization period of galactic exploration.

Kardashev Civilizations

Russian astrophysicist, Nikolai Kardashev, developed a scheme for classifying civilizations in 1964. Known as the Kardashev scale, it identifies the following types:

Type I - A civilization that is able to harness all of the power available on a single planet.

Type II - A civilization that is able to harness all of the power available from a single star.

Type III - A civilization that is able to harness all of the power available from a single galaxy.

Clearly, we have not yet attained Type I status and can therefore be considered a Type 0 civilization. Physicist Freeman Dyson has calculated that, we should reach Type I status within 200 years. However, physicist Michio Kaku points out that we are already on the way because "we see the beginning of a planetary language (English), a planetary communication system (the Internet), a planetary economy (the forging of the European Union), and even the beginnings of a planetary culture (via mass media, TV, rock music, and Hollywood films)". However, to fully make the transition to Type I, we would have to survive significant technological hurdles, not the least of which is to avoid destroying ourselves with technology and technology byproducts that we can't handle (e.g. nuclear, nanotech, runaway greenhouse effect).

Kardashev estimated that at a 1% growth of energy management per year, it would take only 3,200 years to reach Type II status, and 5,800 years to reach Type III

---

status.

For a Type I to transition to a Type II, according to Kaku, they must master space travel, weather modification, survive cosmic disasters (asteroid hits) and planetary disasters (supervolcanos), and depart the planet before exhausting its resources. The Type II to Type III transition is a matter of surviving local solar catastrophes, and getting beyond the limitations imposed by relativity in order to be able to colonize outside of the solar system. Type III civilizations, for all intents and purposes, should be immortal.[24]

3. Add additional factors as necessary, to include the probability of attaining a certain level of civilization. For example, we can define f_{01} as the probability that a Type 0 civilization will make it to Type 1 status, f_{12} as the probability that a Type 1 civilization will make it to Type 2 status, and f_{23} as the probability that a Type 2 civilization will make it to Type 3 status. Current thought is that Type 0 -> Type 1 is the most difficult transition, and essentially boils down to the probability that we won't blow ourselves up. In the book "Our Final Hour", British Astronomer Royal Sir Martin Rees has given a probability of human extinction before 2100 at 50%. So let's set $f_{01}=.5$, $f_{12}=1$, and $f_{23}=1$.

Now comes a very big question. Is the limitation that you can not travel faster than the speed of light a universal, unyielding law of physics? If yes, then f_t must be nearly zero, since it is impossible to travel galactic distances in the lifetime of any living being in our knowledge space. If we restrict travel to manageable distances, even, say, five light years, then f_t becomes 5/50,000, or .0001. There is only one star within 5 light years, so we would have to assume that our ET's have set up camp somewhere either in that star system, or in our own. L might be higher, since, presumably, once a civilization learns to fly at nearly the speed of light, they have become a Type I civilization, which should last for a few thousand years. As a result, perhaps we can estimate N = .025, which is still very unlikely. The only other possibility is that Type III civilizations have been slowly migrating outward from their planet of origin for millions, maybe billions, of years. Plugging in the transition probabilities and 1 billion for L yields N = 80000. Similarly, if the speed of light is not a universal limitation to travel, then f_t may actually approach 1, and L should be more reflective of duration of a Type II & III civilization, which as we have seen above, may be immortal, or millions or billions of years.

Summarizing, if 50% of intelligent life forms can make it to Type III status, there should be thousands of migrating/colonizing/traveling species in our neighborhood. On the other hand, would they even care about us? When we take a walk through a field, do we attempt to communicate with the ants in an anthill? If the field is ready to be leveled in order to make room for a housing development, do we attempt to save the ants? No. Why not? Because they are so far beneath our intellect level or our perceived level of net worth, that such endeavors are simply not worth our time. Now imagine what a Type II or III civilization might be like. Consider how far we have progressed (some might say, regressed) as a society since the hunter/gatherer stage of human evolution 10,000 years ago (note: theories abound that this traditional view of human evolution is incorrect; however, for purposes of this line of argument, it is acceptable to assume the orthodox view of human development). Further, consider that we are accelerating in this progression accordingly to the exponential curves presented in section 2 ("The Acceleration"). Then, for all practical purposes, it is impossible to even imagine where we might be in 10,000 years. Telepathic communication, control of time and space, simultaneous access to parallel universes, full merge with AI? Some futurists predict these things in hundreds of years, not 10,000. Furthermore, since 100 million years represents less than 1% of the lifetime of our galaxy, it is not unrealistic to assume that Type III civilizations may be 100's of millions of years advanced compared to our own society. Given the foregoing discussion, it is easy to make an argument that it is highly unlikely that ETs are zipping about in our atmosphere in vehicles that appear to be no more than 50 years ahead of our technology (they crash, after all). The only possible "True ET" explanation is that extremely advanced species intentionally appear in a form that makes us realize that they are here, not unlike the father figure in the Carl Sagan movie "Contact." We must allow this theory as a logical possibility, which leads into our next theory.

Interdimensional Theory

Rather than being a physical presence, some speculate that UFOs may be objects that dart in and out of our three dimensions, either intentionally or unintentionally. Recall Figure 2-5 and how the higher dimensional sphere briefly entered the plane of the flatlanders. Similarly, UFOs could exist in other dimensions, either in a parallel universe or in other dimensions in our universe (although the distinction is arbitrary). It would certainly explain the category of observations where the objects in question simply appear out of nowhere and disappear just as mysteriously. One could certainly imagine, given the discoveries of dark matter and unexplained forces, experiments being done on teleportation, and the theories of Hilbert space and parallel dimensions, that we might be simply ignorant to the possibilities of mastering these matters and are only discovering the possibilities that sufficiently technologically advanced civilizations might take for granted. In fact, the entire idea of attempting to find ET communications via radio signals seems as ludicrous as something like early Native Americans looking for smoke signals on the moon as evidence of extraterrestrial life. Surely, at the exponential rate of technological acceleration, even civilizations a few hundred years advanced from us would be communicating via telepathy, higher-dimensional (and therefore not restricted to the limitations of light speed) fields, tachyons (faster than light particles) telemetry, or even modulating the quantum entanglement or underlying holographic construct. So, I have to give this theory some likelihood. If the universe is not programmed as I suspect, there is certainly a remote possibility that other highly advanced life forms might have some passing interest in us, perhaps cataloging our existence, checking on our progress toward wiping out our own civilization, or simply toying with us by allowing us to see a slightly advanced artifact and observing humanity's collective response.

The Time Traveler Theory

There are no known physical laws that prevent time travel, either into the future or the past. However, the obvious knock on this theory is that it appears to violate causality arguments; e.g. The Grandfather Paradox – if you were to go back in time, you could kill your grandfather thereby violating your own existence. On the other hand, today's science and science fiction thinkers have come up with all sorts of ways to allow time travel without violating causality. For example, there is Igor D. Novikov's self-consistency principle, which says that it would be impossible for an event to occur that allowed causality to be violated. Physicists Novikov, Kip Thorne, and Joe Polchinski all demonstrated that there are no cases where a mass can be sent back in time and force a paradox. In the parallel universes theories (see the Everett interpretation of Quantum Mechanics, for example), when the murder occurs, the universe is split into one in which the murderer was never born, and the original one with the murderer in it. Other people in the original universe never notice a change and only see the would-be murderer disappear into the time machine. If he succeeded in his dastardly plot, he simply wouldn't ever return to the original universe to tell about it. Therefore, causality is maintained, but in a separate universe.[25] In other theories, there would always be events that would occur so as to prevent the murder and maintain a consistent state, both past and present. So, it seems, for now at least, that science and mathematics allow time travel into the past. And what about our time traveling friends from the future? What could possibly be their purpose? Observation, genetic manipulation, and damage control have all been proposed theories.

Recall the discussion about the technology singularity at the end of Chapter 5. It seems inevitable that we will merge with artificial technology, attain near immortality, and spread our intelligence throughout the universe. The first two components will occur within the next 100 years or so and the timeframe for the third depends on the true limitations of the speed of information transfer. If some other intelligence exists in the universe, then most certainly they will have achieved the singularity, which means one of two things:

Case 1: They have not reached Tipler's Omega Point due to the true limit of expansion being the speed of light. I find this to be unlikely for a number of reasons. Wormholes are theoretically possible and allow the possibility of superluminal transfer of information. Group velocity of a waveform may travel faster than c, the speed of light. Quantum "action at a distance" is not rigorously explained by physics and may be due to information transfer faster than c. The holographic paradigm also provides a theoretical foundation for it as well. There is also evidence, although anecdotal and not scientifically rigorous, of anomalous occurrences that propagate faster than c. Finally, even at near c, it would seem likely that some other singularity civilization would have reached our shores by now. In any case, if Case 1 is true, UFO sightings cannot be due to ETs.

Case 2: Their intelligence is all pervasive in the universe. If so, it would seem very odd that they would present themselves in a tin can with a non-zero probability of crashing.

On the other hand, if we are the first intelligence to reach this level in the universe, UFO's again cannot be evidence of extraterrestrial intelligence.

So what are they and what are the abduction experiences of the millions of people who have reported them?

Cryptozoology

Cryptozoology is a scientific-sounding term for a topic that scientists tend to laugh at, namely, the study of rumored or mythological animals, such as Sasquatch and the Loch Ness Monster. As usual, I am neither a wide-eyed believer in these mysterious creatures nor a closed-minded skeptic, but am positioned smack in the middle of "cautiously open-minded" and "I'll believe it when I see it."

A Gallup Poll reported by Newsweek in June of 1978 revealed that an estimated 30 million Americans believe in Bigfoot and a similar number believe that the Loch Ness monster exists.[26]

The Freedom of Information Act in the UK has revealed records that the "Foreign and Commonwealth Office and the secretary of state for Scotland spent time contemplating whether Nessie should be protected," and determined that the Loch Ness Monster would be protected under the 1981 Wildlife and Countryside Act, according to The Herald newspaper.[27]

In 1977, there were 3 independent sightings of an unearthly creature with an abnormally large head and orange eyes in Dover, Massachusetts. Now dubbed the Dover Demon, there has been no satisfactory explanation for the sightings nor has the credibility of the witnesses been seriously doubted.

In 1966 and 1967 in West Virginia, there were numerous sightings of the so-called mothman, a human sized being with wings and red eyes, also with no satisfactory explanation to date.

The Jersey Devil in southern New Jersey, the Beast of Exmoor in Devon, UK, the Kappa (or water imps) in Japan, the Yeti in the Himalayas, the Chinese Wildman in Hubei, China, the Chupacabra in Latin America, the Nandi Bear in Africa – it seems that all cultures have their own versions of cryptids. Why? Is it due to some deep-seated need to have fearful unknown enemies, perhaps due to a survival advantage? Or is it that every culture has these because they are meant to, perhaps to create controversy and keep life interesting. Cryptozoology has many parallels to the UFO phenomenon. In fact, in many cases, sightings are accompanied by UFO events. Large hominids and other unknown creatures have similar habits to UFO. They tend to appear out of nowhere and disappear at the most inopportune time. They resist quality photography. And there are many reports of telepathic communication and an awareness of being observed. In fact, I would go so far as to say that they are two sides of the same coin and probably have the same origin in our lives, whether it is mass psychology, or the gods messing with us.

Evolution or Devolution

This is a thorny topic, worthy of an entire book. Creationists say there's no anomaly here. "It's obvious that the Darwinists are wrong." "No one has ever observed a species-changing evolutionary event." "If we descended from apes, why are apes still here?" Evolutionists say there's no anomaly here. "Evolution has been observed with microscopic organisms." "The fossil record proves that humans descended from apes." "Over 98% of our DNA is common to a Chimpanzee." "Intelligent design is pseudoscience." And so on. The anomaly is that both sides can be convincing, but both can't be right, at least not in all aspects of the debate.

Intelligent design advocates aren't all non-scientists. Recall the late Cambridge University astronomer Sir Fred Hoyle's statement presented in Chapter 1 that the probability of producing life anywhere in the universe from evolutionary processes, was as reasonable as getting a fully operational Boeing 747 jumbo jet from a tornado going through a junkyard. Lehigh University professor of biological sciences Michael Behe claims that certain biological structures are so "irreducibly complex" that they cannot statistically be accounted for by natural selection and random mutations, the cornerstones of Darwinism. As an example, the clotting of blood requires at least 20 specific proteins to work in concert to do the job correctly.[28] Dr. Stephen C. Meyer, Director of Discovery Institute's Center for Science & Culture, has argued that evolution cannot account for the Cambrian Explosion 530 million years ago, when there was a sudden appearance of new animal body plans that required a vast new set of cells and "complex specified information" regarding genetics. Essentially life went from 3 billion years of simple bacterial forms to a vast variety of complex animals "overnight," in geological terms.[29]

Then there is a category of IDers called Interventionists (not to be confused with the Keynesian economic policy) – people who believe that the intelligent designer intervened with natural (possibly evolutionary) processes to produce humans and, perhaps even crops and domesticated animals via genetic engineering. Scientists generally dismiss this idea out of hand as a convenient and easy explanation for those who don't understand evolution. However, the arguments that the interventionist commonly puts forth can be thought provoking. Some examples:

- *Our supposed predecessor, Homo Erectus, went extinct 300,000 years ago, 100,000 years before the onset of Homo Sapiens. The Neanderthals, by the way, who evolved from Homo Erectus, have been dismissed as potential evolutionary ancestors to Home Sapiens, due to conflicting mitochondrial DNA. So there is a clear missing link.*

- *Humans differ from all other primates in many respects: we have significantly lighter bone density, are 5-10 times weaker per pound, have different brains, different throats (other primates can drink and breathe at the same time), and different body covering (no pelts, reversed thickness pattern). Unlike all other primates, we don't regulate salt intake, we have no estrus cycle, we cry, and have a fat layer attached to our skin.*

- *Humans can't have evolved directly from other primates because our closest supposed primate cousins have 48 chromosomes and we only have 46, which would be a devolution instead of an evolution. The missing chromosomes are actually spliced together.[30]*

Note: Darwinists will point out that chromosome count does not correlate to biological advancement, as the black mulberry plant has 308. But most would probably agree that to lose a chromosome pair is an unlikely evolutionary process. They account for the difference between chimps and humans by the assertion that each evolved along a different branch from a common ancestor. Which puts us back to square one – who is our immediate ancestor?

Evolution and Intelligent Design are two theories that have minimal overlap. On the one hand, a godless universe could simply be following the biological processes that underlie evolution.

Alternatively, the gods may have created each species and started the clock for humans after everything else was set in place, per the book of Genesis. These are the two extreme viewpoints. However, both theories can coexist. For example, it is theoretically possible for the gods to have created the universe, wound the clock (metaphorically speaking), and let it run, allowing it to follow the evolutionary biological processes thereafter. The fact is that there is not sufficient evidence to determine without a doubt which scenario actually played out.

OOPArt

American zoologist Ivan Sanderson coined the term OOPArt, for "out-of-place artifact," an archaeological or paleontological object that appears to be out of place in time or location. Archaeologist Jonathan Gray and other investigators such as Michael Cremo and Richard Thompson have identified thousands of archaeological finds that seem to defy explanation, including the following[31, 32] (except where noted).

- *The 1050 metric ton Baalbek stone block from Lebanon. 3 others, weighing 800 tons each (as much as 2 Boeing 747s), were fitted together into a wall.*

- *An apparent battery, found in Baghdad, dating from the time of Christ*

- *Hundreds of metallic spheres, each with 3 parallel grooves running around its equator, have been found in 2.8 billion year old rock strata in South Africa*

- *Drills used in ancient Egypt for boring into granite – drills that turned 500 times faster than modern drills*

- *An iron nail was found in Scotland in 1844 embedded in a block of stone that dated to about 400 million years ago.*

- *A 10-inch gold chain was found embedded in coal in an Illinois mine. The coal was dated to 300 million years ago.*

- *Raised letters were carved into a block of marble found in a Philadelphia quarry that came from strata dating back 500 million years.*

- *A 20,000 ton stone block in Sacsahuanman, Peru was moved into position. Today's largest cranes can lift about 3,000 tons.*[33]

- *Excavations from the early 20th century in Mohenjo-Daro, India, revealed an ancient town that was destroyed by tremendous heat, along with large deposits of clay and green glass. Modern analysis set the temperature of the catastrophe at 1500 degrees Celsius. Green glass is also know to have been also created in the Nevada deserts as a result of each above ground nuclear test. Dozens of skeletons found in the Mohenjo-Daro area have radioactivity levels 50 times above normal. Regional Indian legends tell of a mysterious weapon capable of leveling towns and burning thousands of people.[34] Coincidental?*

There isn't really much wrong with the "ancient advanced civilization" theories, such as Atlantis. Archeological evidence supports it. Paleontological evidence at best supports it, at worst doesn't falsify it. Think about what would happen if our civilization were to be completely wiped out by some sort of man made or natural catastrophe, leaving only small clans of humans to carry on our civilization. We are so dependent on technology that we wouldn't be able to cope very well without electricity, medicine, energy sources, communications infrastructure, or grocery stores. Imagine going back to growing our own food and creating our own shelters and clothing. Within a few generations, the memories of our glorious past would be greatly faded. Evidence of our past would also start to fade. We haven't really built much that would stand up to entropy and the decaying force of nature. Books would decompose over hundreds of years. Anything metal (vehicles, building frames) would turn to rust and then dust. Even synthetics, like plastics and CDs, would be gone in a thousand years. Our history would simply be a legend handed down generation to generation by Neo Homo Sapiens. So, how do we really know this hasn't happened before?

Taken as a whole, these discoveries, and our evolutionary past, certainly have significant anomalous aspects to them. But, of course, there is nothing that isn't easily explained by the great cosmic reality program.

> "My theory of evolution is that Darwin was adopted."
> - Steven Wright

Eggs and Psi

Paranormal. The mere mention of the word is enough to ruin scientific careers, to invoke the giggle factor, or to render a book unpublishable. Ooooohhhh.

Then again, there is actually significant scientific evidence for paranormal phenomena.

Over a period of 12 years, for example, Robert G. Jahn, Engineering professor and dean emeritus at Princeton University, and associate Brenda J. Dunne, conducted over 1000 experiments where subjects concentrated on the outcome of a random event generator and created a statistically significant effect on the results toward the direction of the subjects intent.[35] While the effects were generally small for each experiment, when taken collectively, the probability of the results occurring naturally were approximately 1 in 3,000,000,000,000. According to Jahn…

> "it appears that once the illegitimate research and invalid criticism have been set aside, the remaining accumulated evidence of psychic phenomena comprises an array of experimental observations, obtained under reasonable

protocols in a variety of scholarly disciplines, which compound to a philosophical dilemma. On one hand, effects inexplicable in terms of established scientific theory, yet having numerous common characteristics, are frequently and widely observed; on the other hand, these effects have so far proven qualitatively and quantitatively irreplicable, in the strict scientific sense, and appear to be sensitive to a variety of psychological and environmental factors that are difficult to specify, let alone control. Under these circumstances, critical experimentation has been tedious and frustrating at best, and theoretical modeling still searches for vocabulary and concepts, well short of any useful formalisms."[36]

In the mid 90's, at the University of Göteborg in Sweden, the department of psychology conducted experiments where subjects underwent mild sensory deprivation while "senders" concentrated on randomly chosen videos. In two studies, a very high hit rate of 37% was achieved. Higher hit rates were noticed in subjects with a predisposition toward the belief in paranormal effects.[37]

British biologist and author Rupert Sheldrake, in his well known experiments involving the "sense of being stared at", found that there is a statistical significance to the effect; that is, that on the average, people can sense when they are being stared at, even when all possible influences are removed. At Our Lady's College in Drogheda, Ireland, for example, in a double blind experiment involving over 2000 randomly chosen test points, 57% of the subjects were correct in their guess when being stared at. This might not sound like much, but, like our penny flipping example, when you have this kind of statistical deviation over so many test cases, it is highly significant. In fact, the chance of this occurring by chance alone is approximately 1 in 1,000,000,000. And, these tests were repeated with similar results at the University College School Junior Branch (UCS), a boys' school in Hampstead, London, at South Connecticut State University, and at schools in Stuttgart, Hamburg, Bremen, Boca Raton, and Stockholm.[38]

Braud and Schlitz conducted 37 studies of direct mental interactions with living systems (DMILS), whereby biological processes were remotely influenced through thought alone. The statistical significance of the results was 1 in 40,000,000,000,000.[39]

From 1981 to 1995, five different US government organizations investigated the validity of psychic phenomena and all concluded that certain forms merit serious study.[40]

Dr. Dean Radin conducted a comprehensive "meta-analysis" of thousands of independent experiments in telepathy, clairvoyance, perception through time, and other psychic phenomena and compiled all of the results. While any given experiment might not yield remarkable results, when taking as a whole, the body of experimental evidence that supports the existence of a bona fide phenomenon is astounding. Considering telepathy for example, across 2549 sessions from 1974 through 1997, the overall "hit rate" was unlikely with "odds against chance beyond a million billion to one." Very few other scientific fields require that level of certainty before accepting a theory as fact.[41]

None of this is a huge surprise to most people. A Gallup poll in June 2001 found that 60 percent of Americans believe in extrasensory perception and 65 million Americans have personally experienced ESP. Personally, I have witnessed my very "intuitive" wife work out a non-trivial 9-character password that was only in my head. I have seen her have eerie premonitions about the impending death of relatives of acquaintances, all of which subsequently and invariably came true. And I have seen her have clairvoyant episodes with no other possible explanation. The Gallup poll also showed that the tendency to believe in ESP increased with intelligence. Catholic priest Andrew Greeley, a sociologist at the University of Arizona, said that "people who've tasted the paranormal, whether they accept it intellectually or not, are anything but religious nuts or psychiatric cases. They are, for the most part, ordinary Americans, somewhat above the norm in education and intelligence and somewhat less than average in religious involvement." Furthermore, he found that "two thirds of college professors accepted ESP, and more than 25% of "elite scientists" believed in ESP."[42]

Global Consciousness and Eggs

At Princeton University, there has been a long running study of the effects of world consciousness on physical systems called the Global Consciousness Project. The project consists of an international network of "EGGs," which are computer-based random number generators, continuously running. If the world were truly random, the random numbers would follow a normal distribution, or bell curve. And, most of the time, they do. However, at times when the world's attention is synchronized, such as during a catastrophe or international news event, a truly remarkable thing happens. The EGGs display a slight but distinctly non-random pattern, as if some cosmic control center were synchronously influencing the outcome of the generated numbers. Shared worldwide emotions during events such as Princess Diana's funeral, Columbine, Embassy bombings, Y2K, and Winter Olympics seemed to actually impact the mechanized generation of random numbers. In many cases, the effect was noted a short time prior to the actual event itself. Taken as a whole, the data for 209 events "chosen a priori" occurring from 1998 through 2005 departed from randomness by an amount that would be likely to occur by chance 1 in 10,000 times. What could possibly cause this? [43]

So clearly, psi is a strong anomaly with no strong explanation. That is, of course, until chapter 7.

Quantum Mechanics and the Nature of Time

We delved into quantum mechanics in much more detail in section 2. As a review, here is some of the high strangeness found in Quantum Mechanics (QM).

It is possible to create an experiment where a living being is neither alive nor dead until someone actually observes them.

Teleportation experiments now demonstrate either a fundamental interconnectedness among various separate objects, or the transfer of information at rates substantially beyond the speed of light.

It is possible, although highly improbable, that you could disappear on one side of a solid door and instantly reappear on the other side.

One interpretation of QM says that at every instant, a mind-numbingly huge number of universes are spawned. In some of them you are not reading this book, in some you have green skin, and in most, life does not exist.

If one were able to view space with a microscope with a power of 10^{35}, one would see a frothy see of foam, with particles continuously flicking in and out of existence. Further, there are spaces and times that simply aren't even defined. There is one school of thought that the origin of the universe came from such a fluctuation of space.

Time is a deep mystery. Physical equations work as well if time flows in either direction – however, our day to day experience is that time only flows from past to present to future. Time paradoxes abound, including time travel paradoxes and relativistic time paradoxes. Some physicists even believe that time does not exist, but is just a set of states of the universe.

Metaphysical thought is that there is no time in the afterlife. Also, time appears to be no object in remote viewing or past life regression as it is just as easy to travel or view deep into past, far into the future, or yesterday.

There is a never-ending flow of scientific theories that attempt to explain the apparent strangeness of our quantum world. Many dimensional theories, string theory, parallel universes, the craziness of universe bifurcations, invisible matter and energy, to name a few. Could there be a simpler all encompassing explanation? Yes, next chapter!

The 100th Monkey

Hey, what's an urban legend doing in this book? For those who have not heard of it, the story has its origins in the 1979 book Lifetide by Lyall Watson, in which he describes scientific observations of monkey behavior on a Japanese island in 1952. Apparently, one monkey learned that washing sweet potatoes made them taste better and other monkeys soon learned this behavior and followed suit. As the story goes, however, at some point, a sort of critical mass of knowledge was reached (the 100th monkey to learn the behavior) and the knowledge spontaneously jumped to monkeys on different islands. Upon further research, however, it was found that while the sweet potato cleaning was true, the knowledge jumping effect has been debunked, although many new age writers still reference it. But what a cool effect if it were true, no?

Rupert Sheldrake is one who believes that, while the 100th monkey story may not be entirely true, he has seen a similar effect in learned behavior in rats in a Harvard study, which may have spontaneously jumped to rats who subsequently demonstrated learning the same behavior faster in Scotland and Australia.[44] According to Paul H. Smith, the Rubik's cube was much more difficult to master when it was first introduced than it was after many people had mastered it, even by someone who had no previous experience with it.[45] Remote viewing instructors have noticed a significant decrease in the amount of time that it takes an initiate to learn the skill as compared to the days when it was first being taught. While this could also be due to better teaching methods, it may also be due to Sheldrake's so-called morphic field, Jung's collective subconscious, or Bohm's Holographic Universe. You actually don't have to look far to see different faces of the anomaly – the amazing feats that freestyle skiers perform today and how fast they learn them and the many examples of near-simultaneous identical scientific discoveries from around the world, to name two.

Black Gold, Texas Tea

Is anybody else bothered by the whole concept of oil?

Although shallow oil wells were drilled in China as early as the 4th century, the first commercial oil well was drilled in Canada in 1858 at the height of the industrial revolution. Since then our use of and reliance upon it has skyrocketed. Also since then has been a continuous debate on the origin of oil. In one corner, weighing in at 25 billion barrels a year, we have the biogenic theory, aka dead plants and animals. In the other corner, weighing in at 900 billion gallons a year, we have the abiotic theory, aka chemical reactions inside the Earth. We shall set aside the conspiracy theories for a moment (*the global elite, or Illuminati, want us all to believe in biogenic, because then we would understand that "fossil fuels" are a limited resource, and hence scarce, and so we don't mind paying $3 a gallon at the pump, which makes the global elite fabulously wealthy. Hmmm – doesn't it seem like Exxon-Mobil are frequently announcing record quarterly earnings?*) and briefly outline each theory.

The "fossil fuel" theory was first proposed by Russian scientist Mikhailo Lomonosov in 1757 who suggested that bodies of animals from prehistoric times were buried in sediments and were transformed into hydrocarbons due to extreme pressure and temperature forces over millions of years. The argument is supported by sound biochemical processes, such as catagenesis. In addition, the evidence of organic pollen grains in petroleum deposits implies (but does not prove) organic origin.

The abiogenic or abiotic theory actually has its origins the 1800s, when proposed by French chemist Marcellin Berthelot and Russian chemist Dmitri Mendeleev. According to their theory, hydrocarbons are primordial in origin and were formed by non-biological processes in the earths crust and mantle. The theory received a modern boost by Russian geologist Kudryavtsev, studying Canadian oil sources in the 1950s and Ukrainian scientist Chekaliuk, based on thermodynamic calculations in the 1960's, who both arrived at the same conclusion. Esteemed planetary scientist Thomas Gold from Cornell University, added to the evidence in his book "The Deep Hot Biosphere." The theory has also attained laboratory support via experiments at Gas Resources Corporation in Houston, Texas which produced octane and methane by subjecting marble, iron oxide, and water, to temperature and pressure conditions similar to that 60 miles below the surface of the earth.[46] Also, there is the fact that some hydrocarbons, like methane, are known to occur throughout the solar system on supposedly lifeless planets. And, finally, deep drilling around the world has discovered oil at depths and in places where there should never have been biological remains. Referring to natural gas wells drilled by the GHK Company in Oklahoma at 30,000 feet and Japanese wells at 4300 meters, Dr. Jerome Corsi (political scientist with a Ph.D. from Harvard University) noted:

"Even those who might stretch to argue that even if no dinosaurs ever died in sedimentary rock that today lies 30,000 feet below the surface, might still argue that those levels contain some type of biological debris that has transformed into natural gas. That argument, a stretch at 30,000 feet down, is almost impossible to make for basement structure bedrock. Japan's Nagaoka and Niigata fields produce natural gas from bedrock that is volcanic in nature. What dinosaur debris could possibly be trapped in volcanic rock found at deep-earth levels?"[47]

Some oil reserves even seem to have the ability to be automatically refilled, like a drink at a burger joint. Gulf of Mexico oil field Eugene Island 330, for example, saw its production drop from 15,000 barrels a day in 1973 to 4,000 barrels a day in 1989, and then suddenly spontaneously reversed and was pumping 13,000 barrels of a "different aged" crude in 1999.[48] In fact, according to Christopher Cooper of the Wall Street Journal, "between 1976 and 1996, estimated global oil reserves grew 72%, to 1.04 trillion barrels." Considering the doubling of reserves in the Middle East alone, University of Tulsa professor Norman Hyne noted that "it would take a pretty big pile of dead dinosaurs and prehistoric plants to account for the estimated 660 billion barrels of oil in the region"[49]

The argument is all very interesting and gets quite political as one might imagine. But my interest revolves more around the basic question of why oil is even there at all. Both sides propose some fairly complex theories to account for the very existence of petroleum, let alone its uncanny ability to refill known reserves automatically. Doesn't it almost seem like it was placed there just for our use?

CHAPTER 7

Are we Living in a Programmed Reality?

Here it is. Chapter 7. Finally. 7. The magic number. The number of the days of the week. The seven deadly sins. The seven sisters of the Pleiades. Seven notes of the musical scale. The seven wonders of the ancient world and the seven natural wonders of the world. Shakespeare's seven ages of man. Seven dwarves. Akira Kurosawa's "The Seven Samurai." The Magnificent Seven. Seven games in the World Series. There are seven seas. In ancient Egypt, seven was the sacred number of Osiris and there were seven houses of the underworld. The Greeks had seven sages, Pan had seven pipes. The Buddhists had seven steps for the seven cosmic stages. Seventh Heaven comes from the Muslim belief that Allah created seven heavens. There were Jesus' famous last seven words on the cross. And in Hebrew tradition, every seventh year was sabbatical, and purifications lasted seven days. Harvard University psychologist George A Miller found that most people could only remember seven chunks of information at a time. For this reason, American phone numbers were originally chosen to be seven digits because any more is too difficult to remember, any fewer can't address enough subscribers. University of Glasgow professor Simon Garrod has concluded from his research that group sizes larger than seven people have difficulty making decisions.[1] When asked to chose a number between 1 and 10, the number most often chosen is 7. And, of course, there is the seven-year itch and Seven Minute Abs.

> " Seven chipmunks twirling on a branch, eating lots of sunflowers on my uncles ranch."
> - The hitchhiker in the movie "There's Something About Mary" (1998)

OK, enough of that! The goal of this chapter is to present all of the arguments for the thesis of this book, which is: that we *live in a programmed reality.* Put simply, we are talking about intelligent design. There had to be some entity that created our reality. Furthermore, the reality seems to be programmed, not unlike a well-designed video game, in the following ways (which is by no means an exhaustive list):

- *The parameters of our world are tuned for our existence.*

- *There is a non-random, or pre-planned aspect to the events in our reality.*

- *Temporal and spatial resolutions are chosen as a tradeoff between realism and performance.*

- *The programmers make frequent modifications to fine-tune the program and its data structures.*

- *They have included "easter eggs" for our enjoyment.*

I will now present the four major categories of evidence:

- *Quantization*

- *The improbability of the world timeline*

- *The tuning of our reality*

- *Anomalous occurrences*

None of these can be considered proof, but remember that there is no such thing as proof in science, only in mathematics. I submit, however, that the evidence combined is more compelling than any other theory of life, reality, or the universe out there!

Evidence – Our Discrete World

Recall our discussion in section 3 about the quantum mechanical version of reality. Assuming the accuracy of the QM theory (and, again, there is a great deal of evidence supporting it), our world is not continuous, but rather quantized, or granular. Setting aside any discussion about the *implications* of such a basis for reality, instead ask the question *why*? Why might reality be quantized and not continuous? One possible answer is…

It takes an infinite amount of resources to create a continuous reality, but a finite amount to create a quantized reality.

By resources, I refer to bits, the information that it takes to model reality. What do I mean by model? I am taking a leap here, but one that I think you will agree makes some sense. If we consider the possibility that our Universe is a creation (whether by God, or by purely physical processes), it has to be created out of something. That something may be superstrings, bits, or quantum states. Building a reality from such raw constituents is the physical manifestation of creating a conceptual model of reality from the information that represents those constituents. If a superstring can be anywhere in a continuous space, it would theoretically take an infinite number of bits to encode its position. If you are creating a model of reality on a computer, for example, an infinite number of bits would cost an infinite amount of money, take an infinite amount of RAM and disk, and take an infinite amount of CPU power to process.

Consider again the task of creating a virtual reality video game. Objects in the virtual reality must be modeled, or represented by data. Take a tree, for example. A tree at full 32-bit (4 bytes) color resolution on a 1024x768 monitor may take up a maximum of 10% of the screen and thus require 1024*768*4*.1 = 330KB to store as a bitmap. This may drop to 30KB, with compression. However, if you want your user to be able to see the tree from any angle, you will need to model the tree in 3 dimensions rather than 2. This raises the number of dimensions from 2 to 3, and the model size may now be $30KB^{1.5}$ = 5MB. A 5MB file, with current technology, takes a few seconds to load and render, which would make the operation of the game a little clunky. The game designer might decide to avoid this by preloading many objects when the game is first run, so that generating new scenery as you move around happens more quickly. In any case, the model of the tree is always a tradeoff in terms of size. Make the model too small, and the tree won't look like a tree because it won't have sufficient resolution. Make the model too big and the game won't run smoothly. This is why first generation video games (e.g. Space Invaders, circa 1978) had low-resolution 2-dimensional characters that only took a few bits to encode. Processors back then ran very slow and memory speeds and sizes were extremely limited, so the amount of data needed to encode the characters had to be equivalently limited. 25 years later, and 12 doublings of Moore's law hence, we have very high-resolution 3D characters in our games, because PC technology can process 4000 times faster now.

I wonder – how does the resolution of the state of the art in video gaming compare to the resolution of our reality and what does that say about our progress toward modeling the *real* world? There are actually a few different kinds of resolution or granularity of our reality that are worth considering:

Observable Granularity
The first type of granularity we will examine is granularity of the world that is necessary for us to perceive with our standard senses. I call this observable granularity. Let's take the sense of sight as an example. According to the NDT resource center, at 12 inches, the normal visual acuity of the human eye is 0.00349 inch^2. Given that the surface area of a sphere is $4\pi r^2$, and assuming that one can typically perceive a third of a full spherical field of view, encoding a view into 50 million pixels would be sufficient. Conventional wisdom is that 24 bits of color resolution is enough for most people –

that is, a deviation of color of 1 part in 16 million is imperceptible. So, we need a total of 150 MB of data to provide a visual scene that would have enough resolution to reach the limits of human perception. Futurist Ray Kurzweil argues that simply following Moore's law, it will be likely that we will have the technology to emulate our reality to a resolution equivalent to the observable granularity that we have defined here by the year 2020.[3]

Instrumental Granularity
Then there is the granularity of our world that is necessary when we allow scientists to pry matter into the smallest constituents and peer into the deepest depths of space. For the former task, we need to consider the resolution of the worlds most powerful particle accelerators. Particle accelerators allow us to explore the constituents of subatomic particles, like protons and quarks. For the latter, we would consider the world's best telescopes. I call this instrumental granularity. Don Lincoln at Fermilab has estimated that physicists can measure objects down to a size of 10^{-18} meters.

Quantum Mechanical Granularity
Finally, there is the actual quantum mechanical granularity, which I call, uh, quantum mechanical granularity. Recall that the granularity of reality is 1.6×10^{-35} meters and 10^{-43} seconds. Considering observable granularity in terms of Planck lengths, the resolution of the human eye at 12 inches is 5×10^{30}. So, there is clearly plenty of excess resolution in QM compared to our physical senses. For instrumental granularity, we are still at a resolution 10^{17} times larger than the Planck length. An interesting exercise would be to calculate Moore's Law as applied to particle accelerators, and then estimate when we might hit the limits of QM granularity in terms of energies. As the table below shows, the energy capacities of particle accelerators doubles about every 3.3 years (hereafter please refer to as *Elvidge's Law*).

Accelerator	eV	Year
Lawrence Cyclotron	1.20E+06	1932
University of Chicago's Betatron	3.15E+08	1949
Stanford Linear Collider	2.00E+10	1989
CERN LHC	7.00E+12	2006
calculated doubling period = 3.29 years		

That means that in about 186 years, or the year 2191, we will hit the limits of quantum mechanics. Interestingly, this is about 130 years after the technological singularity identified in Chapter 2. Maybe not so interesting since it is 130 years off, but maybe interesting because in the grand scheme of things (4 billion year evolution of the planet), it is fairly close to other accelerating limits.

Notice that quantum mechanics by its very nature puts some very significant limitations on the universe...

- A limited number of states of matter
- A finite size to the amount of information required to fully describe the universe
- A limitation to the age of technology before we reach a limit to how deep we can probe reality.

I propose that these limitations are very important clues to the nature of reality. Specifically...

The very fact that our reality is quantized may be considered strong evidence that reality is programmed.

In order to program a virtual reality, there must be quantization. It is impossible to develop a program with unlimited resolution. This does not prove that our reality is programmed, but it might explain why it is quantized. What other reason could there be?

One possibility is that there is a physical law in our Universe regarding the equivalency of information and energy. And since it would be impossible for a source of infinite energy to exist, so would it also be impossible, were such a relationship valid, for infinite resolution in the universe, because that would require infinite information to describe. Similar to Einstein's famous e=mc^2, one could imagine a relationship between energy and information that looks something like e=iα, where e=energy, i=information in bits, and α is the constant relating the two. In fact, in the field of thermodynamics, information has been related to energy in the following manner. Entropy, or the measure of disorder in the universe, is usually expressed in terms of joules/degree Kelvin, or energy per unit of temperature. But it is also related to the number of unique states in a system by the equation Entropy S=k*ln(Ω), where k is called Boltzman's constant (after the dude who discovered the relationship) and Ω is the number of states that a system can be in. Ω, of course, is infinite if the resolution of the universe is infinite, but it is bounded if the universe is quantized. So, in a thermodynamic sense, a non-quantized universe has theoretically infinite entropy and energy. Still, that doesn't make it impossible to exist. So, other than this infinite energy argument it is difficult to imagine a real reason for quantization.

For additional insight, let's go back to our virtual reality video game example – when we left off, our tree model was 5MB. What if you allow your players to zoom in on the tree by a factor of 100? Now, to avoid graininess, you will need to create a higher resolution model by a factor of 100, so it may take about 500MB to model the tree. And then what if you now allow the user to cut into the tree and examine it? Now you need to model the inside of the tree, effectively adding yet another dimension. Suddenly, the tree model jumps to 90GB, which is too unwieldy even by today's standards. Clever algorithms like dynamic resolution (increasing resolution only as you zoom in) and dynamic loading (only loading a model of the inside of the tree when it is actually cut into) can help optimize the performance of the game. In fact, in a MMORPG, before the game developers provide the tools for the players to do their "zooming" and "tree cutting", modules must be added that increase the resolution of the tree and model the insides of the tree. Then, the players are free to "discover" the zoom feature and the chain saws randomly lying around and they will never be any wiser.

Scientists Jahn and Dunne (see Chapter 2) from Princeton's PEAR lab, have suggested that physicists may actually be creating subatomic particles through intent. Certain recently discovered particles, called anomalons, have been observed to have different properties in different labs. There are many cases of theoretical predictions resulting in confirming experimental evidence many years later, but this might be expected from good theoretical physicists. However, it sometimes seems as if the mass consciousness of science is creating its reality. Michael Talbot, in his "The Holographic Universe," notes how Wolfgang Pauli predicted the discovery of a neutrino to solve a particular physics anomaly. 27 years later, the neutrino is discovered. Then, to solve another physics anomaly, some scientists start predicting that neutrinos may have mass. Lo and behold, in 1980 evidence starts to come in that they have mass, but only in Soviet labs, not in US labs. It seems as if different properties of particles are due to "changing expectation and different cultural biases of the physicists who searched for them."[4] Once you are aware of the possibility of such a concept, you see evidence of it all over the place – quantum physics, medicine, cosmology.

Question: Do you notice the striking similarity between these ideas and the clever algorithms added to our hypothetical Virtual Reality game just in time to allow the users to zoom in on and cut into the tree?

What about time? Recall our discussion about time in Chapter 2. I said then that Julian Barbour was right and that there is no time. But not because of Loop Quantum Gravity. Because we live in a programmed universe. Here's why:

In a computer game, there is no time. The game appears to have movement and progression due to two effects. One is the nature of our minds to process changing images into the concept of movement. The other is the progression of states of the game in terms of computer cycles. As of 2006, modern computers are clocked at 3 GHz or so. This doesn't mean 3 billion instructions per second, but actually somewhat more – 3.6 GHz Pentiums run at about 7 billion instructions per second. The intervals between each instruction are essentially a state of the game. Nothing can happen during those intervals. This is exactly how time works according to conventional physics; that is, quantum mechanics. Only, instead of 7 billion different states per second, reality operates at 10^{43} states per second. In other words, it's just a matter of scale!

Evidence – The Simulation Timeline

Nick Bostrom, Director, Oxford Future of Humanity Institute, Faculty of Philosophy at Oxford University, asks the following question in his paper "Are you Living in a Computer Simulation?": "If there were a substantial chance that our civilization will ever get to the posthuman stage and run many ancestor-simulations, then how come you are not living in such a simulation?" By "posthuman", he refers to an evolutionary stage whereby humans have mastered most forms of technology that are consistent with the laws of physics.

He argues that "at least one of the following is true:

1. The human species is very likely to go extinct before reaching a "posthuman" stage;

2. Any posthuman civilization is extremely unlikely to run a significant number of simulations of their evolutionary history (or variations thereof);

3. We are almost certainly living in a computer simulation. It follows that the belief that there is a significant chance that we will one day become posthumans who run ancestor-simulations is false, unless we are currently living in a simulation."[5]

The first consideration is the question of when it would be possible to generate a reality via a computer simulation that is consistent with our observations. In the Quantum Mechanical Argument section above, we noted that this is likely to occur by the year 2020.

Given our technological history, it certainly seems unlikely that humans will ever be presented with a fascinating and feasible line of inquiry and not pursue it. Consider the atomic bomb, cloning, genetic modifications, AI pursuits, nanotech, to name but a few. Does anyone really believe that the entire world would make a conscious effort not to continue to push the virtual reality envelope, especially considering the jump start that the technology already has in the gaming industry? So, Bostrom's second posthuman possibility is very unlikely, leaving only the first and the third. Essentially, that says that…

Either we are currently living in non-simulated reality and will fail to reach posthuman status, or we have already reached it and are living in a simulation.

Is there any way to determine which is more likely? Possibly, using the following timeline argument (see Figure 7-1, which includes a coarse 100,000 year timeline and an expanded view of the next 600 years)

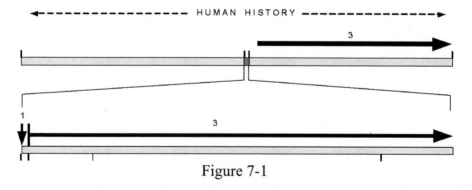

Figure 7-1

Let's assume a 100,000-year period of human evolution (admittedly, this is somewhat arbitrary – conventional science has protohumans at 7 million years ago, abstract thinking at 50,000 years ago[6], development of civilization at 6000 years ago) – 50,000 years into the past and 50,000 years into the future. Nick Bostrom's posthuman phase is identified in the timeline by the number 3, which stretches all the way from 2020 to the year 50000. Our apparent reality at year 2007 is identified on the expanded timeline by the number 1. We determined above that we are likely to be either in section 1 (the apparent reality) or section 3 (living in a simulation that was kicked off in the posthuman era) of the timeline, and that there is no way to tell the difference. Just from glancing at the timeline, it seems clear that it is more likely that we are in the big broad "3" era, rather than the tiny little "1" era. Statistically, one might come up with the probabilities by considering the odds of picking at random a point on the timeline by, say, throwing a dart at the timeline. We neglect the period prior to 2007, because we know we can't be living in that period. The probability that the dart lands in the current era (2007-2020) is 0.0003. The probability that the dart lands in the posthuman era (2020-50000) is .9997. So, by this argument, we are almost certainly living in a simulation. Again, you sharp-minded readers are no doubt thinking, this is entirely dependent on the choice of 50000, which is fairly arbitrary. It came from assuming that we might be in the middle of an evolutionary epoch that began when traditional science says that humans developed abstract thought. One might argue that the timeline should really end at the point that our civilization is likely to end. For the pessimists, that would be sooner rather than later since they would believe that we will never make it to Type I. 2012 per the Mayan calendar? 2020, when we create an AI that outsmarts us (the "Terminator" scenario)? 2029, when asteroid 2004 MN4 does its flyby of planet earth? 2060, per the technical singularity argument? 2191, when Moore's Law allows us to hit the Planck energies. The pessimist's options are endless. Even by averaging out the common doomsday scenarios, we stand roughly a 50% chance of living in a simulation right now. If you take the optimistic point of view and assume that we are capable of making it past the Type I transition, odds are good that we would continue on for millions of years, in which case the probabilities of our reality being a simulation are very nearly 100%.

It is clear how this relates to programmed reality. If it is likely that we are living in a simulation, then by definition, we are living in a programmed reality. However, it is also possible that we are living in a programmed reality that is *not* a simulation. Chapter 8 examines such possibilities.

Evidence – The Fine-tuned Universe

To review some of the examples of our seemingly perfectly tuned universe:

- *Universal constants cancel out all of the vacuum energy to an amazing accuracy of 1 part in 10^{115}.*

- *A deviation in the expansion rate of the early universe of 1 part in a billion in either direction would have caused the universe to immediately collapse, or fly apart so fast that stars could never have formed.*

- *A tiny difference in the ratio of the electric field strength to gravitational field strength would have prevented any kinds of molecules to form.*

- *If the ratios of the masses of protons to electrons were not precisely what it is, chemical reactions could not take place, rendering life impossible.*

- *The strength of the strong nuclear force could not have differed by more than 2% without either preventing hydrogen from being the only element in the universe, or from being too rare to allow the formation of stars.*

- *The number of electrons in the universe must equal the number of protons to an accuracy of 1 part in 1037 in order for gravity to work.*

- *A slight difference in the ratio of the number of photons in the universe to the number of baryons would preclude star formation.*

- *A small deviation in the value of the electromagnetic coupling constant would prevent molecular formation.*

Having a universe perfectly tuned for the development of matter and life, having a planet perfectly tuned for the development of life, being at the perfect place in history to ponder these questions in the context of our future, are all very easily accomplished in a program, but all extremely difficult and unlikely to happen by chance. Recall our two competitive "mainstream" theories: the Anthropic Principle and Flexi-laws. Doesn't Occam's Razor apply here? Which theory is more likely? That zillions upon zillions of universes are spawned every second with every conceivable configuration simultaneously existing, thereby accounting for the anthropic principle? That through 13 billion years of quantum uncertainty we are able to influence the past in such a way as to reverse-evolve existing laws of physics and chemistry via the Flexi-laws concept? Or, the universe was intelligently designed utilizing a technology that should be available to us within this century. Considering that a century is an incredibly small unit of time in the scope of cosmic evolution, it certainly seems plausible, no, almost certain, that someone has done this by now. If I were a betting man, I'd put my money on intelligent design. Which only leaves the questions of who, when, why, and how.

Evidence – Anomalies Revisited

Note that the following examples of possible explanations for various anomalies do not prove the existence of a programmed universe. However, they represent strong circumstantial evidence for it. The more anomalies that can easily be explained by the programming model, the harder that model is to ignore.

The Truman Show

I showed in Chapter 6 how anomalous it is that life always seems to have an evening effect to it. If there was a way to objectify my subjective observations and they retained their patterns, we would have to conclude that life was not truly random, but rather planned in some way. Programming is the perfect explanation. In fact, there are many examples of software systems that contain a stabilizing function called negative feedback, which ensures that temperature stays within a desired range (thermostats), an amplifier doesn't go into oscillation, a missile doesn't go off course, etc. It would be a fairly simply matter to apply the same technique to a reality generating program. Moreover, all of those funny events that make one feel like Truman are easily explained by the processes that automatically intervene to create a pattern in each characters life in the reality program. Need Truman to feel like he shouldn't travel? Just put a heavier weight on the "`CreateFearOfTravel`" method in Truman's configuration file. The underlying functions ensure that back channel processes plant fears in his brain and that events occur to reinforce those fears.

Coincidences

So, if we assume that synchronicity is real and not an effect of the statistics of numerous experiences, what the heck is it?

Laurence Boldt, in the "Tao of Abundance" states that "meaningful coincidences are not coincidences at all but spontaneous realizations of the underlying interconnectedness of all things within the Universe." To Deepak Chopra, "coincidences are not accidents but signals from the universe which can guide us toward our true destiny."[7]

Once again, don't we feel like players in a video game? Coincidences can certainly be programmed. And, if the programmers are going to attempt to communicate with the players, it has to be in an extremely subtle manner, so as to avoid arousing suspicion that the whole thing is put on. It would certainly take away from the experience of the MMORPG online experience, for example, if a player were to receive a message like "hey chief, look under the rock next to the slaughterhouse for the key to the treasure chest." Instead, it will be a rock that *coincidentally* has an identical curious shape to the rock next to the treasure chest. Similarly, you are not going to hear a voice during a dream that says "hey slugger, the girl you are supposed to date is Ramona Lapinski in your Biology class." Instead, you might run into her in the hallway, knocking a CD out of her backpack, which is *coincidentally* your favorite CD.

The Acceleration

At some point, it seems like The Acceleration will get out of control, doesn't it? There are only three possibilities. One is that some heretofore unexpected effect will surface and reverse the acceleration, defying all of the projections of the futurists, and defying our common sense. Seems unlikely, but also not inconsistent with the programmed reality theory. Think about how some creative books, movies, and TV shows have a way of putting the protagonist into a seemingly impossible situation, and just when the viewer is thinking "there's no way out of this," out pops a miraculous (but consistent with universal laws) way out. Two, we do evolve into a silicon-based entity that spreads its intelligence throughout the universe. And we are the first to do so, out of the trillions of solar systems out there? Also very unlikely. Three, the program simply ends at some point in the future, we reset, and start over. In this case, it is no coincidence that we are living in the age of the crazy acceleration because it is by design. It is what makes the game worth playing.

Little Green Men

> "Human beings are simply pawns in the games of alien minds that control our every move."
> - Dr. Fred Hoyle, renowned astrophysicist

As discussed in Chapter 6, the only two reasonable explanations for the millions upon millions of UFO sightings and abduction reports are:

1. *Advanced intelligence has pervaded the universe, is monitoring us, and is either toying with us by presenting*

themselves in a slightly futuristic manner, or coaxing us along developmentally.

2. *It is a mass cultural phenomenon related to the collective consciousness.*

Actually, with a slight twist, both explanations are encompassed by the programmed model, which perfectly fits all observations. The advanced intelligence may be, in reality, our programmers, coaxing us along in the game. We all have a collective awareness of the phenomenon because it is programmed into our reality. A random event generator process ensures that the phenomenon is not so widespread that it ever moves beyond cult status. Even in a particular sighting, only some may be given the ability to see and it is certainly easy to generate a programmatic anomaly that appears to violate our conventional expectations of manned-craft movement, and even violate known physics. It is easy, for example, to make an object suddenly appear or disappear in a program. To cause that effect outside of a program requires all kinds of creative physics (parallel universes, multiple dimensions, etc.)

Cryptozoology

The same argument applied to UFOs can easily apply to unexplained creature sightings. How simple is it to generate an unusual creature in the program, ensure that very few people ever see it, and even make it disappear if the hunters get too close.

Evolution or Devolution

Recall the three scenarios for life – intelligent design, evolution, and the "wind the clock and let it run" hybrid. Each of the three scenarios can easily be programmed. Easiest perhaps is the classic creationist version, where the program need only create the environment and the rules for interaction that the human avatars follow. Pure evolution requires a bit more planning to program, requiring a creation event and a set of very finely-tuned physical laws that will inevitably lead to the formation of life and a variety of species. The hybrid theory is, of course, a hybrid of the two programming models. The conflict that we see today between evolutionists and intelligent design advocates would then simply be the result of a carefully created world without sufficient evidence to prove either position.

Why do we not have an immediate ancestor? Because we did not evolve from anything. Our image was created in the program – as arbitrarily close to our nearest primate relative as the programmers felt like making it.

In the programmed reality model, OOPArt anomalies are nothing more than planted objects. As we shall see, the program most likely began well after prehistoric time, making it very easy to leave fascinating traces of an anomalous past for scientists, theologists, and philosophers to argue about. In fact, it is artifacts like these that cause people to think, to evolve scientifically and philosophically, which may be an important aspect to the program. Otherwise, what's the fun in playing?

Eggs and PSI

Recall the similarity of the Akashic Record and the Holographic Paradigm from the discussion in Chapter 2. Both theories are equivalent and excellent explanations for paranormal events. A Medium contacts people no longer alive because he is "tapping into" the Akashic Record. Telepathy occurs because both parties' thoughts are imprinted on the holographic fabric and one only has to read it to hear what the other is thinking. The remote viewer is able to do her job because she is reading the Akashic Record, which holds a description of everything everywhere. A precognitive psychic feels a distant event occurring because it is encoded into the hologram. Yoda felt a disturbance in the force because "The Force" is just another name for the holographic fabric of space. People can create their own reality by modulating the Record and then living it. The rationale by which the Akashic Record, The Force, or the Holographic fabric of reality can explain all paranormal events is flawless, although the mechanism is certainly not clear. Are these all explanations for the same thing? If so, what is that thing? Ervin

Laszlo has made perhaps the best attempt at a scientific theory to explain the Record:

Consider the properties of superconductivity or superfluidity. The former represents absolute zero resistance to the flow of electrical current and can be made to occur at extremely low temperatures. At these temperatures, for virtually zero voltage, an infinite amount of current flow is possible. Superfluidity is analogous in fluid mechanics. Fluid flow is analogous to electrical current in that the rate of flow is inversely proportional to the resistance of the medium in which the fluid flows. Again, at extremely low temperatures, for virtually zero force, an infinite amount of fluid flow is possible. It is resistance that causes things to slow down; current, moving objects, flowing liquid. Since the vacuum has a sufficiently low temperature, and no resistance to energy flow, a pattern of energy in the vacuum would theoretically propagate indefinitely, and never be dampened. Laszlo's idea is that all events leave imprints in the vacuum that form interference patterns that never disappear. Paranormal events are simply ways of extracting the information that is encoded in these imprints.

However, it does seem that such patterns must be incredibly minute, given that no one has ever been able to measure them. With millions of events superimposing their patterns upon each other every instant, it seems as if it would take an astronomically sensitive and selective system to pull out specific patterns and ignore all of the rest. Admittedly, this is exactly how a radio works. The air is filled with millions of signals from broadcasters, ham radio operators, cell phones, police radios, satellite signals, pagers, marine radios, microwave links, etc. A radio must be an amazingly sensitive and selective device to pull one particular signal out of the noise. Why not apply the analogy to a living being's ability to extract information from the patterns stored in the quantum vacuum? Certainly an interesting possibility, although there do appear to be a few problems with the concept. First, how does it explain precognition? It would seem that events that haven't occurred yet couldn't be stored in the Record. However, from our discussion of the nature of time, it is possible that time doesn't flow like a river. Instead all events may have already occurred and we are just following a sequence of states already imprinted in the vacuum. OK, but what about the sensitivity and selectivity required? Our consciousness must be able to pull a single event out of an encoding of every single event that occurred past, present, and future. Using the mysterious deja-vu experience as a yardstick, we can define an event as a state that occurs in your immediate environment (perhaps 10 square meters, ignoring a 3rd dimension for convenience because not much memorable happens above you?) for, say, five seconds. Then, the earth, which has a surface area of about $5*10^{14}$ square meters, contains $5*10^{13}$ events at a time, or $6*10^{14}$ events per minute, or $2.5*10^{22}$ events per 80 year time span (average human lifetime). For our consciousness to pick one out of that many events requires selectivity well beyond what might be typical for electromagnetic circuitry to be sure, but not necessarily beyond the capacity of a sufficiently advanced intelligence.

But there is another explanation. In information theory, there is the concept of "out of band" signaling. It is actually something that occurs every time you make a phone call. "In band" refers to the communications channel that you speak over; the pair of wires or the channel of bits that encodes your voice that are sent as you are communicating with the person at the other end of the "line." In the early days of telecommunications, the signaling of the number to be called was carried over the same pair of wires. As the network became digital, it was found to be far more scalable and flexible to send the signaling data (phone number, or address of the person being called) over a completely separate network. This was referred to as "out of band" signaling. In the movie "The Matrix," the agents wore earpieces that told them what was going on at all times in the matrix. That communication was an out of band channel in that it was not being sent through the standard reality that they were in. For another example, consider the MMORPG virtual reality game. Your character communicates with other characters by typing or speaking. The communication occurs in the game reality. There may be rules that allow you to speak directly to and only to another character, or it may be that every character that wants to listen is capable of hearing any given communication. Imagine that you want to speak to another character without being monitored by any other character. How could you do it? If you know the phone number of the person playing that character, you could simply call them up, send an email, IM, chat, or use any other valid communication mode that is outside of the game world. What you have done is communicate "out of band."

It may be so that a paranormal event can be completely described by such a mechanism. We are living in a programmed reality. But, sometimes, we can step outside of that program and use another channel to communicate with another entity or to experience another place or time. It doesn't require any complex theory involving space-time and the quantum vacuum. It doesn't require ridiculously sensitive and selective extra senses. Let's say you have an overwhelming foreboding of a particular event happening in the near future. What have you done? Perhaps you simply stepped outside of the program momentarily to look ahead at the upcoming sequence of events and found the one that you were anticipating. Or rather, (because the preceding would imply intent) you were given a hazy bit of the back channel. How could that be possible? Easy, if you think about how the programmed reality might be working. It has access to our consciousness via standard senses, but also via direct, or back channel mechanisms. Think of the hypnotists' ability to plant suggestions in your mind. Or subliminal advertising techniques. Or a swarm of invisible nanobots encoding a hazy thought into your brain. This is why we can't control these abilities at will. They are not skills that we are meant to master at this point. We can only be given glimpses into the possibilities, tantalizing clues that the back channel exists. Otherwise, we would just win the lottery every night, tell the world about the back channel, thereby upsetting the balance of the whole human community. As an aside, there are remote viewers, such as Aaron Donahue, who claim the ability to do that and support their families on their lottery winnings. They also claim that such a power is "allowed", but they are not permitted to "hit it big." Such a view is consistent with Edgar Cayce's readings and the many cases of communications with the "spirit guides" reported during in-between-lives states by patients undergoing past life regressions.

Recall Tom's experience with the hypnotist in Chapter 4. How was it that he was able to see the watch through his daughter's body? Simple. The program simply removed his daughter from his sensory view. Imagine an Everquest scene. How easy would it be to program it so that certain characters (or, certain characters at certain times) simply don't see certain other characters or objects? The game can be programmed, for example, so that player A can see werewolves all the time, player B can only see them during a full moon, and player C can never see them. As a result, they simply won't exist in player B's view when the moon isn't full, nor in player C's view no matter what time it is – they will effectively see through the werewolves. Is the werewolf there? Yes, in the database. Yes, in player A's world. Yes, in player B's world at certain times only. Never, in player C's world. Anomalous in the perceived reality, but entirely consistent with the laws of the program.

Quantum Mechanics and the Nature of Time

This is another easy one. The anomalies are just byproducts of a program with different rules than the reality that we think we area in. Teleportation? Simple. Remove object from place A, position object at place B. Action at a distance? Easy. How hard is it to program two objects in two different scenes to be entangled forever? Quantum foam, both spatial and temporal, is just a necessary aspect of the discrete nature of program processing and data modeling. Half alive – half dead cat? No different that a bit of data that is stored on a disk. Until someone observes it, it is impossible to tell whether it was stored as a 1 or a 0. What about from the cat's perspective? Assuming that the cat is being played by an entity with free will, the state of the cat will be whatever the program decided it to be based on the outcome of the random number generator that drives the radioactive particle's decay. We don't need no stinkin' collapsing wave functions.

The 100th Monkey

This is another classic example of back channel communication. Perhaps the logic in the program is such that once enough people learn how to master the Rubik's Cube, everyone else will be given the skills to master it via the back channel mechanisms outlined above.

Black Gold, Texas Tea

This is straight out of MMORPG Gaming 101. Give the players a way to develop their technology, to travel, to screw up their environment. Guide them to discovering it. Leave just enough to get them to the next phase of the game. If they run out without getting to the next level (e.g. safely mastering the power of the nuclear force), let the oil fields refill a little bit.

Evidence – Summary

In summary, I have presented four distinct classes of evidence that we are living in a programmed reality.

1. The strong evidence (supported by most physicists) that our reality is quantized is best explained by the programmed reality model. I can think of no other reason for such quantization.

2. The simulation timeline argument is strong and flawless logical evidence for the high likelihood that we are living in a programmed reality.

3. By Occam's Razor, the unbelievably finely tuned universe is best explained by intelligent design, which in turn, has its most likely explanation in a programmed model.

4. The huge set of well-studied anomalies facing us in fields as varied as metaphysics, physics, philosophy, geology, anthropology, and psychology can all be explained ONLY by the programmed reality model, providing very strong evidence for the hypothesis.

CHAPTER 8

How to Build a Universe (The Dummies Guide)

> "In the beginning, the universe was created. This made a lot of people very angry, and has been widely regarded as a bad move."
> - Douglas Adams (from "The Restaurant at the End of the Universe", 1980)

OK, so maybe reality is programmed. How did this happen? This chapter will explore a variety of possibilities.

Simulated Reality

I've shown that not only is it possible that we are living in a simulation, it is likely. The Virtual Reality chapter explains very clearly how easy it is to be fooled by a mechanism that intercepts the sensory receptors in your brain. And the technology is straightforward and will be easily available within our lifetimes. The state of the art in virtual reality gaming is well on its way to such a scenario. This is the most obvious method of programming a reality. However, the programming might not be computer based. Read on...

Physical Programming of Reality

There are several methods of creating a programmed reality for us to live in, which are not computer simulations...

Molecular Assemblers

Consider the concept of the "molecular assembler", detailed in Eric Drexler's nanotech foundation book "Engines of Creation" (also popularized as a "matter compiler" in Neal Stephenson's nanotech book "The Diamond Age,") and considered by NASA to be a viable technology for research.[1] A "molecular assembler" is a device capable of creating anything – food, gold, furniture - by building structures at the nanotech scale. It is not hard to envision a molecular assembler being programmed to build a cage for laboratory mice, complete with food, water, and exercise wheel; essentially a full environment for the animals. What would it take to build an environment for a housecat? Just a bigger assembler! And for humans? It would seem to be only a matter of scale, although at scales large enough to create planets, conceptual difficulties must be overcome. Where would such a "cosmic" molecular assembler sit? Is it outside of our known universe? Or is it here but effectively cloaked by dark matter (see Chapter 3, Theories on the Origin of the Universe)?

A molecular assembler doesn't necessarily have to look like a big machine. It could be a distributed cosmological system in "dark matter" space that creates "normal matter" constructs. Recalling the discussion about the Steady State Theory of the universe, it could be that dark matter is the engine behind it. And, with billions of years to create the cosmos, the physical universe could be created so gradually that it is not perceptible in our time frames. Thus, it is not inconceivable that we live in a physical world created by an enormous molecular assembler. This is a non-simulated form of a programmed reality.

Utility Fog

In chapter 2 we described the concept of utility fog, from the future world of nanotechnology. The fog consists of trillions of intercommunicating nanobots with the ability to move and to create light and sound in any direction. As such, they can form any sort of virtual reality for which they are programmed and we would never be the wiser. How do we know that space isn't just a fabric of nanobots (or, perhaps orders of magnitude smaller, like femtobots or attobots) under intelligent control?

Universe in a Lab

> "On the evidence, our universe was created not by a divine being, but by a physicist hacker."
> - Andre Linde, Professor of Physics, Stanford University

If physicist Andre Linde's chaotic inflation theory of the universe is accurate, it really doesn't take much to create a big bang. According to Linde, a mere hundred-thousandth of a gram of matter could be the seed for a "big bang in a lab." If the energy fluctuations from the quantum foam vacuum exceed a certain level, according to his theory, a bubble universe will form and undergo a period of expansion into a full universe.[2] That vacuum can theoretically be created from the small amount of matter mentioned above by a not too advanced civilization. While the point of his theory is that the universe may actually be expanding fractally in this manner, there appears to be nothing in the laws of physics that would prevent someone from also creating a big bang artificially. Of course, just creating a universe isn't enough to achieve our programmed reality. The universe has to also be controlled and it appears at first glance that it might be physically impossible to control, or send information to, a runaway big bang universe. However, physicists believe that the initial conditions can be specified, which could account for the curious set of highly improbable physical parameters that seem to be just perfectly tuned for life.

Materialization

Figure 8-1 shows a sort of paranormal "ladder of psychic evolution." Starting at the bottom of the diagram is a category of phenomena called "Psychic reception" that refers to effects that are passively received by the observer. This includes telepathy, clairvoyance, and precognition. Such effects are typically reported by people who experience them spontaneously and unpredictably, which makes them notoriously difficult to validate and characterize. However, as mentioned in chapter 2, there is also a statistically significant paranormal effect across all such experiments, which demonstrates that it is a subtle effect that is experienced by most people consistently. While the debate still rages, the weight of the evidence leans toward scientific proof and certainly toward general acceptance by the global public. [Note: Despite the fact that the author is well schooled in the scientific method and very knowledgeable about probability and statistics, he has first hand experience of a small number of paranormal effects, some of which were previously mentioned, which are conclusively inexplicable by generally accepted Western science. Therefore, he does not doubt the validity of the bottom of this ladder]. If one were to accept that such effects are real, it must also be considered that with sufficient understanding and practice, it might be possible to control the effect to a greater level than is apparent today. There is a school of thought that animals, and possibly even prehistoric man, have or had greater psychic abilities that humans do today. Thousands of years of socialization, increasing reliance on tools, and schooling in logical and scientific thought have perhaps "devolved" the psychic abilities out of us. So, it must be considered a possibility that the quality lies dormant within us, and may someday be understood and controllable.

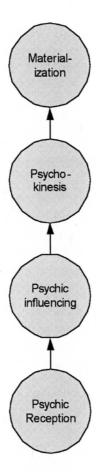

Figure 8-1

If one accepts psychic reception as a real human capability, it is not a stretch to imagine that such effects can also be sent the other way, or transmitted. In fact, in some cases, it is not clear whether the effect is actively received (subject reaches out and remotely reads the mind of another person) or transmitted (the other person reaches out and places the information in the mind of the subject) – experimental evidence supports both concepts. For lack of a better term, we refer to this category of effects as "psychic influencing." As an example, experiments were performed in 1971 by parapsychologists Gertrude Schmeidler and Larry Lewis at City College, New York where the subject, Ingo Swann, successfully influenced the temperature of thermistors in insulated thermos bottles from a remote position.[3] Also fitting neatly into this category is the rapidly growing hands-on practice of Reiki as an effective pre- and post-operative treatment in hospitals around the world. And, of course, Princeton University's remarkable Global Consciousness Project.

Taking the next step up the ladder, if one accepts that both psychic reception and psychic influencing can occur, it is not hard to imagine that a subject, who can influence the mind of another subject, can also influence physical reality, also known as psychokinesis. After all, if we believe that the mind is just a set of chemical bits and synapses, then it follows that psychic influencing is effectively psychokinesis. If we believe that the mind is something different, it is still a small step from influencing the mental state of another to influencing the physical state of an inanimate object. Many reports of this category of phenomenon are anecdotal, rather than the results of rigorous scientific studies. For example, Nobel Laureates Pierre and Marie Curie reported conducted experiments involving a medium and psychokinetic phenomena. According to researcher Michael Cremo, Pierre Curie came to believe that the phenomena were genuine.[4]

And now, if psychokinesis is real and can be controlled, not far behind is the coup de grace of psychic effects: materialization, or the spontaneous generation of physical material based on thought alone. Controversial Indian holy man Sathya Sai Baba has been materializing ashes, rings, candy, oils, and other assorted objects for many years according to thousands of eyewitnesses. In the West, skeptics would be quick to dismiss him as a clever magician, but there are also well educated individuals who are convinced that there is no trickery, such as psychologist Erlendur Haraldsson of the University of Iceland, who studied the man for many years and documented his findings in the book "Modern Miracles: An Investigative Report on Psychic Phenomena Associated with Sathya Sai Baba."[5] Ultimately, if materialization could really exist as a genuine effect or power, then it would be possible for a sufficiently adept master to be able to control the power and generate aspects of reality, such as anomalous figures or objects. Or the heavens and the earth.

Programming Reality

I am a software dinosaur. Back in the day, I wrote lots of digital signal processing code and could make programmable filters do amazing things. I've written some pretty gnarly real time assembly code for audio processing and building compilers, and used a wide assortment of largely obsolete 3GLs like PL/1, Basic, Fortran, and C for trading systems, automated chip layout processing, and network management. But, today, my C and Visual Basic are rusty, C++ even worse, and my Java, JSP, and Perl mojo is pretty much non-existent. So I will not subject myself to embarrassment by pretending to be a software developer (and thus incur the wrath of hackers pointing out where I forgot a semicolon). I figure, once you learn a few languages, the next one is all about syntax and I really think it is a lot more fun to put together higher level systems with components that some smart people have already honed. So, what I will present here is something called pseudocode, a form of software outline, with no encumbering syntax or formatting.

A basic form of the reality Program could look like this (note: I will use the convention of the capital "P" when referring to the Program of the universe, as opposed to some statistical analysis program. Similarly, Programmers will refer to those that programmed the universe, as opposed to the guys who created some eCommerce billing program. The Programmers, therefore, could rightfully be considered our Gods.):

```
SetInitialConditions()

while(time!=EndTime) {
      CurrentState=AcquireState(StateofUniverse);
      IntentMatrix=CollectIntent(AllPlayers);
      NextState=CalculateNextState(CurrentState,IntentMa
trix);
      StateofUniverse=ApplyNextState(NextState);
```

```
time=time+UniversalTimeInterval;
update(EndTime)
}
```

Essentially, what the Program does is create the universe from a set of initial conditions (SetInitialConditions) and then loop, or repeat itself, almost indefinitely, each time through the loop performing the following functions:

1. CurrentState=AcquireState(StateofUniverse) **Read** the entire state of the universe. This is obviously a huge task, but we are not concerned here with scale (remember, Moore's Law will eventually take care of that) but with the concept. So, this means for every single object, every single cell or component that composes that object, every single particle that composes that cell or component, and every single ultimate constituent of matter and energy that composes that particle, determine its position, velocity and direction.

2. IntentMatrix=CollectIntent(AllPlayers) **Read** the intent (free will) of every player (who has free will). Note that without this step, the universe is just a big pre-programmed machine and every point in the future is based solely on the current state of the universe. Players (us) would have no real control because we have no free will. I think that such a universe and such a program is fatally boring and pointless and so am going to include Step 2, which includes the intent of all those players of the game in determining the next step into the future. Who are the players? Me, you, most of the people we see walking around, most of the animals and plants we see, maybe even some objects that we normally consider to be inanimate. For flexibility, I leave open the possibility that there are sentient programs occupying our universe that have no free will (e.g., soulless robots like Agent Smith from The Matrix, or perhaps something more sinister like viruses, or dark energy). I also leave open the possibility that what we think of as an independent sentient entity with

free will may actually be an organized collection of smaller entities without free will (like the cells of a human)

3. `NextState=CalculateNextState(CurrentState,IntentMatrix)` From the detailed state of the universe, we can work our way up to macroscopic influences like forces and fields and determine what the next state of the universe will be, also taking into account the multitude of "intents" from all free-willed players. This is obviously where all the fun is – where all of realities interesting events are programmed, more about which below.

4. `StateofUniverse=ApplyNextState(NextState)` Next, we apply the newly calculated state of the universe to the actual universe via one of the mechanism described earlier in this chapter.

5. `time=time+UniversalTimeInterval` We increment time by the universal time interval, which, in our case, appears to be a quantum "jiffy", or 10^{-43} seconds. Therefore, each step of this Program gets executed 10^{43} times per second, exactly as is predicted by quantum physicists. Again, note that nothing happens in between each instance of `ApplyNextState`, also as predicted by quantum mechanics. Our illusion of the fluid passing of time is simply due to the fact that the rate of execution of `ApplyNextState` is so much higher than what can be assimilated by our true consciousness.

6. `update(EndTime)` Finally, notice the use of the "EndTime" variable. There has to be a way to finish the program, so this leaves the Programmers a way to end the whole thing. `EndTime` could be a predetermined time, such as, say, 12/21/2012 at 11:11 UTC. Alternatively, it could be set as an initial condition to the Program, but subject to modification at the whim of the Programmers. This goes hand in hand with the concept of free will, or reading the intent of all of the players. Without that variable, everything would be so

predictable that there would be no reason to ever update the EndTime. But with players having free will (not unlike all MMORPG's today), the Programmers can't anticipate things that might cause the program to get out of control. They then have two options. The first option is to modify some of the underlying APIs to adjust for the unexpected turns that reality has taken. The second, and much more drastic, one-time-only option is available for the Programmers to throw up their hands in disgust and say "this thing is out of control, it's time to end it" and adjust the EndTime variable.

Let's talk about some specifics and see how this would all work.

SetInitialConditions() is where the universe gets created. We will consider next chapter when this might have happened and how it's underlying functions will depend on whether the universe is very old or very new. Depending on that, initial conditions may consist of any or all of the following:

- *All astronomical components – galaxies, stars, planets, including our distance from the sun, the moon's distance from us, the energy capacity of the sun, speed of rotation, etc.*

- *All structural components of the planet we live on – core, shell, crust, minerals, oceans, atmosphere.*

- *All seed components necessary to create life, or, alternatively, a set of life forms all ready to go.*

The entire state of the universe must be held in the huge data structure StateofUniverse. But it may be necessary to adjust this data structure as time goes on. For example, until Hans Lippershey developed the first telescope in 1608, there would have been no need for the Programmers to include much detail about other celestial bodies. But, suddenly, with the spectre of humans peering through telescopes, the Programmers would have had to modify the StateofUniverse to include moons on Jupiter, for example. Further

224

modifications would have been made as soon as we flew to the moon and sent robots to Mars. Similarly, it may be necessary to adjust some elements of `CalculateNextState` as time goes on. This happens all the time in MMORPGs. As much as the designers try to anticipate what the players will do, there will inevitably be some behaviors that have the potential to ruin the established direction and goals of the program. So, out comes the patch release which updates the data structures or program modules. For example, maybe oil was programmed into the original release of the universe (Universe 1.0). Alternatively, it could have been patched in as a convenient, easily discovered and easily used energy source once humans reached the technological stage. String theory may have been in Universe 1.0 or added to the model of the underlying construct late in the 20th century, just as quantum mechanics may have been added in the early 1900s.

`CalculateNextState` is obviously the highest programming layer. Underneath comes some very interesting APIs like `CalculateProbabilitiesOfNaturalDisasters`, `CalculateNextStateOfAllPlayersBodies`, `CalculateNextWeatherState`, and `CalculateProbabilitiesOfAnomalousEvents`. Beneath `CalculateProbabilitiesOfAnomalousEvents`, for example, we might have `CalculateProbabilitiesOfUFOs` and `CalculateProbabilitiesOfBigfootSightings`. `CalculateProbabilitiesOfUFOs` would easily be programmed to generate UFO sightings of various sorts (saucers injected into the Program in the 50's, black triangles in the 90's, and balls of light only recently) and of various probabilities at different times (highest at 3am) and places (higher in New Mexico, USA).

Physical laws, evolutionary biology, chemistry, fluid dynamics, etc. would be programmed into the rules that are followed in `CalculateNextState`. They will, by necessity, be perfectly tuned to allow for the development of life, as we observe in our world today. Subtle energies may have been part of Universe 1.0, a mystery to be unlocked once the players reach certain levels and/or the society as a whole reaches a certain level. As with MMORPGs, certain players may have a proclivity to experience subtle energies, just as they may have the capability to run fast, or lead large organizations. The Programmers may watch to see how their players develop new scientific theories and either support or discourage such theories depending upon the desired direction of the Program. Ideas for new theories may even be subtly injected into the minds of key players during `CalculateNextState`.

So there you have it – all known anomalies and all known scientific theories easily explained by the programmed reality model, which is predicted by the simulation timeline. The apparent fine-tuning of the universe makes total sense, as it is a requirement of the model. And quantized space and time are merely its artifacts.

Universe Solved!

CHAPTER 9

Waking up to a New Reality

Putting it all together

So here it is. Now that we've shown how it is well within the realm of logical thinking that we are living in a programmed reality, let's explore the questions we raised at the beginning of the book. This is really the fun stuff although clearly purely speculative. I offer some ideas and opinions here just to complete the picture, although it is likely that no one in our reality would have the answers or definitive experimental means to determine the answers. If someone did, it probably wouldn't matter since the rest of us have all been programmed to consider him or her a nut case. Had we not been programmed that way, the answers would spell out the end of the program, which is clearly no fun for anyone.

A note on nomenclature: what shall we call the participants and the act of participating in the reality program? I hesitated to use the respective words "character" and "play" as that seems odd in the case of scenarios that are not truly games, e.g. "The Matrix." However, those terms are still probably the best fit overall. So, we shall refer to the participants as "characters" or "players", and the act of participating as "playing."

How did it get programmed?

Any or a combination of the mechanisms outlined in Chapter 8 are possible. The most compelling answer that accounts for everything that we perceive could easily be accomplished by a combination of computer simulation and utility fog. Again, both technologies will be possible this century, and it is actually likely that we are already experiencing them.

There are two distinct categories of programs, each of which model the virtual reality games that we know and love. In one case, which I shall call the Solipsistic Program, I am the only person in the world with true consciousness. Everyone else is an NPC (non-player character), or a programmed entity. This, of course, perfectly matches the philosophy of solipsism, hence the name. It is really kind of pointless to discuss such a possibility because I would really only be writing this book for myself. I'd hate to think that nobody really bought and read this book even though my NPC publisher says it's flying off the shelves. It is not pointless to consider it, however. Perhaps there are many of us simultaneously playing Solipsism games simultaneously. Maybe the games overlap, like lines that intersect in space. Imagine each line as the sequential states of a particular players program. And imagine the lines of two players. If their lines never intersect, then their players' lives never occupy the same reality (see figure 9-1).

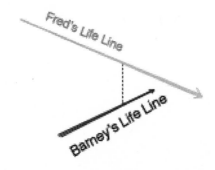

Figure 9-1: Non-Intersecting Lifelines

However, if they intersect for a moment, then they occupy the same reality for that moment only (figure 9-2). You're in a meeting at work and Fred sitting across from you is just an NPC in your reality program. But Fred is based on a real Fred who is busy in his own reality program. For an instant Fred pops into your reality and you into his. Neither of you would notice anything because the only difference between NPC Fred and "real" Fred is free will or consciousness. So, for an instant Fred has free will in your program and then its gone. And vice versa for you in his program.

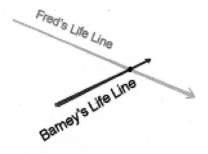

Figure 9-2: Intersecting Lifelines for an Instant

Or, the lifelines may merge for a while (days, years) and then split off (figure 9-3). The similarities between such a concept and the many worlds interpretation of quantum mechanics are strong.

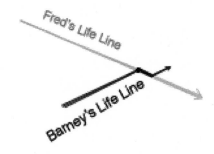

Figure 9-3: Intersecting Lifelines for a Period

The other type of reality game is the MMORPG, which allows for other players. In that case, who are the other players? Is every human a player? Or are there some soulless zombies at your work? (You probably know a few) What about other living things? Did animals choose to play their roles? Are animals separate forms of consciousness? Or are all consciousnesses the same and, per the Hindu philosophy, we may occupy the body of an ant. On the surface, this seems very odd. Not that I believe that animals do not have souls. But what is the point of applying a consciousness that is at least complex enough to fully occupy a human into the nervous system of an ant or bacterium that can only hold the tiniest fraction of a percent of it? Then again, isn't that similar to the days when we reveled in 2D severely pixilated video games? Given that ants live for a very short time, perhaps it is not unreasonable to have a desire to experience being an ant. Or, alternatively, have that lesson thrust upon our consciousness for any particular reason. Extending this thought further, it is not unreasonable to suppose that our consciousness is far far beyond the capabilities of the human nervous system. *I was once a galaxy...*

Here's another twist. According to William Whitman, a microbiologist at University of Georgia, there are about 5×10^{30} bacteria and archaea living on the planet.[1] That means that if we take the position that all living things have consciousness, there are about 8×10^{20} instances of bacterial consciousness for every human on earth. And if you believe that reincarnation can occur between species, the logical conclusion is that for every time you get to spend a life as a human, you would have to spend 8×10^{20} lives as a bacteria, on average. Seems kind of ridiculous to me. Ah, but there is another explanation. Can a consciousness split? Just as trillions of living cells combine to form a human that has an individual human consciousness, or thousands of pieces of software can combine together to form a single operating program, or colonies of bees can display hive mind behavior, so too, perhaps, can a consciousness be split into many constituents. Perhaps the billions of bacteria in your gut form a single consciousness. Or all of the bacteria on the planet. Leading to an ultimate conclusion, could all of our human consciousnesses be constituents of a single larger one, aka the earth, or God?

Self-referential Systems and Recursion

Does it seem odd that we might be living in a program in which we write programs similar to that in which we live? This is an example of a self-referential system, a system that refers to itself in some way. Not so odd, really. Seinfeld fans will recall the entire season about two guys who wrote a show for NBC about nothing. It is perfectly logical to write about what you know about. That is why MMORPGs model life – they have currency, evil characters, various physical settings, rules of physics, and hot women. An MMORPG that allows a character to write an MMORPG would be doubly self-referential. Triply self-referential if you count the MMORPG that we live in. Theoretically this can nest indefinitely, a concept familiar to programmers as recursion. I point this out only to dissuade any arguments that it would be unlikely that we live in a reality that is similar to the programs that we write and play.

For the non-sequitor of this chapter, fans of the writer Douglas Hofstadter will recognize some of the following self-referential sentences:

> "This sentence no verb."
> "is a sentence with no subject" is a sentence with no subject.
> "This sentense contains exactly three errors."
> "This sentence is a !!!! premature punctuator"

Who programmed it?

There are many possibilities...

1. Earthlings - It could be a company that creates reality games here on earth. Our entire history may have been a fabrication, at least up to a point, with the game engine taking over from there. Perhaps we are actually immortal consciousnesses, or, live a very long time. So the idea of playing out an 80-year scenario might not be as crazy as it seems to someone who only has an 80-year lifespan. It would be tempting to give a little less likelihood to this scenario because our consciousness is clearly not aware that it is playing a game. However, perhaps we suspend reality prior to starting the game by downloading our memory set, clearing our mind, and starting from scratch. Upon death in the virtual world, the suspended memories can be restored. Alternatively, rather than being a product of a company, the program may have been generated by a highly advanced earthbound entity, who has the capacity to create a virtual world. Scientists of the future, politicians from the 1984/Matrix school of governing, or a bald scar-faced James-Bondian villain. The possibilities are really endless.

2. Artificial Intelligence – Here, I am referring to AI as a pure machine-based intelligence, unoccupied by any sort of "spirit" or "consciousness." Already, machines are the biggest users of the Internet, in terms of numbers of transactions and volume of data used. Already, machines can create intelligent programs. Given our state of technology, it is not at all unreasonable that the creation of artificial intelligence will ultimately result in a world where machines are capable of extremely rapid development and will therefore have the

ability to generate a virtual reality program in which the stage for us biological players is one of the constructs outlined earlier.

3. Biological Extraterrestrials - Alternatively, the programmers may be entities from elsewhere in the universe. The universe may be completely different that what our reality tells us. The ET's may be evil (which I doubt because advanced beings implies advanced thought and socialization) or benevolent. The purpose of the program may be to create an intelligent species by helping us to develop values and intelligence. Or, it may be simply for the fun of playing God. We think it is human nature for us to play god with animals, with dolls, with MMORPGs, with simulated baseball games. Maybe it is *Blonkian* nature to play god via fabricated universe bubbles, nanobot swarms, or virtual reality simulations.

4. The Gods - Or, the programmers may be higher-level entities, true spirit beings, per the new age vernacular. They may exist on a completely different plane or dimension of reality and only interact with us in between lives, as consistently reported by such diverse sources as regression hypnotherapists, Edgar Cayce, shamans the world over, new age philosophers, modern Buddhists, and NDE experiencers. The "gods," as I shall call them (leaving it plural for flexibility), developed the program and the reality construct, in which we carry out our lives and ultimately die. At that point, we meet with spiritual guides to plan our next lives, which may be analogous to designing our character and choosing our next scenario in an MMORPG. The fact that this "memory" can be accessed may be due to an incomplete suspension of memories at the start of the current player's scenario. Or, it may also be part of the program, designed to make us question reality.

Who are you?

Actually more of an existential question, let's clarify "you" as meaning "the seat of your consciousness". Who we are probably depends on the answer to the first question, "Who programmed it?"

1. In the Earthling scenario, we are likely to also be earthlings, but probably living in a very different reality than the one to which we are accustomed, since the programmers are local and in the future compared to our perceived reality. Virtual Earth may be based on real earth, or it may be a close facsimile.

2. In the AI scenario, we are either earthlings (if the AI programmers chose to maintain a consistent environment between the real world and the virtual world), or some other lesser-developed entities. Theoretically, we may have been kidnapped as a species a la the movie The Matrix, either against our will for evil purposes or for our own good (e.g. to pull us out of our developmental rut). The AI would have created our world, but we may be exactly what we think we are – a consciousness occupying and controlling a biological entity living in this reality. Or, we may be occupying a different body and, like the drug "soma" of Aldous Huxley's "Brave New World," virtual reality may be all that we do in the future, by choice, since machines will take care of everything else. Alternatively, our consciousness could simply be occupying a machine, making us hybrids of a sort. In fact, the distinction between biological and machine gets very blurry in the near future anyway. So unless society finds a way to segregate us, we can safely assume that what holds for biological entities also holds for bio-machine hybrids.

3. In the ET scenario, we are also either earthlings or ET's ourselves. We may be unknowing subjects in the program or, we may be willing knowledgeable participants who agreed to a grand training plan in order to join the cosmic community. The various possibilities of who we are would be the same as with the AI scenario.

4. In the God scenario, we are spiritual entities ourselves, but members of those who learn rather than those who teach or lead. It makes sense that we are following a quest, which takes us through many experiences via human lives in order to achieve some ultimate goal. The goal may be to become spirit guides, or to become "one with the creator." Or, perhaps that is only the next level of the program, and "the creator" is just another level of entity in a never-ending nest of programmable realities. Since there is really no need

for a complex redirection, like a simulated reality, we are probably what we think we are - a consciousness occupying and controlling a biological entity living in this reality. Again, it is likely from the evidence that the seat of our consciousness is not our body.

When did it start?

This is an interesting question, and the one that, on the face of it, might most make one doubt the entire thesis. Here's why:

We have assumed that a significant portion of humans (maybe all) have true consciousness, are playing a role in the program, and are thus not program entities (NPCs). Let's use the term "real" for entities with that true consciousness. What about our parents? If we agree that at any given point, everyone is real, then several generations are real at the same time. 50 years ago, many of those real people were living, presumably with other real people. Going back in time, was there ever a point when people weren't real and were just echos of the program – historical characters that never truly existed?

But, recall our discussion about Jessica in Chapter 5. It is impossible to tell the difference between memories and when we truly existed. In such case, the program could have started at any time. 1307? 1947? Yesterday? There is no way to tell and no reason to assume that any starting point is more logical than any other. Regarding our three scenarios:

1. Earthling – As a game or as a method of control or education, the program could have started at any time. It is tempting to say that it must have started recently because it is easy to dismiss the need to have characters carry out the dull first billions of years of life, or the first 50,000 years of modern human life, or even the violent and pointless middle ages (or, the big-hair bad-music 80's?). It would also seem pointless to act out a character that is significantly devolved in comparison to the player, which would tend to support the idea that the true players are only slightly advanced compared to us. This implies a player base in the relatively near future (<100

years?), and therefore a reality scenario that projects back only a few hundred years at most.

2. AI – If machines are in control of the program and we are unwilling participants, it could have started at any time in this reality's past. If we are willing participants the Earthling argument would also hold, and the scenario probably started at some point within the past few hundred years.

3. ET - In the evil ET scenario, the program could also have started at any time. In the benevolent training program, it would probably have spanned multiple lifetimes, given the amount of time that it takes people to really learn their lessons and develop their values. Again, however, the lifetimes need not be sequential in VR time. The lessons may occur in separate simultaneous realities, like the lifelines described earlier (remember Neo's training in the movie "The Matrix", which took him into many different programs.)

4. God – Again, the program may have been started at any time and would probably have spanned many lifetimes in terms of human perception, as in the benevolent ET scenario.

How will it end?

1. Earthling – As a game, our reality may be over when someone wins it. Or, like most MMORPGs, there is no predetermined end. However, it could also be all over when somebody hits the wrong switch and resets the server.

2. AI – If we are unwilling participants, the machines have no real reason to shut down the program and might prefer to keep us dumb and happy. But, one wonders, to what end? Why not just kill us off? Better science fiction minds than mine have only come up with lame answers to that question, such as "bio-electric batteries." On the other hand, if we are willing players, our poor VR-riddled minds will probably continue playing ad infinitum, much like the rats that press the pleasure bar until they die of malnutrition.

3. ET – In the case of the evil ETs "putting their thumb down" on us, the interest would presumably be to maintain the game as long as it is necessary to carry out their nasty little objectives, so it is very hard to say when the program would end. Perhaps as long again as it has been going on thus far. For the benevolent ETs, the program should end when we have learned what is needed to complete our training, become galactic citizens, or whatever the ultimate goal may be. Given our behavior as a society, our propensity for war, our treatment of animals, our willingness to ignore the plight of other suffering humans, our disregard for the environment, and the popularity of The Jerry Springer show, I would say that we have a long way to go.

5. God – It would be surprising for there to be, in the God scenario, an end to the program. It somehow seems more satisfying to imagine that there is no end to our development than a hard and fast terminus at which we spend the rest of eternity.

6.

My best guess?

Logic and existing evidence does not favor a few of the scenarios outlined earlier. As already mentioned, we are probably not under the control of evil ET's. Anyone advanced enough to generate a full blown reality program would probably also be advanced enough to have respect for the entities that it is "cultivating." That might not be the case for AI, however. Machines that are not programmed to respect human life would probably exterminate it once they no longer need it and since we are here to ponder the nature of reality, that can't be the case. However, as Ray Kurzweil, Frank Tipler, and others have projected, it is highly likely that we will not remain separate from machines for long, and will ultimately merge with AI. So, the scenario might be that AI-biological hybrids created the program and AI-biological hybrids play it. But again, to what end? Besides, if we are really just playing a game, as in the Earthling scenarios, what fulfills our biological needs while we play a life-long-duration game? (OK, I can think of some scenarios, but what's the point?) And why wouldn't we just be having fantasy sex all the time? Could we really be both so advanced as to no longer desire such a base human need but not so advanced that we still have a desire to immerse ourselves in mostly dull scenarios? And yet, by the simulation argument, we are most likely living in one now.

So, I would have to conclude that we are not biological willing participants but rather spiritual entities occupying an advanced machine somewhere in a universe. The program that generates our reality was created either by AI or my definition of the "gods" (which are ultimately indistinguishable in that whomever creates the known universe can certainly be referred to as a "god.")

The end of the line?

I muse about the possibility that after this book is published, I go to sleep one night and wake up at a galactic awards ceremony. I'm on stage accepting the Zorpfnat Award, which is given out to the conscious entity that figured out the solution to the game. I reach out with my middle arm and accept the Zorpfnat statue. The crowd cheers. The rest of Earth's conscious entities are awakened and told the truth. As in "The Truman Show", the viewers at home reach for the TV Guide.

Let's see what else is on.

NOTES AND REFERENCES

Chapter 1

1. Hoyle, Fred. "The Intelligent Universe," Michael Joseph Limited, London 1983, p 19.

Chapter 2

1. Radin, D. I. "Unconscious perception of future emotions: An experiment in
presentiment." Journal of Scientific Exploration 11 (2) (1997): 163-180.

2. Gopnik, Adam. "Death of a Fish: The passing of a betta and the making of a child's mind." New York Journal vol. 81 Issue 19. 4 July 2005: 42.

3. Taylor, Humphrey. "The Harris Poll® #11, February 26, 2003: The Religious and Other Beliefs of Americans 2003." Harris Interactive. <http://www.harrisinteractive.com/harris_poll/index.asp?PID=359>

4. Dei, Jipei, et al. "Recovery of axonal transport in "dead neurons"." LANCET 351, 14 Feb 1998: 499-500.

5. Brooks, Michael. "Reality Check." New Scientist, June 23-29, 2007: 30-33.

6. Rincon, Paul. "Teleportation goes long distance." BBC News Online, 18 August, 2004.
<http://news.bbc.co.uk/2/hi/science/nature/3576594.stm>

7. Tegmark, Max. "Parallel Universes." Scientific American vol. 288, #5. May 2003: 40-51.

8. Price, Michael Clive. "The Many-Worlds FAQ." February 1995 <http://www.anthropic-principle.com/preprints/manyworlds.html>

9. "Casimir effect." Wikipedia. 10 October 2005 < http://en.wikipedia.org/wiki/Casimir_effect>

10. "Life: Far out: Zero point energy." 17 July 2003. < http://www.redorbit.com/news/display/?id=12269>

11. Greene, Brian. Fabric of the Cosmos. New York: Vintage Books, 2004.

12. Guth, Alan H. The Inflationary Universe. Reading, MA: Addison-Wesley, 1997.

13. Krauss, Lawrence, M. "Cosmological Antigravity." Scientific American, The Once and Future Cosmos, vol. 12, no. 2. 2002: 31-39.

14. Ostriker, Jeremiah P. and Paul J. Steinhardt. "The Quintessential Universe." Scientific American, The Once and Future Cosmos, vol 12, #2. 2002: 40-49.

15. Arkani-Hamed, Nima, Savas Dimopoulos, and Georgi Dvali. "The Universe's Unseen Dimensions," Scientific American, The Once and Future Cosmos, vol. 12, no. 2. 2002: 66-73.

16. Linde, Andrei. "The Self-Reproducing Inflationary Universe." Scientific American, vol. 271, no. 5. November 1994: 48-55.

17. Laszlo, Ervin. Science and the Akashic Field. Rochester, VT: Inner Traditions, 2004.

18. Davies, Paul. "Laying down the laws." New Scientist, 30 June – 6 July 2007: 30-34.

19. Chown, Marcus. "'Phantom menace' may rip up cosmos." New Scientist, 5 March 2003. http://www.newscientist.com/article.ns?id=dn3461

20. Talbot, Michael, <u>The Holographic Universe</u>., New York: HarperCollins, 1991. 31.

21. Talbot, p. 293.

22. Talbot, p. 54.

23. Cromwell, David. "Zen and the art of Theories of Everything," Science Tribune, August 1997.
<<u>http://www.tribunes.com/tribune/art97/crom.htm</u>>

24. "Light can break its own speed limit, researchers say," July 20, 2000.
<<u>http://archives.cnn.com/2000/TECH/space/07/20/speed.of.light.ap/</u>>

25. Van Flandern, Tom. "The Speed of Gravity - Repeal of the Speed Limit."
<<u>http://www.metaresearch.org/cosmology/gravity/speed_limit.asp</u>>

26. Troitskii, V.S. 1987. "Physical constants and evolution of the universe." Astrophysics and Space Science, vol. 139: 389-411.

27. Smarandache, Florentin "There Is No Speed Barrier in the Universe."
<<u>http://www.gallup.unm.edu/~smarandache/NoSpLim.htm</u>>

28. Thorne, Kip. <u>Black Holes & Time Warps</u>. New York: W. W. Norton & Company. 476-477.

29. Smolin, Lee. "Atoms of Space and Time." Scientific American, vol. 15, no. 3: 56-65.

30. Thorne, 483-504.

31. Ori, Amos. "A new time-machine model with compact vacuum core." Department of Physics, Technion-Israel Institute of

Technology, Haifa, 32000, Israel. 19 December, 2005. <
http://arxiv.org/pdf/gr-qc/0503077>

32. Singletary, Michael. University of California, San Diego,
"abstract for a presentation given at the Sixth Foresight Conference
on Molecular Nanotechnology."
<http://www.foresight.org/Conferences/MNT6/Abstracts/Singletary/>

33. Kurzweil, Ray. The Age of Spiritual Machines. New York:
Viking, 1999. 145.

34. Kurzweil, Ray. The Singularity is Near. When Humans
Transcend Biology. New York: Viking, 2005. 25-29.

Chapter 3

1. Roffwarg et al. "Ontogenetic development of the human sleep-
dream cycle." Science, 152:604-619, 1966.

2. Radin, Dean. The Conscious Universe: The Scientific Truth of
Psychic Phenomena. San Francisco: Harper, 1997. 68-73.

3. Bem, Daryl J. and Charles Honorton. "Does Psi Exist? Replicable
Evidence for an Anomalous Process of Information Transfer."
Psychological Bulletin 1994, vol. 115, no. 1: 4-18.

4. Radin, 72.

5. LaBerge, Stephen. Lucid Dreaming. New York: Ballantine, 1985.

6. Kellogg, E. W. III. "Mutual Lucid Dream Event." Dream Time,
14(2), 1997: 32-34.

7. Gittelson, B., and L. Torbet. Intangible evidence. New York:
Simon & Schuster, Fireside Books, 1987.

8. Lange, Rense, Michael Schredl, and James Houran. "What Precognitive Dreams are Made of: The Nonlinear Dynamics of Tolerance of Ambiguity, Dream Recall, and Paranormal Belief." <http://www.goertzel.org/dynapsyc/2000/Precog%20Dreams.htm> and Clericus, J. "Zum Wahrtraum des Bischofs Lanyi von Großwardein." Psychische Studien, 45, 1918: 465-468.

9. Stowell, Mary S. "Precognitive Dreams: A Phenomenological Study. Part I. Methodology and Sample Cases," American Society for Psychical Research, Journal, 91:163, 1997.

10. Moss, Robert. Dreamways of the Iroquois : Honoring the Secret Wishes of the Soul. New York: Destiny Books, 2004.

11. Bhattathiry, M. P. "Neurophysiology of Meditation." < http://1stholistic.com//Meditation/hol_meditation_neurophysiology-of-meditation.htm>

12. Kirkpatrick, Sidney D. Edgar Cayce: An American Prophet. New York: Riverhead Books, 2000.

13. Talbot, 141.

14. Weiss, Brian. Many Lives, Many Masters. New York: Fireside, 1988.

15. Talbot, 231, 232.

16. Puthoff, H.E., Ph.D. "CIA-Initiated Remote Viewing at Stanford Research Institute." Institute for Advanced Studies at Austin, 1996. <http://www.remoteviewinghistory.com/cia-remote-viewing-at-stanford-research-institute.html>

17. Targ, Russell. "Remote Viewing at Stanford Research Institute in the 1970s: A Memoir." Bay Research Institute, Palo Alto, CA, vol. 10 no. 1: 7.

18. Anderson, Jack and Jan Moller. "Military Psychic Unit's 'Hits' and Misses." Washington Post, 30 December 1996.

19. Utts, Jessica. "An assessment of the evidence for psychic functioning." Division of Statistics, University of California, Davis, 1995.

20. Talbot, 240

21. Lear, John. Interview. "Coast to Coast AM", 21 March, 2004.

22. Talbot, 242.

23. Rawlings, Maurice. <u>Beyond death's door</u>. Bantam Books, 1979.

24. Talbot, 68-70.

25. Seaman, Gary, & Day, Jane S. "Ancient Traditions: Shamanism in Central Asia and the Americas." Niwot, CO: University Press of Colorado and Denver Museum of Natural History, 1994.

26. Malmgren, Jeanne. "The Good Friday Marsh Chapel Experiment, THEN -- Rev. Mike Young – NOW, "TUNE IN, TURN ON, GET WELL?" St. Petersburg Times, 27 November, 1994.

27. Arthur, James. "Mushrooms and Mankind." <http://www.jamesarthur.net/mm_01.html>

28. Min, K.W., Seo, I.S. and Song J. "Postnatal evolution of the human pineal gland. An immunohistochemical study." Laboratory Investigation 57, 1987: 724-728.

29. Strassman, Rick. <u>DMT: The Spirit Molecule</u>. Rochester, VT: Park Street Press, 2001. xvii.

30. Sting. <u>Broken Music: A Memoir</u>. The Dial Press; 1st edition, 2003. 46-47.

31. Pickover, Clifford A. Sex, Drugs, Einstein, & Elves. Petaluma, CA: Smart Publications, 2005. 83-109.

32. "Kundalini" Wikipedia. 15 November 2005 <http://en.wikipedia.org/wiki/Kundalini>, and Sovatsky, Stuart. "Words from the Soul : Time, East/West Spirituality, and Psychotherapeutic Narrative." Suny Series in Transpersonal and Humanistic Psychology. New York: State University of New York Press, 1998.

33. 4 August, 2005. <http://www.lorientrust.co.uk/>

34. 4 August, 2005. <http://www.doai.co.uk/>

35. "Sony Online Entertainment Launching Game Auction Site", ecommercetimes.com, 20 April, 2005. < http://www.ecommercetimes.com/story/42464.html>

36. Kent, Stephen L. "Making an MMOG for the Masses." gamespy.com, 10 October, 2003 < http://archive.gamespy.com/amdmmog/week3/>

37. "Addicted: Suicide Over Everquest?." CBS News @ www.cbsnews.com, October 18, 2002.

38. "S Korean dies after games session." BBC News – World Edition, 10 August, 2005. <http://news.bbc.co.uk/2/hi/technology/4137782.stm>

39. "Virtual Trader Barely Misses Goal." Wired News, 16 April, 2004. <http://www.wired.com/news/games/0,2101,63083,00.html>

40. "Chinese gamer sentenced to life." BBC News – World Edition, 8 June, 2005. <http://news.bbc.co.uk/2/hi/technology/4072704.stm>

41. "Computer characters mugged in virtual crime spree." NewScientist.com, 18 August, 2005. <http://www.newscientist.com/article.ns?id=dn7865>

42. Lee, James. "From sweatshops to stateside corporations, some people are profiting off of MMO gold." 5 July, 2005.
<http://www.1up.com/do/feature?cId=3141815>

43. "Blizzard bans 1,000 World of Warcraft gamers." 16 March, 2005.
<http://www.macworld.com/news/2005/03/16/wow/index.php?lsrc=mcrss-0305>

44. "EverQuest: 77th Richest Country." 4 July, 2007.
<http://www.flatrock.org.nz/topics/info_and_tech/game_theories.htm>

45. "Second Life." Wikipedia. 4 July 2007
<http://en.wikipedia.org/wiki/Second_Life>

46. "Businesses and organizations in Second Life." Wikipedia. 4 July 2007
<http://en.wikipedia.org/wiki/Businesses_and_organizations_in_Second_Life>

47. "Product Launch in Second Life - April 26 Event." 4 July 2007
<http://www-03.ibm.com/developerworks/blogs/page/InsideSystemStorage?entry=product_launch_in_second_life>

Chapter 4

1. "The Industrial Era." The History of Computing Project.
<http://www.thocp.net/timeline/1947.htm>

2. Idem

3. "The FORTRAN Programming Language." University of Michigan College of Engineering and Computer Science.

<http://www.engin.umd.umich.edu/CIS/course.des/cis400/fortran/fort
ran.html>

Chapter 5

1. "High-Speed Love Connection," Wired News, 24 June, 2004.
<http://www.wired.com/news/games/0,2101,63963,00.html?tw=wn_
1techhead>

2. Sharp, F.R. and M.F. Gonzalez. "Fetal frontal cortex transplant
(14C) 2-deoxyglucose uptake and histology: survival in cavities of
host rat brain motor cortex." Neurology 1984 34: 1305-1311.

3. Lehman, M.N., R. Silver, W.R. Gladstone, R.M. Kahn, M. Gibson
and E.L. Bittman. "Circadian rhythmicity restored by neural
transplant. Immunocytochemical characterization of the graft and its
integration with the host brain." Journal of Neuroscience, vol. 7,
1987: 1626-1638.

4. Graham-Rowe, Duncan. "World's first brain prosthesis revealed."
New Scientist, 12 March 2003.

5. Kurzweil, Ray. The Age of Spiritual Machines. 101-156.

6. Kurzweil, Ray, The Singularity is Near. 25-29.

7. Kurzweil, Ray, The Singularity is Near. 21.

Chapter 6

1. Crease, R. P., C.C. Mann. The Second Creation: Makers of the
Revolution in Twentieth-Century Physics. Rutgers University Press,
1996.

2. Matthews, Robert A. J. "Facts versus Factions: the use and abuse of subjectivity in scientific research." ESEF Working Paper, February 1998.

3. Beaty, William. "Ridiculed Discoverers, Vindicated Mavericks" 2002. < http://www.amasci.com/weird/vindac.html>

4. Hancock, Graham. <u>Supernatural – Meetings with the Ancient Teachers of Mankind</u>. Canada: Doubleday, 2005. 136-146.

5. Plotkin, Marc J. "Cold Fusion Heating Up -- Pending Review by U.S. Department of Energy." Pure Energy Systems News Service, 27 March, 2004.

6. Lungold, Ian Xel. "The Mayan Calendar Applied." <http://accessnewage.com/articles/mystic/mayancal.htm>

7. "Population Growth & Migration." Gaia Watch of the UK. <http://www.population-growth-migration.info/>

8. "CNN Poll: U.S. hiding knowledge of aliens." 15 June, 1997. http://www.cnn.com/US/9706/15/ufo.poll/

9. "Summaries of Some Recent Opinion Polls on UFOs." 14 November, 2005 <http://www.ufoevidence.org/documents/doc999.htm>

10. "General / Mass Sightings." 14 November, 2005 <http://www.ufoevidence.org/topics/generalsightings.htm>

11. Mack, John, M.D. "The UFO Abduction Phenomenon: What Does it Mean for the Transformation of Human Consciousness?" Primal Renaissance: The Journal of Primal Psychology, Vol. 1, No. 1, Spring 1995: 96-110.

12. Sparks, Brad. "Comprehensive Catalog of 1,500 Project BLUE BOOK UFO Unknowns: Work in Progress (Version 1.6, June 18, 2003).

13. "Physical Evidence Related to UFO Reports." The Proceedings of a Workshop Held at the Pocantico Conference Center, Tarrytown, New York, September 29 – October 4, 1997.

14. Marrs, Jim. Alien Agenda. New York: Perennial, 1997. 30-35, 61-64.

15. Idem

16. Anderson, Bruce Roger "An Interview with Retired Sergeant-Major Robert Dean." Excerpted from UFO Update AZ. 23 July, 2005 < http://home.pacbell.net/joerit/docs2/crash/bobdean.htm>

17. "Lt. Walter G. Haut, Roswell base public information officer, "Deathbed" affidavit to seeing spacecraft & bodies." 17 July, 2007 <http://roswellproof.homestead.com/Haut.html>

18. "In Their Own Revealing Words," 9 July 2007, <http://www.mega-genius.com/editorial_no_23.htm>

19. Strassman, Rick, DMT: The Spirit Molecule

20. Davies, Paul. The FIFTH MIRACLE: The Search for the Origin and Meaning of Life." London, England: Penguin, 2000. 145.

21. "Life on Mars." 1 November, 2005 <http://aerospacescholars.jsc.nasa.gov/CAS/lessons/L9/21.htm>

22. Hoooper, Rowan. "Scientists: Life on Mars Likely." Wired News, 2 May 2005. < http://www.wired.com/news/space/0,2697,67315,00.html>

23. David, Leonard. "NASA Scientist: 'Mars Could be Biologically Alive'." space.com, 19 April 2005. http://www.space.com/scienceastronomy/050419_mars_methane.html

24. Kaku, Michio. "The Physics of Extra-Terrestrial Civilizations."
23 November, 2005
http://www.mkaku.org/articles/physics_of_alien_civs.shtml

25. Thorne, Kip, 508-521.

26. Cazeau, Charles J. and Stuart D. Scott, Jr. Exploring the
Unknown. New York: Da Capo Press, 1979.

27. Forrest, Jean. "Protection of Nessie perplexed men from the
ministry." The Herald, Web Issue 2446, 9 January, 2006. <
http://www.theherald.co.uk/news/53911.shtml>

28. Orr, H. Allen. "Why intelligent design isn't." The New Yorker,
30 May, 2005.

29. Meyer, Stephen C. "Intelligent Design: The Origin of Biological
Information and the Higher Taxonomic Categories." Proceedings of
the Biological Society of Washington, November 30, 2005.

30. Pye, Lloyd. "Darwinism vs. Creationism: A Checkered History, A
Doubtful Future." http://www.lloydpye.com/

31. Gray, Jonathan. Dead Men's Secrets. Bloomington, IN:
AuthorHouse, 2004.

32. Cremo, Michael A., and Richard L. Thompson. Forbidden
Archeology. Los Angeles, CA: Bhaktivedanta Book Publishing,
2003.

33. Noorbergen, Rene. Secrets of the Lost Races: New Discoveries of
Advanced Technology in Ancient Civilizations. Tennessee: Norcom
Publishing, 1977.

34. Childress, David Hatcher. Technology of the Gods: The
Incredible Sciences of the Ancients. Adventures Unlimited Press,
2000.

35. Jahn, R.G., B. J. Dunne, R. D. Nelson, Y. H. Dobyns, and G. J. Bradish. "Correlations of Random Binary Sequences with Pre-Stated Operator Intention: A Review of a 12-Year Program." Journal of Scientific Exploration, Vol. 11, No. 3: 345–367, 1997.

36. Jahn, Robert G. "The Persistent Paradox of Psychic Phenomena: An Engineering Perspective." IEEE, Proceedings, 70:136, 1982.

37. Parker, Adrian. "Report on Work in Progress on the Ganzfeld Project - January1996-June1997." University of Göteborg Department of Psychology. <http://psi-sweden.org/artiklar/ganzfeld.html>

38. Sheldrake, Rupert. "Experiments on the Sense of Being Stared at: The Elimination of Possible Artifacts," Journal of the Society for Psychical Research Vol. 65, 2001: 122-137. <http://www.sheldrake.org/papers/Staring/artefacts_elim.html>

39. Delanoy, D. "Experimental Evidence Suggestive of Anomalous Consciousness Interactions." 2nd Gauss Symposium, Munich, August 1993. <http://www.tcm.phy.cam.ac.uk/~bdj10/psi/delanoy/node5.html#SECTION00050000000000000000>

40. Radin, Dean, The Conscious Universe: The Scientific Truth of Psychic Phenomena.

41. Radin, p 89.

42. "Information & explanations, latest texts & monographs on Parapsychology" 9 July 2007. <http://real-estate-properties.com/primary/psychology/Parapsychology.html>

43. "Global Correlations in Random Data." 23 July, 2005. <http://noosphere.princeton.edu/>

44. Sheldrake, Rupert. <u>A New Science of Life</u>. Park Street Press, 1995. chapter 11.

45. Smith, Paul H. "Mormonism and the 100th Monkey." Paul H. Smith, submitted for presentation at the Sunstone Theological Symposium X, August 1988.

46. Clarke, Tom. "Fossil Fuels Without the Fossils: Petroleum: Animal, Vegetable or Mineral?" Nature News Service, 14 August, 2002.

47. Corsi, Jerome. "At 30,000 feet down, where were the dinosaurs?" WorldNetDaily.com, 29 November, 2005.

48. Cooper, Christopher. "Odd Reservoir Off Louisiana Prods Oil Experts to Seek a Deeper Meaning," Wall Street Journal, 16 April, 1999.

49. Idem

Chapter 7

1. Briggs, Helen. "Magic number seven for decision making." BBC News Online, 3 September, 2001
<<u>http://news.bbc.co.uk/1/hi/in_depth/sci_tech/2001/glasgow_2001/15 23755.stm</u>>

2. "Visual Acuity of the Human Eye," NDT Resource Center.
<<u>http://www.ndt-ed.org/EducationResources/CommunityCollege/PenetrantTest/Introduction/visualacuity.htm</u>>

3. Kurzweil, <u>Age of the Spiritual Machine</u>

4. Talbot, <u>The Holographic Universe</u>

5. Bostrom. Nick. "Are You Living In a Computer Simulation?" Philosophical Quarterly, 2003, Vol. 53, No. 211: 243-255.

6. Rincon, Paul. "Evidence of earliest human burial." BBC News, 26 March, 2003. http://news.bbc.co.uk/1/hi/sci/tech/2885663.stm

7. Chopra, Deepak. "Coincidences – "Clues from the Universe." <http://www.beliefnet.com/story/134/story_13425_1.html>

Chapter 8

1. Globus, Al, David Bailey, Jie Han, Richard Jaffe, Creon Levit, Ralph Merkle, and Deepak Srivastava. "NASA applications of molecular nanotechnology."
The Journal of the British Interplanetary Society, vol. 51, 1998: 145-152.

2. Holt, Jim. "The Big Lab Experiment, Was our universe created by design?" 19 May, 2004. <slate.msn.com>

3. Schmeidler, G.R. "PK Effects Upon Continuously Recorded Temperature." Journal of the American Society for Psychical Research, no. 4, Oct. 1973
<http://www.rviewer.com/IngoSwann_encyclopedia.html>

4. Cremo, M.A. "Famous scientists and the paranormal: Implications for consciousness research." Presented at Toward a Science of Consciousness, April 27-May 2, 1998, Tucson, Arizona. < http://www.mcremo.com/paranormal.html>

5. Talbot, 150-152.

Chapter 9

1. Tenenbaum, David. "Microbial Population Explosion." 23 December, 2005. <http://whyfiles.org/shorties/count_bact.html>

NOTES AND REFERENCES

About the Author

Jim Elvidge holds a Master's Degree in Electrical Engineering from Cornell University. He has applied his training in the high-tech world as a leader in technology and enterprise management, including many years in executive roles for various companies and entrepreneurial ventures. He also holds 4 patents in digital signal processing.

Beyond the high-tech realm, however, Elvidge has years of experience as a musician, writer, and truth seeker. He merged his technology skills with his love of music, developed one of the first PC-based digital music samplers, and co-founded RadioAMP, the first private-label online streaming-radio company.

For many years, Elvidge has kept pace with the latest research, theories, and discoveries in the varied fields of subatomic physics, cosmology, artificial intelligence, nanotechnology, and the paranormal. This unique knowledge base has provided the foundation for his first full-length book, "The Universe-Solved!".